Portugal

WORLD BIBLIOGRAPHICAL SERIES

General Editors:
Robert L. Collison (Editor-in-chief)
Sheila R. Herstein
Louis J. Reith
Hans H. Wellisch

VOLUMES IN THE SERIES

VOLUME 71

– Portugal –

P. T. H. Unwin
Compiler

CLIO PRESS

OXFORD, ENGLAND · SANTA BARBARA, CALIFORNIA
DENVER, COLORADO

© Copyright 1987 by Clio Press Ltd.

British Library Cataloguing in Publication Data

Unwin, P.T.H.
Portugal.—(World bibliographical series; 71)
1. Portugal—Bibliography
I. Title.   II. Series
016.9469   Z2711
ISBN 1–85109–016–9

Clio Press Ltd.,
55 St. Thomas' Street.
Oxford OX1 1JG, England.

ABC-Clio Information Services.
Riviera Campus, 2040 Alameda Padre Serra.
Santa Barbara, Ca. 93103, USA.

Designed by Bernard Crossland
Typeset by Columns Design and Production Services, Reading, England
Printed and bound in Great Britain by
Billing and Sons Ltd., Worcester

THE WORLD BIBLIOGRAPHICAL SERIES

This series will eventually cover every country in the world, each in a separate volume comprising annotated entries on works dealing with its history, geography, economy and politics: and with its people, their culture, customs, religion and social organization. Attention will also be paid to current living conditions – housing, education, newspapers, clothing, etc. – that are all too often ignored in standard bibliographies; and to those particular aspects relevant to individual countries. Each volume seeks to achieve, by use of careful selectivity and critical assessment of the literature, an expression of the country and an appreciation of its nature and national aspirations, to guide the reader towards an understanding of its importance. The keynote of the series is to provide, in a uniform format, an interpretation of each country that will express its culture, its place in the world, and the qualities and background that make it unique.

SERIES EDITORS

Robert L. Collison (Editor-in-chief) is Professor Emeritus, Library and Information Studies, University of California, Los Angeles, and is currently the President of the Society of Indexers. Following the war, he served as Reference Librarian for the City of Westminster and later became Librarian to the BBC. During his fifty years as a professional librarian in England and the USA, he has written more than twenty works on bibliography, librarianship, indexing and related subjects.

Sheila R. Herstein is Reference Librarian and Library Instruction Co-ordinator at the City College of the City University of New York. She has extensive bibliographic experience and has described her innovations in the field of bibliographic instruction in 'Team teaching and bibliographic instruction'. *The Bookmark*, Autumn 1979. In addition, Doctor Herstein co-authored a basic annotated bibliography in history for Funk & Wagnalls *New encyclopedia*, and for several years reviewed books for *Library Journal*.

Louis J. Reith is librarian with the Franciscan Institute, St. Bonaventure University, New York. He received his PhD from Stanford University, California, and later studied at Eberhard-Karls-Universität, Tübingen. In addition to his activities as a librarian, Dr. Reith is a specialist on 16th-century German history and the Reformation and has published many articles and papers in both German and English. He was also editor of the *American Society for Reformation Research Newsletter*.

Hans H. Wellisch is a Professor at the College of Library and Information Services, University of Maryland, and a member of the American Society of Indexers and the International Federation for Documentation. He is the author of numerous articles and several books on indexing and abstracting, and has also published *Indexing and abstracting: an international bibliography*. He also contributes frequently to *Journal of the American Society for Information Science, Library Quarterly*, and *The Indexer*.

To the people of the Minho

Contents

Contents

Contents

Preface

This bibliography provides an annotated list of selected books on Portugal written in English, and is designed to present English-speaking readers with an introduction to the country which will enable them to identify sources from which they can then find further material on their own specialized interests. In line with the nature of the *World Bibliographical Series*, material in languages other than English is generally excluded, although some bibliographies in Portuguese are listed. The bibliography also includes some articles in periodicals where these are felt to provide different information from that available in books. The introduction provides a brief descriptive overview of the country in terms of its geography, history, politics and economy, against which the detailed annotations noted in the bibliography can be viewed.

The choice of works to include on the countries that once formed Portugal's overseas empire proved to be difficult. In general the works that have been included are those that are concerned more with the effects of Portugal's empire and colonial policy on mainland Portugal itself, rather than with the effects of Portugal on her overseas possessions in Africa, Asia and South America.

Place- and personal-names mentioned within the annotations have normally been left in the same form as that in which they are mentioned by the authors in question. In general, Portuguese place-names have been left in their Portuguese spellings apart from names in common English usage such as Lisbon, Oporto and the Azores. Authors have been listed and indexed according to the Anglo-American Cataloguing Rules in which personal names are entered under the part of the name following the prefix.

Numerous people have helped me in my compilation of this bibliography, and in my visits to Portugal. For financial support I am particularly grateful to the UK Branch of the Calouste Gulbenkian Foundation, to the Central Research Fund of the University of London, and to the Departments of Geography at the University of Durham and at Royal Holloway and Bedford New College, University of London. Library staff at the British Library, the Library of Congress, and the library of the Hispanic and Luso-Brazilian Council at Canning House all deserve special thanks for their labours on my behalf, as does Valerie Allport in the library of Royal Holloway and Bedford New College who obtained several items for me through the inter-library loan scheme. Many thanks are due to Kathy Roberts who turned my illegible scrawl into a clear manuscript with great speed, skill and patience. Without her this book would never have seen the light of day so quickly. Likewise I am particularly grateful to Susan Haberis of Clio Press for her detailed editorial work on the volume. Mike Drury, Jim Lewis, Janet Townsend and Allan Williams first inspired me to become interested in Portugal, and so this book owes much to them. My greatest debt, though, is to my friends in Portugal, and especially to John and Janet Burnett, Maria Cálem, Luis Filipe Cunha, and Concha Feijó – without them my knowledge of Portugal would be far less than it is, and I hope that this book will repay some of the debt that I owe them. Above all, however, I must thank my wife, Pam, for putting up with long absences during my research in Portugal, and for sharing some excellent times exploring Portugal's towns and countryside.

Tim Unwin
Englefield Green
1 May 1986

Introduction

To most people in the English-speaking world, Portugal springs to mind for two main reasons: on the one hand for the beaches and tourist resorts of the Algarve, and on the other for its wine and in particular its port. These interests are well-reflected in the literature about Portugal written in English, but the country has very much more of interest than just these two characteristics. It is a country with a long and important history, culminating in the great maritime explorations of the 15th century written about by Luís de Camões in his epic poem *Os Lusíadas*. It is also a country of considerable diversity, in which the wide, open expanses of the Alentejo, with their wheat fields and cork-oaks, contrast markedly with the densely-settled, irrigated green of the Minho.

The links between Portugal and England go back well into the mediaeval period and were first formalized in the Anglo-Portuguese alliance of 1373 and substantiated by the Treaty of Windsor which the two countries signed in 1386. The year of the 600th anniversary of this treaty has also seen Portugal embark on a new era of its political and economic life as it joined the European Community on 1 January 1986. It remains the poorest country in western Europe, with the Gross Domestic Product (GDP) per head being estimated in 1985 at only $1,950, and it is the only country in western Europe to have undergone a radical left-wing revolution.

Geography and geology

Portugal, with a population of about ten million, forms the south-westernmost extremity of Europe, with its western and southern shores washed by the Atlantic Ocean. It has an area of 92,000 square kilometres and includes the offshore island groups of Madeira and the Azores (*Açores*). To the north and east it borders on Spain, and as such its geology largely represents an extension of that of the Iberian *meseta* (plateau).

The north of Portugal is geologically the oldest part, formed from a pre-Palaeozoic block which is covered in places with metamorphosed Palaeozoic sediments. This area is mainly granite, with schists being found in the Upper Douro valley, in a band to the east of Oporto running from north-west to south-east, and in a zone in the centre of the country between Coimbra and Castelo Branco. In the west of the country there is an extensive Mesozoic and Cainozoic border between the Iberian massif and the sea, with the very varied rocks lying in strips broadly parallel with the coast. A similar but narrower series of rocks is also found in the Algarve, running from west to east along the coast. Three small Tertiary basins form coastal plains along the lower courses of the River Tagus (*Tejo*), the River Sado, and in the area centred on the rivers Mondego and Vouga. These are bordered by Mesozoic and Palaeozoic deposits, and some patches of the Tertiary are still found covering the ancient massif itself. Recent alluvium deposits from the Tagus, the Sado and the Mondego are found along the lower reaches of these rivers, and on the west coast these have been redistributed to form extensive areas of coastal sand-dunes. During the Tertiary much of the central plateau was dislocated into a number of small massifs, such as the Serra da Estrela and the Serra do Marão. The faults and fissures deriving from this period have given rise to the many thermal and mineral springs to be found particularly in the north of the country. Tectonic activity was similarly responsible for the scattered mineral deposits in the north and vulcanism has also given rise to ranges such as the Serra de Monchique and the Serra de Sintra in the south and west of the country. The fault-lines and structural basins resulting from these orogenic movements have continued to be active in recent times, with the Lisbon (*Lisboa*) earthquake of 1755 being the most violent. Other, smaller tremors, such as that occurring in the north of the country in 1958, have continued into this century.

The main mountains of continental Portugal are found in the north of the country in the Serra da Estrela, which rises to 1,991 metres, in the Serra do Marão and in the Serra do Gerês. However, the country's highest peak is Pico Alto in the Azores, which reaches a height of 2,351 metres. Most of the country's rivers flow broadly from east to west, and many of them rise across the border in Spain. The two most important rivers are the

Tagus in the centre of the country, which flows out to the Atlantic at Lisbon, and the Douro in the north, which reaches the ocean at Oporto (*Porto*). The longest river entirely within Portugal, however, is the Mondego, which rises in the Serra da Estrela and flows 225 kilometres to the Atlantic at Figueira da Foz.

Lying at the western edge of Europe, Portugal receives relatively more rain than does Spain to its east, with the pattern of rainfall being considerably influenced by its mountain ranges. Portugal's highest rainfall is thus found in the north-west, where the mountains force the Atlantic air masses upwards, and provide annual averages of between 1,000 and 2,500 millimetres of precipitation. The north-east, lying behind the mountains, is much dryer with rainfall on average below about 800 millimetres a year. Annual rainfall figures of between 500 and 800 millimetres prevail over much of the remaining centre and south of the country, apart from over the few ranges of hills, such as the Serra de Monchique and the Serra de Sintra, where rainfall rises to about 1,250 millimetres a year.

In terms of temperature, Portugal can also be seen to benefit from a markedly maritime climate, and the isotherms for the coldest and warmest months both reflect a general gradation from west to east. The January isotherms range from a cold north-east at about 7°C near Bragança to a much warmer 12°C in the south-western Sagres peninsula. Most of the country, though, at this time of year lies between the 9°C and 11°C isotherms. In July the isotherms run much more closely parallel to the coast, where the cooling influence of the Atlantic is clearly noticed. The western edge of the country thus has a steep gradient of isotherms ranging from about 17°C at the coast to 22°C along a line running from Lagos through Lisbon and Coimbra to Braga in the north. Further east, the increase in temperature of the July isotherms is more gradual, generally reaching 27°C at the Spanish border.

Human interaction over the centuries in this varied physical environment has given rise to a variety of very distinct landscapes, which in many cases can be closely identified with the historic provinces of the country. The Minho in the north-west, with its relatively higher rainfall and its granite hills, has a dense rural population scattered throughout a dispersed pattern of rural settlement. The fields are extremely small and are often surrounded by vines trained over arbours, with maize, beans and potatoes providing the main ground crops. Much of the Minho remains as woodland consisting principally of maritime pine and eucalyptus trees. By contrast, the north-east of the country, Trás-os-Montes, presents a much more barren landscape with settlement nucleated into villages and small towns. Here gorse-clad slopes lead up to barren rocky summits, and agriculture is dominated by potatoes and wheat, with chestnuts and oaks being the dominant trees. Further south, the River Douro is the artery of port wine, down which countless barrels have travelled from the precipitous schist slopes of the upper valley where the grapes are grown. Across the river the provinces of Beira Litoral and Beira Alta encompass the most mountainous part of the country where the high granite peaks and once-glaciated valleys of the Serra da Estrela still have enough snow in winter to permit a little skiing. In the centre of this region, around the town of Viseu, is found one of the country's main demarcated wine regions, that of Dão, and to the west lies a flat coastal plain around Aveiro. Southwards again, the lands become increasingly dryer in summer and across the River Tagus in the Alentejo there are large expanses of wheat fields and cork plantations. Settlement here is highly nucleated, with famous walled towns, such as Évora, Estremoz and Elvas, standing out on the skylines. In the west, at the mouth of the Tagus, lies the capital, Lisbon, with its wealthy suburbs stretching out towards the open Atlantic. Nearby, the popular tourist haunts of the Serra da Sintra and the Serra da Arrábida provide welcome oases of greenery. Further south the vast expanses of the Alentejo continue until the Algarve, the southernmost province of the country, is reached. Here, groves of almonds, figs and oranges are to be found in the hinterland, and along the coast the old fishing harbours and nearby sandy beaches have now become the centres of a thriving tourist industry.

History and politics

Portugal's history prior to 1974 can be divided into five broad periods: the formation of the country and its reconquest from the Moors; the great discoveries and the rise of the empire; crisis and domination by Spain; the restoration and the constitutional monarchy; and the Republic and New State.

The emergence of Portugal

Considerable archaeological evidence of prehistoric cultures has been found throughout Portugal from the Palaeolithic to the Roman periods. Phoenician and Greek influence can be identified around the southern coasts of the country, and when the Romans arrived in the 2nd century BC they found a number of different groups of people living in what later became Portugal. They grouped these, from north to south, into the Gallaeci, the Lusitani, the Celtici and the Conii. The Romans also introduced the first main towns and comprehensive road network into the country, and impressive ruins of the deserted Roman towns of Conimbriga, Cetobriga and Mirobriga can still be seen near the modern towns of Coimbra, Setúbal and Santiago do Cacém. Under the Romans the modern area of Portugal formed part of the two provinces of Gallaecia in the north and Lusitania in the south, and these were united by a road running south from Braccara (Braga) through Potucale (Oporto) and Conimbriga to Olisipona (Lisbon) and thence to Ossonoba (near Faro).

At the beginning of the 5th century Iberia was conquered by a number of Germanic tribes, with the Suevi eventually achieving dominance. In their turn, however, the Suevi were invaded by the Visigoths in the middle of the 5th century and were finally incorporated into the Visigothic state in 585. During the period of Suevi rule, the country was converted to Christianity, and Braccara (Braga) rose to a position of ecclesiastical prominence. Between the late 6th and early 8th centuries, little is known about western Iberia, but in 711 the peninsula was invaded by Muslim forces. By 713 Lusitania and Gallaecia had fallen, and thus within two years of the initial invasion the whole peninsula came under the sway of Islam. For the next two centuries Christian rebellion centred on the north-west of Iberia, and during the 9th century Gallicia formed one of the *terrae* or provinces of the kingdom of Asturias, later known as Leon. Towards the end of the century the land between the rivers Minho and Douro was split off to form a new province, that of Portucale, and by the early 10th century its administration seems to have been centred on the towns of Guimarães, Braga and Portucale. It was this area that formed the basic hearth from which the remainder of the country of Portugal was reconquered. During the late 10th century the caliphs of Cordoba again attacked the Christian north, but with the collapse of the caliphate in 1031 and the subsequent disintegration of Muslim Spain into the small *taifa* kingdoms, the scene was set for the eventual Christian reconquest of Iberia. In 1096-97 Alfonso VI, King of Leon, Castile, Galicia and Portugal, gave the land lying in the county of Portugal, as it had by then become known, together with the land to the south centred on Coimbra to his son-in-law Henry of Burgundy.

The first half of the 12th century saw Henry's son, Afonso Henriques, gradually move Portugal towards independence from Leon and Castile. In 1143 a permanent peace settlement was arranged and in 1157 the division of Leon and Castile into two separate kingdoms considerably strengthened the position of Afonso Henriques. However, during the first quarter of the 12th century the land to the south of the River Mondego remained firmly in Muslim hands. It was not until 1147, when Afonso Henriques captured Santarém, that the expansion of the new Portuguese kingdom really began, and by 1160 with the capture of Alcácer do Sal the frontier had been pushed as far south as the River Sado. The emergence of Almohad power in north Africa in the 1150s, and their subsequent offensive in Iberia in the 1180s forced this frontier back temporarily to the Tagus. Meanwhile, in 1179 the Papacy had recognized Afonso Henriques as King of Portugal and the continuity of the new Portuguese monarchy was already assured through his son Sancho. The strength of Almohad power prevented any major Christian advances until they were able to conquer the Alentejo between 1226 and 1238. However, by 1249 in the reign of Afonso III (1245-79) Faro had been taken and with it the reconquest of modern mainland Portugal became complete. Much of this reconquest was undertaken by the various military orders, and in return the King granted them vast tracts of land. The Knights Templar thus received most of Beira Baixa together with land between the Mondego and Tagus; the Hospitalers received land in the eastern Alentejo; the Order of Calatrava, later known as the Order of Avis, received most of Alto Alentejo; and the Order of Santiago was given most of Baixo Alentejo, the peninsula of Setúbal, and much of the Algarve. It was these massive land grants that formed the basis of the large estates that came to be such a characteristic feature of southern Portugal in later centuries.

At the beginning of the 13th century the broad distinction between the north and south of the country, split by the River Tagus, had already come into existence. In the south large urban settlements, such as Lisbon, Évora, Santarém, Elvas, Beja and

Faro continued to exist, separated by wide expanses of virtually uninhabited countryside. By contrast, the north was characterized by a dense rural population, scattered in numerous small villages, with the only real towns being Oporto, Braga, Guimarães and Coimbra. Commerce and trade both within the country and also overseas was expanding, and by the 14th century Portugal was exporting a variety of goods including fruit, salt, wine, olive oil, wax, cork, leather and skins to the remainder of Europe. In exchange the Portuguese were importing considerable amounts of textiles, particularly from England. The 13th century also saw the emergence of a more formalized structure of government, with the establishment of the cortes in the 1250s. This served as the Portuguese parliament until the end of the 17th century and in its early years was mainly concerned with the provision of taxation to finance the machinery of government once the flow of tribute and booty from the Muslims had ceased.

During the reign of Afonso IV (1325-57) the great plague ravaged the country in the autumn of 1348, coinciding with a period of growing economic and social crisis. Afonso had married a Castilian princess, and had also arranged for his heir, Pedro I (1357-67), to marry likewise. Dom Pedro, however, fell in love with Inês de Castro, one of his wife's ladies-in-waiting, and this story, dramatized by António Ferreira, has become one of Portugal's most famous national legends. Afonso IV, fearing that his son was becoming increasingly influenced by her Castilian relatives, arranged for Inês to be killed, and this resulted in a brief civil war. Soon afterwards Portugal became embroiled in the wider political conflict between Spain and England, with Pedro's son, Fernando I (1367-83), initially backing John of Gaunt, the English pretender to the Castilian throne. In 1382, when the Castilians again invaded Portugal, however, Fernando made peace, and promised that his daughter Beatriz would marry Juan I of Castile thus making Juan his successor as King of Portugal.

When Fernando died in 1383, Juan I invaded Portgual, but was resisted by the middle and lower ranks of the bourgeoisie who had rallied under the leadership of João, Master of Avis, an illegitimate son of Pedro I. In April 1385 João had himself proclaimed King, and in August the smaller Portuguese army, assisted by English archers, defeated Juan and the Castilians at the Battle of Aljubarotta. In fulfilment of a promise he had made on the eye of battle, João then began the construction of the monastery at Batalha, which remains today as the finest example of Gothic architecture in Portugal. João's success in the war with Castile ranks as one of the decisive events of Portuguese history, and ensured the country's independence for the next two centuries. His victory resulted in a new dynasty, the House of Avis, and also a new ruling class, as João I brought into important political and social positions people who had formerly belonged to the bourgeoisie, the lower aristocracy and even artisans. Renewed negotiations with England were formalized in the Treaty of Windsor which provided for an eternal, solid and true league of friendship, alliance and union between the two nations, and this alliance was sealed by João I's marriage to Philippa of Lancaster, the daughter of John of Gaunt.

The Great Discoveries

At the beginning of the 15th century, João I (1385-1433) together with his sons, particularly Dom Duarte, Dom Pedro and Dom Henrique, set in motion the wheels that would soon lead to the Great Discoveries. The wars had been financially draining, and João was uneasy about the political ambitions of many of the old nobility. Overseas exploration was thus seen as a way of overcoming many of the problems that beset the country, through the hope of relieving the economic crisis, by keeping the nobility active outside Portugal itself, and by distracting attention from internal social problems. At the far western edge of Europe, with its shores washed by the Atlantic, Portugal was also fortunately placed to begin exploration overseas.

The first Portuguese foray overseas was the capture of Ceuta in Morocco in 1415. One of the main goals inspiring exploration, though, was the quest for the gold of west Africa, which was reputed to supply all of the needs of Islam. By 1419 a Portuguese expedition had reached the islands of Madeira in the Atlantic, and then in 1427 Diogo de Silves found the Azores. Many of the subsequent voyages of discovery were sponsored by João I's son, Dom Henrique, known to the English as Prince Henry the Navigator, who had been made governor of Ceuta and the Algarve, and who was also governor of the Military Order of Christ. It seems probable, however, that his main interest in these voyages was to increase his financial resources, and although he did gather around him a considerable number of sailors, navigators and knights keen on exploration, it must be noted that at least as many voyages of discovery were sponsored by the King or other nobles. In 1437 Dom Henrique, against the advice of the cortes of Évora, sent an expedition to Tangiers, but this failed dismally. His younger brother Fernando was captured and died later in captivity. The new King, Duarte, who had succeeded his father in 1433, died soon afterwards in 1438 and was in turn succeeded by his young son Afonso V, who was only six years old. A brief civil war ensued over the regency, with Dom Pedro, João I's second son, eventually becoming Regent from 1441-48. When Afonso came of age he turned against his uncle Dom Pedro who then rose in arms against the King and was killed in battle in 1449.

During the 1430s and early 1440s various exploratory voyages pushed southwards along the coast of Africa, with Cape Bojador being passed by Gil Eanes in 1434 and Cape Verde being reached in 1444. In 1443 Dom Henrique had managed to obtain a monopoly of all trade carried out on the African coast south of Cape Bojador, and by the time of his death in 1460 his ships had reached as far south as Sierra Leone. On the death of Afonso V, his son, João II (1481-95), reasserted the power of the crown, and following his grandfather's policy supported the African explorations. In 1482 Diogo Cão reached the mouth of the Congo river and Angola, and on a second voyage in 1485-86 he almost reached the Tropic of Capricorn. As well as exploration by sea, João II was also interested in establishing contacts by land with the fabled Christian kingdom of Prester John in Ethiopia, and in 1487 he sent out two emissaries, one of whom, Pero da Covilhã, travelled to India and after having sent João II a detailed report finally reached Ethiopia. At the same time Bartolomeu Dias was sent on an attempt to discover a seaway to India to unlock the source of spices and wealth there to be found. Dias reached the Cape of Good Hope in 1488, but was unable to proceed further, mainly because of the tiredness of the crew, and returned to Lisbon in December 1488 with the news that he had reached Mossel Bay.

By the end of the 15th century Lisbon had achieved a position of undoubted predominance among the urban settlements of Portugal, and it was here that much of the wealth derived from the overseas expeditions of the 16th century found its way. Increasing competition with Castile concerning the possession of newly-discovered lands was settled by the Treaty of Tordesillas in 1494, by which the earth was split into two zones of influence along a meridian line 370 leagues to the west of the Cape Verde Islands, with lands to the east belonging to Portugal. The choice of this specific meridian has given rise to speculation that the Portuguese had some knowledge of South America before the treaty, and it seems possible that an expedition had indeed been sent out to explore the west of the Atlantic in the early 1490s. By the time of João II's death in 1495, however, the Portuguese had not yet reached India. With João's only son dying in 1491, the crown passed to the Queen's younger brother Manuel (1495-1521), and it was during his reign that the east was really opened up to the Portuguese. On 8 July 1497 Vasco da Gama set sail from Lisbon and by Christmas of that year he had passed Dias's limit of exploration and reached Natal. From there he sailed to Moçambique, Mombassa and Malindi where the fleet obtained a pilot who led them to Calicut in India. Following lengthy negotiations da Gama obtained the spices which formed the goal of his expedition and after considerable hardships on the return voyage he reached Lisbon in September 1499. Six months later a fleet of thirteen ships was fitted out under the command of Pedro Álvares Cabral, and set sail in the wake of Vasco da Gama's expedition. However, Cabral sailed further to the south-west and reached Brazil in April 1500. From there he continued to India, where he arrived later in the year, and after loading up with spices he returned to Portugal in the summer of 1501 having made a considerable profit. From then on discoveries continued apace in South America, Africa and Asia, with the Portuguese reaching the Pacific in 1511, China in 1513 and Japan in the 1540s.

Until the beginning of the 16th century Portuguese interests overseas seem mainly to have been concerned with establishing contacts and trade, but when Francisco de Almeida was appointed Viceroy of India in 1505 the Portuguese embarked on a policy of building key fortresses in Africa and Asia. This policy was expanded under his successor Afonso de Albuquerque (1509-15) who conquered Goa in 1510 and made it the seat of Portuguese administration in the East. This activity brought the Portuguese into direct conflict with the Muslim forces which had previously monopolized the spice trade, and several wars were fought during the 16th century against the Egyptians and the Turks who were allied to the numerous small Islamic states in the region.

Manuel I's reign saw the influx of wealth from overseas transformed into lavish buildings and an extravagant courtly lifestyle. The architecture, known as the Manueline style, with its elaborate decoration incorporating maritime symbols, finds its best expression in the Jeronimos monastery at Belém, the Convent of Christ at Tomar, and in some of the decoration at

Batalha. Under Manuel I contacts with Spain became closer, with his son João III (1521-57) marrying the sister of Emperor Charles V, and Manuel's daughter Isabel marrying Philip II of Spain. In 1529 territorial disputes between the two countries in the Far East were settled by the Treaty of Zaragoza, and by the 1530s both economically and socially the two countries were becoming increasingly interdependent. Following the earlier establishment of the Inquisition in Spain in 1478, João III sought permission to install the Inquisition in Portugal in 1531, but this was initially resisted by the Papacy.

Under João III a governor of Brazil was appointed for the first time in 1549, and, following the establishment of firmer political control, the country's sugar production, based on plantations using African slave labour, increased appreciably. In 1555 the Portuguese also established a small trading settlement at Macão in China. João III's son had died in 1554, and when João III himself died in 1557 his grandson Sebastião (1557-78) was only a child. Consequently it was necessary to appoint a Regent, and his grandmother, the Queen of Spain, took over this role between 1557 and 1562, to be followed as Regent by Sebastião's great uncle Cardinal Henrique until 1568. Sebastião was a sickly child, fired by religious fervour, and when he took over the reins of power in 1568 he set his sights on the conquest of Morocco. Surrounding himself by a group of young flatterers he prepared the Portuguese for war, and in 1578 he embarked for Africa only to be routed by the Sultan 'Abd al-Malek at the battle of al-Qaṣr al-Kabir (Alcázar Quibir). Here the flower of the Portuguese nobility was killed, along with Sebastião himself. However, rumours began to circulate that Sebastião had mysteriously disappeared during the battle, and later in the century this was to give rise to the belief that one day he would return and claim his throne. When news of the disaster reached Lisbon the ailing Cardinal Henrique, Sebastião's great-uncle, was crowned King. Two years later, however, when he died, Philip II of Spain invaded Portugal and claimed the throne. Just before Philip II entered the country, Portugal's most famous poet, Luís Vaz de Camões, also died, and with him the great period of discoveries, about which he wrote so eloquently in his poem *Os Lusíadas*, can also be seen as coming to an end.

Domination by Spain
The Spanish conquest was initially extremely unpopular, but Philip II was nevertheless able to cajole the Church and the

nobility into supporting him, and in practice under his rule the Portuguese maintained a large degree of autonomy, particularly in the field of administration. Resistance to the Spanish Crown initially focused around the issue of Sebastianism, and several pretenders, claiming to be the returning King Sebastião, emerged during Philip II's reign (1580-98). None were sufficiently convincing, and by the end of the 16th century the Spanish had achieved considerable domination over Portugal. Under Philip II's successors, Philip III (1598-1621) and Philip IV (1621-40), however, increasing attempts by Spain to exploit Portugal, particularly through new taxes and military service, led to growing dissatisfaction. At the same time the Dutch were becoming increasingly powerful as a maritime force, and were challenging Portugal's hegemony of power in Africa, Brazil and the Far East. Within Europe the Spanish were also increasingly in conflict with France, and when João, the Duke of Bragança, emerged as the focus for Portuguese national independence, to be acclaimed King as João IV in 1640, virtually the whole country rallied to his support. A cortes was then assembled at Lisbon in 1641 to raise money for the defence of the kingdom against Spain and to make legitimate João IV's accession.

The Restoration and the Constitutional Monarchy
João IV's reign was beset by problems from the very beginning. Dissension split the Portuguese people with many of the nobility, merchants and clergy still supporting the Spanish claimant to the throne, and a frontier war continued throughout his reign. Overseas the Dutch were making deep inroads into Portugal's possessions with Malacca falling in 1641 and Portugal's Arabian possessions being lost in the 1650s. However, in Brazil, following ten years of rebellion, the Portuguese were able to gain a complete victory over the Dutch in 1654.

When João IV died in 1656 he was succeeded by his son Afonso VI who was both paralysed and also of unsound mental health. Consequently the Queen Mother, Luisa, was appointed as Regent. The lack of strong leadership at this time gave rise to the loss of further overseas territory, a Dutch blockade of Lisbon in 1657, and considerable internal discord within Portugal. In 1661 a peace treaty was eventually drawn up with Holland, and, France having made peace with Spain in 1660, Portugal once again turned to England for military assistance. This coincided with the Restoration in England, and on 6 June 1661 a treaty was agreed between the two countries by which Catarina of Bragança

João IV's daughter, would marry Charles II of England, and England would in turn help to defend Portugal against the Spanish. In Catarina's dowry Bombay and Tangiers were also ceded to the English, thus further weakening Portugal's hold on its remaining territories in Asia. The renewed Spanish offensive of 1661, which led a year later to the loss of Borba and then Évora, culminated in the removal of Luisa from power as Regent, and the reins of government being taken over by the King and a group of nobles led by Luís de Vasconcelos e Sousa, Count of Castelo Melhor. Soon afterwards the Portuguese recaptured Évora after the Battle of Ameixial in June 1663, and when Philip IV of Spain died in 1665, a few months after another Portuguese victory at Montes Claros, conditions were ripe for a formal peace settlement between the two countries. In 1667 Afonso VI's brother, Pedro, forced the removal of Castelo Melhor from power, took the title of Prince Regent, imprisoned Afonso VI, and restored the traditional power of the nobles. This acquisition of power by a new government led to further negotiations with Spain and a peace treaty was eventually signed in 1668.

The peace with Spain inaugurated a century of relative political stability. Overseas most of Portugal's empire in the Far East had been lost, but Brazil and the Atlantic islands of the Azores and Madeira remained firmly in Portuguese hands. When Afonso VI died in 1683 Pedro took the title of King, as Pedro II, and sought to establish new economic links within Europe. In 1703 Portugal joined England, Holland and Austria in the Grand Alliance against France and Spain, and associated with this a commercial agreement known as the Methuen Treaty was also signed. This provided for increased trade between Portugal and England, with Portugal permitting the regular import of English woollen textiles, and England agreeing to allow the import of Portuguese wines at a rate of customs duty no higher than that paid by French wines. Pedro II died soon afterwards in 1706 and was succeeded by his son João V (1706-50), during whose long reign Portugal's economy expanded rapidly, but not as a result of the Methuen Treaty which was seen by many as creating severe constraints for Portugal's own textile industry.

The new source of wealth for Portugal resulted from the discovery of gold in Brazil at the end of the 17th century. The first gold shipments to Portugal started at the turn of the 18th century, and by 1720 it is estimated that they had reached a peak of more than 25,000 kilogrammes. Thereafter gold production declined and by the early 19th century only very small quantities were being shipped. In addition to gold, considerable amounts of diamonds were also exploited, and these two sources of revenue enabled João V to embark on an extravagant display of opulence. The court vied with that of Louis XIV of France for splendour, and numerous churches and mansions were built by the nobility, the most famous of these being the monastery at Mafra begun by command of the king following the birth of his heir. With the profits from Brazil's mines being spent on conspicuous consumption, insufficient attention was paid to Portugal's internal economy, and, although glass, paper and leather production received some royal support, the dearth of industrial investment was clearly visible by the time of João V's death in 1750.

The new King, José (1750-77) appointed Sebastião José de Carvalho e Melo as Prime Minister, raising him to Count of Oeiras in 1759 and to Marquis of Pombal in 1770, and under Pombal's rule the power of the Church and old nobility waned, while that of the bourgeoisie grew markedly. Five years after the start of the new reign Lisbon was hit by the devastating earthquake of 1755 and this provided Pombal with the opportunity to rebuild the capital in a grand style. Three years later anger amongst the nobility against Pombal and his measures culminated in a plot led by the Duke of Aveiro to kill the King. The discovery of this plot provided Pombal with the opportunity to arrest and banish many of the nobility, and also to expel the Jesuits who were closely implicated in the plot. Under Pombal Portugal's tax system was thoroughly reformed, and the power of the merchants rose appreciably with exports of wine reaching new records. Increased imports of raw materials, particularly from Brazil, also led to some real industrial expansion within Portugal and this focused mainly around the ports. Pombal's power, however, lasted only as long as José's reign, and upon the King's death in 1777, Pombal was summarily dismissed by his daughter Maria I.

Maria I ruled first with her husband, and then by herself until 1791 when she was declared insane, and her son João took over as Regent. Although Pombal's enemies were rehabilitated, the social reforms that he had introduced proved to be lasting. On the political front Maria I and her son abandoned the clear alliance with Britain and played a delicate game of diplomacy with the other great powers of the day, France and Spain. In 1801 Spain and France nevertheless declared war and forced Portugal to close her ports to the British fleet and also to pay a heavy indemnity. Trade with Britain, though, seems to have continued, and in 1807 Napoleon ordered the Portuguese to declare war against Britain. This they were unwilling to do, and with French armies under Andoche Junot consequently invaded Portugal. As they did so, the royal family and court left Lisbon and sailed for Brazil, where the new capital was established at Rio de Janeiro.

The French and Spanish invaders were universally unpopular, and a guerilla war began immediately. In June 1808 open revolution broke out in the north with a Provisional Junta being established in Oporto. In July the British under Sir Arthur Wellesley came to their assistance entering Portugal from Galicia, and together with Portuguese forces Wellesley then defeated the French at the battles of Roliça and Vimeiro. However, in the truce that followed, which was ratified at the Convention of Sintra, Junot was able to leave Portugal with all his troops. They were also permitted to take with them most of their booty without having to pay for any of the damages that they had inflicted on Portugal, and this gave rise to considerable anger within Portugal. The following year the British General William Beresford became a Field Marshal in the Portuguese army and set about reorganizing the country's defences.

Early in 1809 the French under Soult again invaded, this time from the north, but they were rapidly driven out by the combined Anglo-Portuguese army. The French campaign of 1810 was then placed under the command of Marshal Masséna who attacked across the eastern border from Spain. In September the French were beaten by Wellesley at the Battle of Buçaco, but they were nevertheless able to push on to the lines of Torres Vedras which formed a defensive ring around Lisbon. Here the Anglo-Portuguese army held firm, and gradually wore down the French who eventually ran out of supplies and were forced to retreat, being defeated again at Redinha before being pushed back into Spain and then to France itself.

The four years of war had severely damaged the Portuguese economy, and in the political sphere had also left the country in an unusual position, being both a British protectorate and a Brazilian colony between 1808 and 1821. In 1815, when Maria I died, her son, the Regent, became King as João VI. He declared Brazil a united kingdom with Portugal and the Algarve, but showed no desire to return to Europe. As a result Beresford, who was fully in charge of the army, became virtual ruler of the country. Economically weak, Portugal was unable financially to support the army, and a growing crisis erupted into a revolution in 1820, beginning in Oporto and leading to the introduction of Liberal Constitutionalism. João VI returned to Portugal in 1821, leaving his son Pedro as Emperor of Brazil, and in 1822 a new Constitution based on the Spanish Constitution of 1812 was accepted. The 1822 Constitution, however, proved to be highly unpopular and with the independence of Brazil anti-liberal feeling focused on Dom Pedro's brother Dom Miguel and the Queen, Carlota Joaquina. In 1826, when João VI died, his eldest son became Pedro IV of Portugal, but with neither the Brazilians nor the British being prepared to accept the reunification of the two crowns he quickly abdicated on behalf of his seven-year-old daughter Maria II, with the proviso that she marry her uncle Dom Miguel who would act as Regent. This attempt by Dom Pedro at achieving a compromise between the liberal position and the extreme views of his brother, was further enhanced by his introduction of a much more conservative Constitutional Charter in 1826. When Dom Miguel returned to Portugal in 1828, however, all attempts at conciliation disappeared, and, firmly attaching himself to the absolutist cause, Dom Miguel convened a new cortes which declared him King in July 1828. In 1829 the Azores revolted against Dom Miguel and upheld the liberal cause, but uprisings in Oporto and elsewhere on the mainland failed until 1831 when Dom Pedro abdicated the crown of Brazil in favour of his son and turned his attention to Portugal itself. In 1832, having gained some English and French support, Dom Pedro landed near Oporto and full civil war broke out between the liberals supporting Dom Pedro and the Miguelites advocating absolutism. The liberals entered Oporto but were then besieged there for a year until the summer of 1833 when liberal forces attacked the Algarve and then marched on Lisbon which they occupied in July. News of the defeat in the south forced Dom Miguel to abandon the siege of Oporto, and following further battles in 1834 Dom Miguel acknowledged defeat in the Treaty of Evoramonte.

In an effort to break the power of the Church and to overcome the financial crisis in which the liberals found themselves, Pedro immediately introduced an act to eliminate all religious orders and to confiscate their property. However Pedro himself quickly became unpopular and when he died later in the year his daughter, Maria II, although still only a child was declared Queen and of age. Initially a conservative régime was introduced, but this was overthrown by the Septembrists in 1836, who abolished the Constitutional Charter of 1826 and returned to a variant of the 1822 Constitution. By 1842 power had again shifted to the right, and the Charter was restored at Oporto. Warfare between the two sides continued until 1851 when the Duke of Saldanha, who had long supported the liberal cause rose up again at Oporto and forced Maria II to entrust him with the powers of government. By this time there was wide agreement that there was a need for a period of peace and reorganization, and in 1852 an amendment to the Constitutional Charter finally brought peace between the Chartists and Septembrists and introduced a period of relative calm in the country's political structure. In 1853, when Maria II died, her son Pedro was not of age and the powers of Regent were taken over by his father until 1855. Pedro V, however, died of typhus in 1861, and the succession thus passed to his brother Luís I who reigned until 1889.

This period of stability lasted until the late 1880s, and was followed by a severe political and economic crisis, provoked by the British ultimatum of 1890 that Portugal should give up its African territories. Over the previous twenty years there had been a growing tide of Republicanism in Portugal, and when the Brazilians rejected Pedro IV's son and declared themselves a Republic, the financial repercussions for Portugal exacerbated an already fragile situation. In 1889 Carlos I took over the throne of Portugal on his father's death, and two years later the first Republican uprisings occurred in Oporto. The new King did not enjoy the support that his father had held, and in 1908 after a period of considerable unrest both the King and the heir to the throne, Luís Filipe, were shot and killed in Lisbon. Carlos I was succeeded by his younger son Manuel II, and an attempt was made to appease the Republicans. However, it became clear after two years in which six different governments were appointed, that by 1910 the monarchy was at an end. In August the Republicans did well in the general elections, winning seven seats in Lisbon and four in other parts of the country, and by October the royal family was forced to flee the country as a Republican revolution overthrew the last vestiges of the monarchy.

The Republic and the New State
At the beginning of the First Republic Portugal's economy was dominated by her agriculture, with wine, cork and fruit being the main exports. However, despite attempts to improve agriculture in the 19th century, including the suppression of entailed estates in 1863, grain production remained low and considerable food

imports were necessary. Lacking major deposits of coal and iron ore, industrial production focused on textiles and fish canning. No sooner had the Republic been declared, however, than Portugal, being fearful of German interests in her African territories, became embroiled in the First World War on the side of the British and the French. After the end of the war, increased social disturbances, the disintegration of the Republican party into six branches, and growing economic chaos, provided the background against which a military coup took place in May 1926. The Republic was overthrown and the scene was set for the emergence of a particular blend of Portuguese Fascism, based on Lusitanian Integralism, a Catholic revival, and increasingly nationalist sentiments.

In 1928 General Carmona was formally elected President, and he immediately appointed Dr. António de Oliveira Salazar, Professor of Economics at Coimbra University, as Finance Minister with a brief to reform the economy. For the next forty years Salazar was to dominate Portugal's political scene, becoming Prime Minister in 1932 and remaining in office until he suffered a cerebral haemorrhage in 1968. In 1933, during the depths of the Great Depression, Salazar promulgated the Constitution which laid down the principles for his New State based upon a corporatist ideology. Under the New State both employers and workers were organized together into guilds and syndicates. Strikes were prohibited, and the power of labour organizations was minimized. There was to be extensive state management of the economy, but at the same time the means of production were to be held in private hands. Individual freedom was to be sacrificed to the benefit of the nation, and all political parties and secret societies were disbanded. Strict censorship was introduced, and during the 1930s a secret and political police force, the PVDE (Polícia de Vigilância e Defesa do Estado), was established. This changed its name after 1945 to the Polícia Internacional e de Defesa do Estado (PIDE) and its activities were later to play a significant role in leading to unrest within the country.

In the early stages of the New State, Salazar's fiscal policies were able to convert the country's previous heavy deficits into surpluses, and throughout his régime considerable stability was ensured through a balanced budget. In the Second World War Portugal remained neutral, but in the period of regeneration following the war its economy was unable to grow as fast as that of the other poor European countries. Perhaps more significantly, the social and cultural restrictions imposed on the

Portuguese people and their relative isolation from the mainstream of European affairs added to the growing tensions within the country. Until the 1960s Portugal's economic policy remained inward-looking, but with the beginning of the independence movements in the African territories, which started in Angola in 1961, Guinea in 1963 and Moçambique in 1964, attention became increasingly focused overseas. In an attempt to retain the position by which these territories were an integral part of the Portuguese State, it became essential to try and develop their economies. As guerrilla activity expanded, increased numbers of troops had to be sent overseas to keep order, and by 1968 more than 100,000 Portuguese forces were on active duty in Africa.

The relative stagnation of Portugal's domestic economy also gave rise to extensive emigration from the poorest areas of the country in the north and east to the cities and to other countries of Europe in search of better employment prospects. Between 1961 and 1970 more than 1,300,000 people thus emigrated overseas, particularly to France, seeking greater prosperity. As the economic and political crisis deepened, internal dissension was met with swift retribution by the PIDE, and as Salazar increasingly lost touch with the situation the practical running of the state came to lie more and more in the hands of the secret police and the censors. In 1968 the leader of the opposition, Mário Soares, who eventually became Portugal's President in 1986, was deported overseas, and by the time Salazar suffered his cerebral haemorrhage it was evident that the New State was in imminent danger of collapse. When Salazar's incapacity was confirmed President Tomes appointed Marcello Caetano, Rector of the University of Lisbon, to be his successor as Prime Minister. In many ways Caetano was caught in a cleft stick, unable to continue the repressive régime that had been maintained under Salazar and yet at the same time being unwilling radically to move to the left.

Increasing expenditure overseas, inflation running at thirty per cent, discontent with the African wars, increasing social unrest, and a weak agricultural sector all exacerbated an already tense situation. The immediate cause of the 1974 revolution, though, lay with the doubts instilled in the minds of the troops in Africa who came face to face with the communist doctrine of the liberation movements they were fighting. This had given rise to the formation of the Movimento das Forças Armadas (MFA) by a group of disillusioned army officers with the expressed aim of bringing down the Caetano régime.

Introduction

The 1974 revolution and its aftermath

On 25 April 1974 the MFA, acting with the support of the underground Communist and Socialist parties, made their move, and in the early hours of the morning captured key targets in Lisbon. Army units mutinied throughout the country, and by the afternoon Caetano was forced to hand over power. People poured out into the streets of Lisbon and other major cities, and the red carnations carried by the demonstrators and placed in the guns of the soldiers became one of the key symbols of the revolution. Power was placed in the hands of a Junta and on 15 May General Spinola, one of the heroes of the African wars, was appointed President of the Republic. Tensions within the MFA, and between the Communist Party and the Socialist Party, came to a head later in the year, and at the end of September Spinola resigned, to be replaced by General Costa Gomes who then held the titles both of President and of Chief of Staff of the Armed Forces. Meanwhile the process of decolonization had begun, and on 10 September following negotiations by the Foreign Minister, Mário Soares, Guinea-Bissau was granted its independence. In March 1975 Spinola attempted a counter-coup, but this failed, and on 25 April 1975, the first anniversary of the revolution, Portugal held free elections for the first time since 1926. In these, among the major parties, the Partido Socialista (PS) won thirty-eight per cent of the vote, the Partido Popular Democrático (PPD) won twenty-six per cent, the Partido Comunista Portugues (PCP) won thirteen per cent, the Centro Democrático Social (CDS) won eight per cent, and the Movimento Democrático Portugues (MDP) won four per cent.

During 1975 political and economic chaos continued, but, despite this, a programme of nationalization and land reform was set underway, and the remaining African territories were granted their independence, giving rise to an influx of about 650,000 returnees from Africa. On 25 November 1975 a further counter-coup, this time by the far left, failed, and in April 1976 in the Assembly elections the Partido Socialista was confirmed in power, winning thirty-five per cent of the vote and forming a minority government. Just prior to the elections the new Constitution, which attempted to strike a balance between the powers of the President, the government, the Assembly and the military, was approved on 2 April 1976. Some form of stability was eventually achieved later in the year when General Ramalho Eanes was elected President of the Republic and General Chief of Staff of the Armed Forces with sixty-one per cent of the vote.

Introduction

The late 1970s were also characterized by considerable political turmoil and economic upheaval as the country came to grips with the new freedoms of a restored democracy. The lack of unified political direction at this time is reflected in the observation that in the decade following 1974 fifteen different governments were in power. Until the end of the 1970s all of these governments were formed from various left-wing and socialist alliances, but since then there has been a shift to the right, with the Aliança Democrática being in power between December 1979 and April 1983, and the Partido Social Democrático (PSD) under Anibal Cavaco Silva defeating the socialists in the October 1985 elections. In the Presidential elections, Eanes was re-elected for his maximum second period of office in 1980, and at the beginning of 1986 at the next elections Mário Soares was elected President.

The economy

Portugal's economy remains in an uncertain position despite the country's recent accession to the European Community, which is seen by many as offering a real hope of economic improvement. The period of political upheaval in the mid-1970s coincided with the rapid increases of oil prices in 1973 and 1974. Coming on top of the growing economic crisis of the 1960s this gave rise to severe economic problems which would have presented considerable difficulties even without the political turmoil surrounding the events of 25 April 1974. In addition, the return of both soldiers and civilians from the African territories led to greater unemployment within Portugal, high interest rates retarded investment, and considerable political uncertainty reduced international investment in the economy. During 1974 and 1975 it is estimated that about sixty per ent of the country's productive capacity was nationalized, and in 1975 the real Gross Domestic Product (GDP) declined by 4.3 per cent.

Over the next six years, however, between 1976 and 1982, the GDP expanded by an average five per cent per annum as a result of policies aimed at maintaining employment levels and sustaining domestic demand. This was achieved at the cost of an increased government deficit, a growth in external debt, and the maintenance of a large and inefficient public sector. At the end of 1982 Portugal's balance of payment on its current account was thus in deficit to the tune of $3,245 million and the total public debt was

$13,640 million. In 1983, therefore, when the PS under Mário Soares came to power, they introduced an emergency economic programme following a financial package agreement with the International Monetary Fund (IMF). This programme has been based mainly on the close control of domestic demand and on the re-allocation of resources to the export sector. As a result, the deficit on the current account fell from 13.9 per cent of the Gross National Product in 1982 to only 2.7 per cent in 1984, and inflation has also fallen markedly from a peak of 33 per cent in July 1984. Towards the end of 1984 a Plan for Financial and Economic Recovery was introduced, and this seeks to achieve a relatively satisfactory level of economic activity by the end of 1987.

In June 1985, after several years of detailed negotiations, Portugal eventually signed the treaty of accession to the European Community, and on 1 January 1986 formally joined it. Over the next decade a complex series of transition agreements will bring Portugal into line with the remaining countries of the Community, with State aid to the steel industry being phased out over five years, and the State's exclusive marketing rights for petroleum products being phased out over seven years. In agriculture there will be a ten-year phased transition period for cereals and rice, eggs and poultry, beef and veal, milk and milk products, fresh fruit and vegetables, and wine.

The levels of both Portugal's industrial and agricultural production remain well below those of most other countries in western Europe. Within industry, textiles and food processing remain dominant, but increasing investment is leading to the modernization and development of some other sectors such as chemicals, petroleum and shipbuilding. The country's industry is strongly localized, being focused mainly in the north around Oporto, where textiles dominate, and also in the region around Lisbon and Setúbal, where metallurgy, engineering and general manufacturing are of most importance. The oil price rises of 1973-1974 and 1978 forced the country to look to sources of power other than oil, and an ambitious programme has been implemented to switch much of the country's generating capacity to coal. The mid-1980s have seen the textile industry remaining relatively prosperous, but there has been a severe recession in the construction industry, much of which operates outside the formal economy.

Most Portuguese manufacturing firms are very small-scale, with seventy per cent employing less than ten people in 1982. There are nevertheless several large industrial companies, such as the Lisnave ship-repair yard on the Tagus, the Setenave ship construction yard at Setúbal, and several motor vehicle assembly plants elsewhere in the country. In addition a major industrial growth pole including a petrochemicals plant and an oil refinery is being developed at Sines. The 1974 revolution led to certain manufacturing sectors being taken over by the State, and a number of major manufacturing firms in the paper, steel, cement, chemicals, shipbuilding and brewing industries remain State-owned. Most of the smaller firms have, though, been returned to their former owners, and eighty-seven per cent of the country's industrial workforce is now employed in the private sector.

Another characteristic of Portugal's industry is its labour-intensive nature, and with the labour laws introduced after 1974 it is extremely difficult for companies to lay off workers. With the return of many migrant workers who had previously found employment elsewhere in Europe, and the influx of people from the African territories, unemployment became a serious problem during the 1970s, and the need to balance this against the constraints imposed by overmanning has caused severe difficulties for successive Portuguese governments.

The agricultural sector also needs comprehensive reorganization. Agriculture still employs about one-quarter of the country's labour force, but in 1983 it only accounted for 8.4 per cent of the GDP, and Portugal still has to import approximately half its food requirements. In 1983 agricultural imports alone accounted for almost seventeen per cent of the country's total import bill. Average yields for 1982-83 were among the lowest in Europe, with wheat yields of 988 kg/ha, rye yields of 698 kg/ha, maize yields of 1,364 kg/ha and potato yields of 7,493 kg/ha. Portugal's agriculture prior to 1974 could broadly be distinguished into two types. In the north and west thousands of farmers cultivated tiny plots of land in a mixed, and largely subsistence, economy, producing maize, beans, potatoes, a variety of vegetables, cattle and wine. By contrast, in the south large private estates concentrated on the extensive production of wheat and cork. This division has given rise to two different sets of problems in the aftermath of the revolution. One of the first important measures introduced by the new government was a comprehensive agrarian reform programme. By the end of 1975 over 1.5 million hectares of land had been expropriated and a further 700,000 hectares had been taken over illegally by agricultural workers, with the vast majority of both types of enforced change taking place in the south of the country in the Alentejo and Ribatejo. During 1976 the new Socialist government announced that illegally-occupied land should be returned to its former owners, and this process was taken further in the Land Reform Law of 1977. With the shift in political power to the right at the end of the 1970s the pace of handing back land increased, but about 2.5 million hectares still remain in the form of collectives. In the wake of this land reform there was an initial fall in production, coinciding with poor harvests in 1976 and 1978. Since then there has been some recovery, but production of wheat in 1982 and 1983 still remained below the average for the previous ten years.

In the north of the country the fundamental problem limiting increased agricultural production is the small size, and subdivided nature, of the agricultural holdings, with government figures suggesting that in the north-west about half of all holdings are less than one hectare in size. Under these conditions, with most farmers having fields dispersed throughout their villages, it is extremely difficult to see how productivity levels can easily be increased.

Apart from industry and agriculture, tourism also plays an important role in the economy, with tourist receipts reaching more than $1,000 million in 1981, when over seven million visitors, mostly from Spain, came to the country. The main tourist regions are the Algarve and the area around Lisbon, but considerable numbers of tourists also visit Madeira, and efforts are being made to develop the Costa Verde north of Oporto as another tourist region.

Turning to the financial sector, all Portuguese banks were nationalized in 1975, and, following a number of mergers, eight major banking groups emerged. In 1982 the revisions in the Constitution opened the way for renewed private ownership of banks and since then a small number of new banks have been established. High interest rates, introduced as part of the emergency austerity package, have been a characteristic feature of recent years and have placed a considerable constraint on industrial investment.

The outlook for Portugal's economy remains uncertain, but some aspects of accession to the European Community and the dramatic fall in oil prices in 1985 and 1986 provide some grounds for optimism. Appreciable advances have to be made in the agricultural sector, and it would seem that it is here that most problems will be encountered despite the extensive funding for agricultural development which is being made available by the European Community. Industry, which has previously benefited from low labour costs, will have to face an increasingly higher wages bill, and it will also suffer from growing competition from other more efficient European countries as tariff barriers are removed. However, there are already signs of an economic recovery underway, with economic growth in 1986 expected to be around 4 per cent compared with 2.5 per cent in 1985, and inflation down to about 12 per cent as against 19 per cent in the previous year. Much will depend, however, on the ability of the Portuguese government to take advantage of the net inflows from the Community budget, which, in Portugal's first year of membership, are likely to be worth between $200 million and $300 million.

The Country and Its People

1 **Alfama, Lisbon, Portugal.**
Norberto de Araújo, with drawings by Ingeborg von Erlach,
photographs by Armando Serôdio, Herácio Novais.   Lisbon: Lisbon
City Council, [no date]. 84p.
A pictorial celebration of the old city of Lisbon, the Alfama, in drawings and
photographs.

2 **Cavaliers of Portugal, with a glossary of bullfighting terms.**
Huldine Beamish.   London: Geoffrey Bles, 1966. 146p. map.
bibliog.
This illustrated account of Portuguese bullfighting is divided into chapters on the
bulls, the horses, the men, training and technique, the pega, the cavaliers and the
bullrings. It concludes with a short glossary of bullfighting terminology.

3 **Portugal of the Portuguese.**
Aubrey F. G. Bell.   London: Pitman, 1915. 268p. map.
This account of the people, life and culture of Portugal was written in the early
20th century. It provides a succinct historical and geographical survey and in
particular has useful chapters on literature and drama.

4 **Portugal.**
Yves Bottineau, with 166 photographs by Yan.   London: Thames &
Hudson, 1957. 2nd ed., 1962. 304p. map.
Provides an extensively-illustrated account of Portugal in the 1960s which, after
an introductory chapter, is divided into sections on the different regions of the
country: Oporto and the north; Coimbra and its surroundings; Tomar to Nazaré;
Lisbon and the River Tagus; Évora and the Alentejo; and the Algarve in the
south.

1

5 **Portugal.**
   Sarah Bradford. London: Thames & Hudson, 1973. 176p. map.
   bibliog. (New Nations and Peoples Library).

A lucid account of the country and people of Portugal prior to the events of 1974. After an initial chapter describing the provinces of the country, the next ten chapters provide an historical account from the arrival of the Romans to Caetano's period of rule in the late 1960s. This is followed by chapters on economic change, foreign relations, social structure and the prospects for the future. There is also a short 'who's who' of the more important people in Portuguese history.

6 **The land and people of Portugal.**
   Denis Brass. London: Adam & Charles Black; New York:
   Macmillan, 1960. 90p. map.

Presents a short introduction to the history, economy and people of Portugal. An appendix provides limited geographical and economic statistics.

7 **Portugal.**
   Roy Campbell. London: Max Reinhardt, 1957. 206p.

Provides a highly personal account of Portugal and its people based on the author's experiences in the country. After chapters on fruit and trees, wine, underwater fishing, horsemen and horses, and bullfighting, three detailed chapters cover Portuguese poetry, prose and the fado. These include translations by the author of several Portuguese poems. The author asserts that during the 1940s and 1950s Portugal experienced a remarkable rebirth under the guidance of Premier António de Oliveira Salazar, and the book includes numerous anecdotes concerning the author's activities in the Spanish Civil War.

8 **Saudades.**
   Frances S. Dabney. Boston, Massachusetts: Privately printed at
   Merrymount Press, 1903. 103p.

A collection of eighteen short prose pieces relating to the Azores on such subjects as the vintage, the old fig tree, the sierra and night fishing.

9 **The Azores.**
   Claude Dervenn. (pseudonym of Claude le Bayon). London:
   Harrap, 1956. 165p. map.

An extensively-illustrated account of the Azores in the 1950s, divided into chapters on each of the islands. The text provides a general introduction to the history, economy and way of life of the people living there prior to the mid-20th century.

10 **Madeira.**

Claude Dervenn (pseudonym of Claude le Bayon), translated by Frances Hogarth-Gaute. London: Harrap, no date [ca. 1957]. 151p. map.

This illustrated introduction to the Madeira archipelago is divided into chapters on a geographical basis and provides a wide range of information on the lifestyles and customs of the islands' inhabitants.

11 **Portugal.**

Jean Dieuzaide, complete text by Hans Seligo, translated by G. A. Colville. Munich: William Andermann Verlag, 1959. 62p.

Presents a description of Portugal in the 1950s, illustrated by a series of photographs, the majority of which are by Jean Dieuzaide. Specific attention is paid to Lisbon, Coimbra, Oporto, Belém, Costa do Sol, Sintra, the azulejos (decorative tiles) and the monasteries of Alcobaça, Batalha and Tomar.

12 **Portugal: the country and its people.**

John Eppstein. London: Queen Anne Press, 1967. 114p. 3 maps. bibliog.

This short introduction to the country and people of Portugal has chapters on geography, the life of the people, history, the constitution and political life, economic change, education and literature, and foreign relations.

13 **Madeira, Portugal.**

Willy Heinzelmann. Basel, Switzerland: Willy Heinzelmann, 1971. 88p.

This short introduction to Madeira covers its history, geography, habitations, fauna and flora, economy, customs, embroidery, wine and legends of the past.

14 **Coast of the sun.**

Henry C. James. London: Jarrolds, 1956. 176p.

This personal account of Portugal in the mid-20th century provides a general description of the lifestyle and economy of Portuguese people.

15 **The road to Alto: an account of peasants, capitalists and the soil in the mountains of southern Portugal.**

Robin Jenkins. London: Pluto Press, 1979. 158p. 6 maps. bibliog.

An analysis of the relationship between ecology, class structure and the economy in a rural community in the Serra de Monchique. Based upon the experiences of the author when he farmed some rented terraces there in 1976, it provides a fascinating account of the way of life in a southern Portuguese community. It also presents a wide-ranging account of the so-called 'development' of a primitive community, its subordination to the demands of the external world and its consequent rapid decline.

16 **Area handbook for Portugal.**
Eugene K. Keefe, David P. Coffin, Sallie M. Hicks, William A.
Mussen Jr., Robert Rinehart, William J. Simon. Washington, DC:
US Government Printing Office, 1977. 456p. 18 maps. bibliog.

This comprehensive introduction to Portugal is divided into main sections on
social, political, economic and national security affairs. The social section covers
Portugal's history, physical environment, population and living conditions, social
and education systems, religious life and the arts. The political section deals with
the government, political dynamics, foreign relations and mass communications.
In the economics section there is a general chapter on the character and structure
of the economy, followed by a chapter on agriculture and industry, and with
further coverage of trade, transport and services. The final section deals with the
armed forces, public order and internal security. There is a useful glossary and a
comprehensive bibliography including much journal material published in the
USA.

17 **Madeira: old and new.**
W. H. Koebel, with photographs by Mildred Cossart. London:
Francis Griffiths, 1909. 216p.

This wide-ranging historical account of the islands of the Madeira archipelago is
based mainly on the information given to the author by British residents in
Madeira. It provides extensive details on the way of life of the people, the
economy, agriculture, irrigation, health, viticulture, religion and tourism in
Madeira. The 134 photographs provide a fascinating insight into what Madeira
was like at the beginning of the 20th century.

18 **Portugal: its land and people.**
W. H. Koebel, illustrated by S. Roope Dockery. London:
Archibald Constable, 1909. 405p.

Provides a detailed and expansive account of Portugal at the beginning of the 20th
century based on the author's experiences there. The first five chapters deal with
Lisbon and cover its history as well as its buildings, museums, ancient landmarks,
transport and entertainments. Two chapters on the region around Lisbon
including the towns of Cintra and Estoril are followed by a further six covering
various aspects of the Alentejo province and southern Portugal, including details
of a cork forest, a farm, the Quinta do Carmo and various towns in the region.
The next four chapters look at Évora, the far north and the Minho region, with
four more chapters on Oporto and its English residents. These are followed by
two chapters on the Douro valley, concentrating on its wine production, and one
chapter on the market at Arrifana. There is then a chapter on places to be found
on a journey from Oporto to Lisbon, before the book concludes with a
description of a Portuguese bullfight and two chapters on the Portuguese at home.

19 **Madeira: impressions and associations.**
Alan Lethbridge. London: Methuen, 1924. 199p.

An introduction to the history, scenery, customs and economy of Madeira in the
early 20th century.

20 **Palácios portugueses; Portuguese palaces and castles: Palais et châteaux portuguais. 1° volume.**
Edited by Raul Lino. Lisbon: Secretaria de Estado da Informação e Turismo, 1972. [not paginated].

This extensively-illustrated volume in English, French and Portuguese describes the palaces of Sintra, Évora, Guimarães, Vila Vicosa, Mafra, Queluz and Ajuda, and the castle of Pena.

21 **Portugal and Brazil: an introduction.**
Edited by H. V. Livermore with the assistance of W. J. Entwistle. Oxford: Clarendon Press, 1953. 418p.

A memorial volume to Edgar Prestage and Aubrey Fitz Gerald Bell who contributed much to the study of Portugal. The following chapters are concerned specifically with Portugal: 'The Portuguese and Brazilian language', by William J. Entwistle; 'The land', by William J. Entwistle; 'The Portuguese character', by Marcus Cheke; 'Portuguese history', by H. V. Livermore; 'Religion', by William J. Entwistle; 'Institutions and Law', by William C. Atkinson; 'Perspectives of Portuguese literature', by Aubrey Fitz Gerald Bell; 'Portuguese literature in English translation', by Carlos Estorninho; 'Contemporary Portuguese writing', by B. da S. Vidigal; 'Architecture', by J. B. Bury; 'Painting', by Carlos de Azevedo; and 'Music', by Ann Livermore.

22 **Portugal.**
Frederic P. Marjay. Lisbon: Livraria Bertrand, 1967. 246p.

A brief introductory section written in English and Portuguese which covers the following themes: early history; the arts; Oporto; Coimbra; Lisbon; Évora; Algarve; industrial development; and tourism. This is followed by 206 pages of photographs of Portugal and its people, some of which are in colour.

23 **Impressions of Madeira in the past.**
Luis de Sousa Melo, Susan E. Farrow. Funchal, Portugal: English Bookshop, 1983. 60p. 2 maps.

Provides a collection of old photographs showing the lifestyles of the people and the landscapes of Madeira, together with a text covering aspects of the society and economy of the islands in the 19th and 20th centuries. It covers the following themes: the countryside; economic activities; emigration; tourism; social and religious activities; transport; and the old town of Funchal.

24 **A glimpse of Madeira.**
Cecil H. Miles. London: Peter Garnett, 1949. 147p.

This illustrated introduction to the islands of Madeira does not aim to be a guidebook, but rather a 'picture of this island, its people and its customs, against their true background', presenting 'the co-ordinated ramblings of a dreamer's mind'. In passing, it gives details of the country's history, economy, culture and landscapes.

25   **Portugal.**
Henry Myhill.   London: Faber & Faber, 1972. 248p. map. bibliog.

Presenting a general account of the provinces and cities of Portugal, the volume also provides information on the country's history, architecture, arts and economic change. A concluding set of appendixes contains data which were of use to visitors to the country in the early 1970s.

26   **Spain and Portugal.**
Edited by Doré Ogrizek.   New York, London, Toronto: McGraw-Hill, 1953, 484p. 22 maps. (World in Colour Series).

A now somewhat dated, but still useful, introduction to Iberia divided into two sections, one on Spain and the other on Portugal. The latter includes accounts of the art and history of the country followed by a description of each of the provinces by Suzanne Chantal and José dos Santos.

27   **The Statesman's Year-book**
Edited by John Paxton.   London: Macmillan; 1864- . annual.

The section on Portugal within this useful year-book includes sections on the following: history; area and population; climate; constitution and government; defence; international relations; economy; energy and natural resources; trade; communications; justice, religion and education; and diplomatic representatives. Similar topics are covered in the *Europe Review 1986* (Saffron Walden, England: World of Information) which has an informative chapter on Portugal by Jill Jolliffe (p. 158-62).

28   **Portugal: a bird's eye view.**
Lisbon: Directorate-General of Diffusion, 1983. 165p. map.

A broad and quite useful summary of Portuguese society, economy and culture. Following a short statistical survey, it covers: the land and the people, state and politics, education, justice, social policy, labour and foreign policy.

29   **Portugal: a country worth getting to know.**
Lisbon: Edições Panorama, 1972. 182p.

This volume of colour photographs covers the country's physical landscape, its agriculture, industry, colonies, cultural heritage and its tourism.

30   **Landscapes of Portugal.**
Carlos Queiroz.   Lisbon: National Secretariate of Information, [n.d.] [ca.1940]. 65p.

This volume is a translation of the first part of the work *Paisagens e monumentos de Portugal* (Portuguese landscapes and monuments) by Carlos Queiroz and Luís Reis Santos, published in 1940 in Lisbon by SPN. It is divided into three sections: a literary interpretation of the various different landscapes of Portugal; a series of notes on interesting features of the country; and a collection of twenty-six photographs of various parts of the country.

31 **Portugal.**
Gilbert Renault, with photographs by Antonio de Castelo Branco,
Antonio Santos d'Almeida Jr., geographical, historical and
archaeological notes by Magdelaine Parisot.   Paris: Librairie
Hachette, 1957. 127p. maps. (Hachette World Albums).
An extensively-illustrated account of the history of Portugal and the way of life of
the Portuguese.

32 **Atlantic islanders of the Azores and Madeiras.**
Francis M. Rogers.   North Quincy, Massachusetts: Christopher
Publishing House, 1979. 464p. 5 maps. bibliog.
This comprehensive study of the lives and values of the islanders is divided
into two parts. The first of these analyses the islands' economy, politics, and social
structures, while the second looks at the role of religion, education and culture.
Particular attention is paid to the emigration of people from the two archipelagos
to the United States.

33 **Portugal.**
Cedric Salter.   London: Batsford, 1970. 208p. map.
In this general description of Portugal an introduction covers the country's history
and culture. This is followed by chapters describing its main regions. A final
chapter briefly describes port wine and Oporto.

34 **Portugal and Brazil in transition.**
Edited by Raymond S. Sayers.   Minneapolis, Minnesota:
University of Minnesota Press; London: Oxford University Press.
1968. 367p.
This publication emanates from the sixth Colloquium of Luso-Brazilian Studies.
held in 1966. The following papers are concerned specifically with Portugal:
'Portuguese literature', by Jorge de Sena; 'Linguistics in Portugal', by José G.
Herculano de Carvalho; 'Permanence and change in overseas Portuguese
thought', by Alexandre Lobato; 'Social evolution in Portugal since 1945', by João
Baptista Nunes Pereira Neto; 'A case study of the Portuguese business élite, 1964-
1966', by Harry M. Makler; 'Lisbon of 1750-1850', by José-Augusto França; 'The
architecture and wood sculpture of the north of Portugal 1750-1850', by Flávio
Gonçalves; 'Portuguese music and musicians abroad to 1650', by Robert M.
Stevenson; and 'Portuguese activities in public health in the Tropics', by F. J. C.
Cambournac.

35 **Let's visit Portugal:**
Ronald Seth.   London: Burke, 1976. 96p.
A simple guide to the life of people in Portugal set against the history and
geography of the country. It also includes information on industry, agriculture,
religion and education, and has a small section on Portugal's overseas possessions.

36 **Things seen in Portugal. The garden of the west, a land of mountains and rivers, of the vine, the olive & the cork tree, & of ancient buildings richly carved, picturesque peasantry & hardy fishermen.** M. F. Smithes. London: Seeley, Service, 1931. 158p. map.

This descriptive introduction to Portugal is divided into ten chapters, the majority of which are on the main towns of the country. It is illustrated with thirty-two photographs of the country indicating the ways of life of the people in the late 1920s.

37 **Spain and Portugal. Volume II: Portugal.** London: Admiralty, Naval Intelligence Division, 1942. 450p. 78 maps. bibliog. (Geographical Handbook Series, BR 502A).

Provides a detailed account of Portugal in the mid-20th century which is divided into chapters on recent history; administration; population; ports; mining industry and power; agriculture; forestry; the fishing industry; commerce and finance; roads; railways; waterways; mercantile marine; aviation; and postal services and signal communications. Appendixes cover: the Portuguese-Spanish boundary; the Lisbon earthquake of 1 November 1755; the fauna of Portugal; and twenty-one statistical tables. This volume was written mainly by E. W. Gilbert and R. P. Beckinsale.

38 **Spain and Portugal. Volume IV: the Atlantic Islands.** London: Naval Intelligence Division, 1945. 371p. 55 maps. bibliog. (Geographical Handbook Series, BR 502C [restricted]).

Produced by the Naval Intelligence Division of the Admiralty during the Second World War, this handbook provides a wealth of information on the islands of Madeira and the Azores as well as the Canaries. Introductory chapters provide details of the geology, fauna and flora, history, administration and public health, people, commerce and signal communications of the islands, and these are followed by sections on each of the islands in the groups. Each of these island sections covers such items as relief, drainage, water supply, vegetation, coasts, population, industries, ports, towns and communities. Appendixes give details of recent volcanic and seismic activity in the Azores, meteorological tables and wireless and radio stations.

39 **The Azores and the early exploration of the Atlantic.** Egerton Sykes. London: Markham House, 1965. 26p. 3 maps.

Gives a brief account of the early exploration of the Azores and describes the individual islands themselves.

40 **Portugal.** Frank Tuohy, with photographs by Graham Finlayson. London: Thames & Hudson, 1970. 203p. map.

A collection of 117 photographs of Portugal together with an introductory text on the history of the country and comments pertaining to each photograph. It is divided into three general sections: Oporto and the north; Lisbon and its surroundings; and the Algarve and the south.

41 **Madeira.**
John Underwood. London: Sunflower Books, 1983. 144p. map.
A collection of 175 photographs illustrating all aspects of Madeira's varied scenery.

42 **Landscapes of Madeira: a countryside guide for ramblers and picnickers.**
John Underwood, Pat Underwood. London: Sunflower Books, 1980. 64p. 15 maps.
A guide to fourteen main walks, many of which follow the *levadas* or irrigation canals on the island of Madeira. It includes an introduction on general information for walkers on the island, and the main walks can be subdivided into forty rambles of varying length. Following these walks can provide a fascinating insight to the beautiful landscapes of Madeira well off the normal tourist path.

43 **Background notes: Portual.**
United States Department of State, Bureau of Public Affairs. Washington, DC: US Government Printing Office, 1983. 8p. 2 maps. bibliog. (1983-421-410/13).
A short collection of notes providing a profile of Portugal covering its people, geography, history, government, economy, foreign policy, United States-Portuguese relations, travel notes and further information. First published ca. October 1968.

44 **Portugal.**
Hellmut Wohl, Alice Wohl, with an introduction by Alexandre O'Neill. New York: Scala Books, 1983. 196p.
One of the best illustrated introductions to the country of Portugal. It consists of four chapters separated by photographic essays. The first chapter on 'The discoveries' is by John Train, and the remaining chapters are on the land, the spell of the past and traditions and life. The collections of photographs are grouped by regions, the first concentrating on Lisbon and its surroundings, the second on the north and the third on the south.

45 **Lisbon.**
Carol Wright. London: J. M. Dent, 1971. 88p 2 maps.
A character sketch of the city of Lisbon aimed as much at the armchair traveller as at the visitor who wants an insight into what to see and do. Three chapters towards the end also provide brief details on places worth visiting in the environs of the capital.

Portugal old and new.
See item no. 80.

The Country and Its People

Round the calendar in Portugal.
See item no. 81.

Portugal and Gallicia with a review of the social and political state of the Basque provinces: and a few remarks on recent events in Spain.
See item no. 85.

Madeira: pearl of the Atlantic.
See item no. 106.

The Azores.
See item no. 107.

To Portugal.
See item no. 110.

South of Lisbon: winter travels in southern Portugal.
See item no. 113.

This delicious land Portugal.
See item no. 115.

Invitation to Portugal.
See item no. 116.

Portuguese panorama.
See item no. 118.

Portugal and Madeira.
See item no. 119.

Algarve, Portugal: the holiday land for all seasons.
See item no. 126.

A Portugese rural society.
See item no. 399.

Baleia! The whalers of Azores.
See item no. 515.

The Ocean Flower: a poem. Preceded by an historical and descriptive account of the island of Madeira, a summary of the discoveries and chivalrous history of Portugal and an essay on Portuguese literature.
See item no. 596.

Geography
and Geology

46 **Atlas de Portugal** (Atlas of Portugal.)
    Aristides de Amorim Girão. Coimbra, Portugal: Instituto de
    Estudos Geográficos, 1958. 2nd ed. [not paginated].
A comprehensive, if now somewhat dated, atlas of Portugal. It consists of forty-
three pages of maps, with associated text, covering the emergence of Portugal, its
geology, climate, population, agriculture, land tenure, industry, communications,
languages, regions and overseas territories. The text is in English and Portuguese.

47 **Bartholomew world travel map: Spain and Portugal.**
    Edinburgh: Bartholomew, 1985. Scale 1:1,250,000.
A basic map of Iberia showing roads, rivers, railways, areas of hills and marsh,
provincial boundaries and airports.

48 **Geology of the Pomarão region (southern Portugal).**
    Marinus van den Boogaard. Rotterdam, The Netherlands:
    Grafisch Centrum Deltro, 1967. 113p. 9 maps. bibliog.
A thesis on the geology of the region around Pomarão in Baixo Alentejo,
concentrating on the stratigraphy of the region indicated as upper Devonian on
the geological map of Portugal (1952). There are summaries in Dutch and
Portuguese.

49 **The climate of Portugal and notes on its health resorts.**
    D. G. Dalgado. Lisbon: Coimbra University Press, 1914, 479p. 6
    maps.
Provides a thorough account of Portugal's climate together with its relationship to
medical geography and the country's health resorts, written at the beginning of
the 20th century. Each of the main resorts and spa towns is described in some
detail, including chemical analyses of the various waters.

Geography and Geology

50 **Geomorphology of Europe.**
Edited by Clifford Embleton. London: Macmillan, 1984. 465p.

A survey of the geomorphology of Europe written by members of the Commission on Geomorphological Survey and Mapping of the International Geographical Union. Portugal is mainly discussed in Chapter Twelve on the Iberian massif by M. Sala.

51 **The Western Mediterranean World: an introduction to its regional landscapes.**
J. M. Houston, with contributions by J. Roglić, J. I. Clarke. London: Longmans, 1964. 800p. 260 maps and diagrams. bibliog.

Provides an introduction to the landscapes of the Western Mediterranean. Part One presents a general background to the area, covering its climate, the sea, geological structure, soils, vegetation, the activities of man and recent developments in the landscape. Part Two focuses on the Iberian peninsula, with Chapter Thirteen (p. 336-68) concentrating on Portugal. This provides descriptions of each of the main regions of the country. The remainder of the book describes Italy and the peripheral lands of the Mediterranean. Appendixes provide climatic, demographic and land use statistics.

52 **Mapa do estado das estradas.** (Map of the state of the roads).
Lisbon: Automóvel Club de Portugal, Secção de Informações Turísticas, Itinerários e Cartografia, [1975]- . annual. Scale 1:550,000.

Probably the most useful road map of Portugal. It is regularly updated and provides details of the road numbers, distances between places, the quality of the roads, the railways, parks, rivers, tourist facilities, places of interest, and service points for the Automobile Club of Portugal. There are inserts of Oporto and Lisbon, and each year there is a map of a different tourist region of Portugal on the reverse at a scale of 1:300,000.

53 **The thirsty Algarve.**
L. Martin, R. J. Bennett, D. J. Gregory. *Geographical Magazine*, vol. 56, no. 6 (June 1984), p. 321-24.

Evaluates the conflicting water demands of agriculture, tourism and industry in the Algarve following the winter droughts of the early 1980s.

54 **A treatise on the climate and meteorology of Madeira; by J. A. Mason, edited by James Sheridan Knowles. To which are attached a review of the state of agriculture and of the tenure of land by George Peacock and an historical and descriptive account of the island, and guide to visitors, by John Driver.**
J. A. Mason. London: John Churchill; Liverpool, England. Deighton & Laughton, 1850. 388p.

Presents a comprehensive survey of the climate and meteorology of Madeira and also mentions the town of Ponta Delgada in the Azores. There is a chapter on agriculture and land tenure by George Peacock and four chapters by John Driver on the discovery of Madeira; a description of the island; its variety of wine, fruit, manufacture and amusements; and advice for visitors.

55 Failure of the breakwater at Port Sines, Portugal.
Port Sines Investigating Panel (Billy L. Edge, William F. Bird, Joseph M. Caldwell, Virginia Fairweather, Orville T. Magoon, Donald D. Treadwell). New York: American Society of Civil Engineers, 1982. 278p. 3 maps. bibliog.

A report on an investigation of the breakwater failure at Port Sines on 26 February 1978, and a compendium of data and reports relevant to this failure.

56 Granite intrusion, folding and metamorphism in central northern Portugal.
Oen Ing Soen. *Boletin Geológico y Minero*, vol. 81, nos. II-III (1970), p. 157-84.

A comprehensive geological analysis of the intrusion of granite into northern Portugal and the folding and metamorphism associated with it.

57 The Carboniferous of Portugal.
Edited by M. J. Lemos de Sousa, J. T. Oliveira. Lisbon: Direccão-Geral de Geologia e Minas, 1983. 211p. 9 maps. (Memórias dos Serviços Geológicas de Portugal, no. 29).

Provides a comprehensive analysis of the Carboniferous geology of Portugal presented in eleven papers: 'The marine Carboniferous of south Portugal: a stratigraphic and sedimentological approach' by J. T. Oliveira; 'Hercynian magmatism in the Iberian pyrite belt' by J. Munhá; 'Structure of the south Portuguese zone' by A. Ribeiro and J. Brandão Silva; 'Structure of the Carrapateira Nappe in the Bordeira area, S.W. Portugal' by A. Ribeiro; 'Carboniferous volcanogenic sulphide mineralizations in south Portugal (Iberian pyrite belt)' by F. J. A. S. Barriga and D. Carvalho; 'General description of the Terrestrial Carboniferous basins in Portugal and history of investigations' by M. J. Lemos de Sousa and R. H. Wagner; 'The Carboniferous Megafloras of Portugal – a revision of identifications and discussions of stratigraphic ages' by R. H. Wagner and M. J. Lemos de Sousa; 'The palaeogeographical and age relationships of the Portuguese Carboniferous floras with those of other parts of the western Iberian peninsula' by R. H. Wagner; 'The non-marine bivalve fauna of the Stephanian C of north Portugal' by R. M. C. Eager; 'The structure of the intramontane Upper Carboniferous basins in Portugal' by L. C. G. Domingos, J. L. S. Freire, F. Gomes da Silva, F. Gonçalves, E. Pereira and A. Ribeiro; and 'Petrological characteristics of the Upper Stephanian coals in north Portugal (Douro coalfield) and their relevance to coalification studies' by M. J. Lemos de Sousa.

58   **The individuality of Portugal: a study in historical-political geography.**
Dan Stanislawski.   Austin, Texas: University of Texas Press, 1959.
248p. 15 maps. bibliog.
This regional geography of Portugal covers its landforms, climate, soils, vegetation, prehistoric settlement, early central-European influences, contacts with ancient Mediterranean civilizations, the Roman conquest, the Germanic conquest, Muslim domination, the Christian reconquest, the gaining of Portuguese independence, the completion of the Portuguese state, the development of Portuguese international relations, the geography of Portuguese-Spanish boundaries, environment and culture, and the geographical basis of Portuguese political independence.

59   **A geography of Spain and Portugal.**
Ruth Way, assisted by Margaret Simmons.   London: Methuen, 1962. 362p. 52 maps. bibliog.
This traditional regional geography of the Iberian peninsula provides a general introduction to Portugal's geology, landforms, climate and soils, as well as information on agriculture and industry. Chapter Fourteen provides an overall description of the country divided into sections on the following regions: Algarve, Alentejo and Tagus Plains, coastal and Coimbra Plains, Serra da Estrêla and Douro. Appendix B gives details of Portugal's colonial possessions.

A yachtsman's guide to the Atlantic coasts of Spain and Portugal El Ferrol to Gibraltar.
See item no. 563.

Bibliografia hidrológica do Império Português. (Hydrological bibliography of the Portuguese Empire.)
See item no. 745.

Geologia de Portugal: ensaio bibliográfico. (Geology of Portugal: bibliographical essay.)
See item no. 746.

Flora and Fauna

60 **Birds of the Atlantic islands. Volume 2: a history of the birds of Madeira, the Desertas & the Porto Santo Islands.**
David Armitage Bannerman, W. Mary Bannerman. Edinburgh, London: Oliver & Boyd, 1965. 207p. map. bibliog.

Following introductory sections on the ornithological history, natural features and climate of the Madeira archipelago, this illustrated volume provides full details of the breeding and migratory birds of these Atlantic islands.

61 **Natural history of the Azores, or Western Islands.**
Frederick Du Cane Godman. London: John Van Voorst, 1870. 358p. 2 maps.

This volume presents the results of four months' investigation, undertaken in 1865, of the flora and fauna of the Azores. It pays particular attention to birds, beetles, butterflies and moths, the mollusca and the botany of the archipelago.

62 **Flowers of south-west Europe: a field guide.**
Oleg Polunin, B. E. Smythies. London, New York, Toronto: Oxford University Press, 1973. 480p. 12 maps. bibliog.

The definitive, comprehensive and well-illustrated field guidebook of flowers in south-west Europe. Introductory chapters cover landform, climate and vegetation, and the plant-hunting regions. The bulk of the book is then concerned with the identification of plant species. There are eighty pages of colour illustrations and sixty-one pages of line drawings.

63 **The birds of Portugal.**

William C. Tait. London: W. F. & G. Witherby, 1924. 260p. map. bibliog.

Following short introductory chapters on the chief physical features of Portugal and bird migration, this book describes all the birds found in Portugal with many of the descriptions being based on the author's own observations. As well as the English and Latin names of the birds, the Portuguese names are usually given and an appendix provides a list of ringed birds recovered in Portugal between 1910 and 1922. Ten pages of plates illustrate different types of habitat. The birds themselves are not illustrated.

64 **Wild flowers of Spain and Portugal.**

Albert William Taylor. London: Chatto & Windus, 1972. 103p. map.

An introduction to ninety-one species of wild flower which can be found in Spain and Portugal. Each plant is illustrated by a photograph showing it in its natural setting.

Travellers' Accounts

Pre-1900

65 **The journal of William Beckford in Portugal and Spain, 1787-1788.**
Edited and with an introduction by Boyd Alexander. London:
Rupert Hart-Davies, 1954. 340p. 2 maps.

The first transcription of writer William Beckford's journal relating to Portugal
and Spain, together with a short introduction by the editor which provides a short
biography of Beckford. His account of Portugal begins on 25 May 1787 in Lisbon
and ends on 27 November of the same year. In that time he visited many places in
the environs of the capital and his journal also provides a detailed account of his
friendship with the Marquis of Marialva and of court intrigue.

66 **England's wealthiest son: a study of William Beckford.**
Boyd Alexander. Fontwell, Sussex, England: Centaur Press, 1962.
308p.

Provides an account of those aspects of Beckford's life concentrating on what the
author calls his 'baffling and contradictory character'. In 1787 he spent seven
months in Portugal during which time he wrote a detailed journal. His second
visit to Portugal lasted from November 1793 until October 1795 and was recorded
in a volume of recollections, which he began in 1834. These stays in Portugal are
described in Chapter Ten, which is partly based on the letters he wrote from
there. It provides some information on the political and social life of late 18th-
century Portugal. Beckford's third visit to Portugal in 1798-99 is also briefly
mentioned.

67   **From Lisbon to Baker Street: the story of the Chevalier Franchi,**
     Beckford's friend.
     Boyd Alexander.   Lisbon: British Historical Society of Portugal,
     1977. 32p.

An account of the life of Gregorio Franchi (1770-1828) who, Alexander argues,
became the most important man in the life of writer William Beckford. It
provides some references to Portugal in the various correspondences between
Beckford and Franchi.

68   **Sketches in Portugal during the civil war of 1834, with observations**
     on the present state and future prospects of Portugal.
     James Edward Alexander.   London: James Cochrane, 1835. 328p.

Presents an account of the author's visit to Portugal to communicate with the
government there concerning his mission to explore parts of south-east Africa on
behalf of the Royal Geographical Society. It provides a wide-ranging account of
life in Portugal at the time of the civil war led by the two sons of King João VI,
Dom Pedro and Dom Miguel, and pays particular attention to the areas around
Lisbon and Oporto; to military activity in the country; and to the economic and
social conditions therein. Appendixes provide information on trade between
Britain and Portugal, wine consumption and other material pertaining to Portugal
in the early 19th century.

69   **A visit to Portugal 1866.**
     Hans Christian Andersen, translated by Grace Thornton.   London:
     Peter Owen, 1972. 105p. bibliog.

A translation of Andersen's *Et Besøg i Portugal 1866* first published in Danish in
1868. It includes an introduction by the translator on Andersen's life and two
appendixes on Andersen's letters from Portugal and the activities of the O'Neill
family in Portugal. Andersen was in Portugal from May to August 1866, where he
spent much of his time with the family of his friend George O'Neill, and he
describes Lisbon, Setúbal, Aveiro, Coimbra and Cintra in some detail.

70   **Rough leaves from a journal kept in Spain and Portugal during the**
     years 1832, 1833 and 1834.
     Lovell Badcock.   London: Richard Bentley, 1835. 407p.

Notes based on the author's diary when, as a Lieutenant-Colonel, he
accompanied Lord William Russell to Portugal in 1832 on a mission ordered by
the British government to reopen relations between Britain and Portugal. In
addition to a picture of contemporary politics in Portugal the work provides
accounts of Lisbon, Elvas, Oporto, the Douro and Viana during the time of the
conflict between Dom Pedro and Dom Miguel which resulted in civil war. It also
provides scattered accounts of the wines of the Douro, and of British interests in
the wine trade at Vila Nova de Gaia in the north-west. Considerable attention is
paid to the battles which took place around Oporto.

71 **Lisbon in the years 1821, 1822 and 1823.**
Marianne Baillie. London: John Murray, 1825, 2nd ed. 2 vols.

An account of Lisbon as it was in the early years of the 1820s in the form of a number of letters written by Marianne Baillie. Most of the letters in the first volume were written from Cintra while those of the second volume are from Lisbon. They provide useful insights into the society and political intrigues of the time when they were written.

72 **Journey from London to Genoa.**
Joseph Baretti, with an introduction by Ian Robertson. Fontwell, Sussex, England: Centaur Press, 1970. 2 vols.

Presents a new facsimile edition of the critic Baretti's journey from London to Genoa which was first published in 1770. Giuseppe Marc' Antonio Baretti and his companion Edward Southwell arrived at Lisbon on 30 August 1760 and on the way to Genoa they travelled to Badajoz in Spain via Estremoz near Évora. The volume provides an account of Lisbon five years after the 1755 earthquake, his excursion to Mafra and Cintra and his journey via Montemór, Estremoz and Elvas to Spain.

73 **Italy, with sketches of Spain and Portugal.**
William Beckford. Paris: Baudry's European Library, 1834. 338p.

This collection of Beckford's letters includes thirty-four in connection with Portugal dating from 6 March 1787, when he was at Falmouth to 26 November 1787, when he was at Lisbon. It provides interesting descriptions of Lisbon, the valley of Alcantara, Cintra, Collares, Ramalhão, Mafra, Cascais and Belém at the end of the 18th century. Many of the letters also concentrate on portrayals of Beckford's acquaintances in Portugal.

74 **Recollections of an excursion to the monasteries of Alcobaça and Batalha.**
William Beckford, with an introduction and notes by Boyd Alexander. Fontwell, Sussex, England: Centaur Press, 1972. 228p.

A reprint of Beckford's *Recollections*, first published in 1835, together with the diary which he kept during his trip to Portugal in 1794. They provide details and personal impressions of Alcobaça, Batalha and Queluz as well as several other places Beckford visited at the end of the 18th century.

75 **Letters from Portugal on the late and present state of that kingdom.**
[John Blankett]. London: printed for J. Almon, [1777]. 66p.

A collection of seventeen letters written between 26 January and 3 June 1777 from Lisbon and generally attributed to John Blankett. They concentrate on the country's recent history and the activities of the statesman Marquis de Pombal but also cover such items as the country's current economic and political state, trade with England, the Lisbon earthquake of 1 November 1755, the role of the clergy and conflicts with Spain.

19

76 **A description of the Azores, or Western Islands. From personal observation. Comprising remarks on their peculiarities, topographical, geological, statistical, etc., and on their hitherto neglected condition.**
Captain Boid. London: Edward Churton, 1835. 373p. map.

The first part of this 19th–century account of the Azores covers its geography, agriculture, trade and commerce, government and population, customs and architecture, political history, revenues and expenditure, and observations on the navigation of the islands. The second part provides a description of each of the nine islands in the archipelago.

77 **Several years travels through Portugal, Spain, Italy, Germany, Prussia, Sweden, Denmark and the United Provinces. Performed by a gentleman.**
[William Bromley]. London: printed for A. Roper at the Black Boy; R. Basset at the Mitre in Fleet Street; and W. Turner at Lincolns Inn Back Gate, 1702. 280p.

In 1693 the author left England to travel 'for his own private satisfaction' and visited the countries named in the title. The book begins with a description of Lisbon, and then on 6 May 1694 the author began his journey north during which he describes Coimbra, Aveyro, Porto, Villa Nova, Gamarains, Braga, Viana, Camena, Villa Nova de Sylvero and Valencia.

78 **A winter in the Azores and a summer at the baths of the Furnas.**
Joseph Bullar, Henry Bullar. London: John van Voorst, 1841. 2 vols.

A transcript of the journals of Joseph and Henry Bullar, who as invalids visited the Azores in 1838 and 1839. It is illustrated with several small woodcuts, and provides a wealth of information about the different islands of the Azores and the way of life of the people living there in the early 19th century. There is an appendix covering the climate, a chemical analysis of the hot baths and cold springs of the Furnas, and information for visitors to the islands.

79 **Sketches of society and manners in Portugal. In a series of letters from Arthur William Costigan, Esq., late a Captain of the Irish Brigade in the service of Spain, to his brother in London.**
Arthur William Costigan [pseudonym of Major James Ferrier].
London: printed for T. Vernor, 1787, 2 vols.

A collection of forty-four letters written between 1778 and 1779 referring to the people and places encountered by the author. In particular it provides interesting descriptions of Faro, Tavira, Castro-Marin, Évora, Elvas, Porto, Villa de Conde, Braga, Coimbra, Lisbon, Cintra and Oeyras, as well as other general observations on the political, social and economic state of the country at that time.

80 **Portugal old and new.**
Oswald Crawfurd. London: C. Kegan Paul, 1880. 386p. map.
This account of Portugal in the late 19th century by the British Consul at Oporto
is partly made up of contributions to the *Fortnightly Review*, the *New Quarterly
Magazine* and the *Cornhill Magazine*. It pays particular attention to Portugal's
history, poetry, country life, farming, port wine, the ruins of Troia and Citania,
the island of Madeira and the customs of the Portuguese people.

81 **Round the calendar in Portugal.**
Oswald Crawfurd. London: Chapman & Hall, 1890. 316p.
Presents a discursive and romantic account of rural life at the end of the 19th
century in the north of Portugal by the then British Consul at Oporto. It is
divided into chapters relating to each month of the year, and covers a wide range
of material including the flora and fauna of the region, ornithology, agriculture,
games and bullfighting, folklore, rural art, gardening, wine-making, music, diet,
racial characteristics and the arts of Oporto.

82 **Travels through Spain and Portugal, in 1774, with a short account of
the Spanish expedition against Algiers in 1775.**
William Dalrymple. London: printed for J. Almon, 1777. 187p.
map.
Presents an account of the author's travels in Iberia between 29 June and 26
November 1774 in the form of sixteen letters, followed by an account of the 1775
Spanish expedition against Algiers. Having travelled north from Gibraltar
through Spain to St. Jago de Compostella, the author entered Portugal on 15
September at Valenca on the River Minho. He went from there to Braga,
Oporto, Coymbra, Pombal, Leyria, Batalha, Alcobaza, Obidos, Mafra, Cintra
and Lisbon, where he arrived on 12 October. After two weeks in Lisbon, which is
described in some detail, he then had 'a most disagreeable and dismal journey' to
Seville via Montemor, Évora and Elvas.

83 **An account of Portugal as it appeared in 1766.**
[Charles François Duperrier] Dumouriez. London: printed for
C. Law, Ave-Maria Lane; J. Debrett, Picadilly; Elph. Balfour,
Edinburgh, 1797. 274p.
A translation of the French work *Etat présent du royaume de Portugal* first
published at Lausanne in Switzerland in 1775. During 1765 and 1766 the author,
then a captain of infantry, made the tour of Iberia by order of Louis IV's Minister
of Foreign Affairs. It is divided into four main books: the first is a geographical
description of Portugal: the second is an account of the Portuguese colonies; the
third is a survey of the army, including details of rivers, mountains and fortified
places; and the fourth is a wide-ranging survey of national character and
government.

84 **Jonathan Wild and the journal of a voyage to Lisbon.**
Henry Fielding. London; Toronto: J. M. Dent, 1932. 286p.
(Everyman's Library).

The second part of this collected volume is an edition of Fielding's journal of his voyage to Lisbon in 1754. Towards the end it describes the coasts near the mouth of the Tajo and very briefly mentions his landing in Lisbon which he describes as 'the nastiest city in the world, though at the same time one of the most populous'.

85 **Portugal and Gallicia with a review of the social and political state of the Basque provinces; and a few remarks on recent events in Spain.**
[Henry John George Herbert, Earl of Carnarvon]. London: John Murray, 1836, 2 vols.

In these volumes the author aims to make the reader 'acquainted with the fairy fields of the Minho, with the gloomy superstitions of the wild districts of Alentejo, with the feudal state of society still existing in the Tráz os Montes, and to give him some insight into the peculiar habits of the virtuous but almost unknown Gallicians'. It provides much information about the people and places of Portugal early in the 19th century.

86 **An overland journey to Lisbon at the close of 1846; with a picture of the actual state of Spain and Portugal.**
T. M. Hughes. London: Henry Colburn, 1847. 2 vols.

Portugal is mainly described in volume two (from Chapter Fourteen onwards) of this 19th-century account of the author's travels from Spain to Elvas, Estremoz, Évora, Montemôr and then Lisbon. It provides information relating to the regions surrounding his route, and in particular on the places of interest around Lisbon.

87 **Fair Lusitania.**
Catherine Charlotte Lady Jackson. London: Richard Bentley & Son, 1874. 406p.

An account of Portugal in the second half of the 19th century based on a collection of extracts from a diary kept by the author, together with letters written during a visit to the country. Particular attention is paid to Lisbon and Oporto, although chapters also cover visits to Cintra, Mafra, Setúbal, the Minho, Coimbra, Bussaco, Batalha, Alcobaça and Leiria. It includes numerous anecdotes concerning Portuguese life during the last century.

88 **Lusitanian sketches of the pen and pencil.**
William H. G. Kingston. London: John W. Parker, 1845. 2 vols.

This account of Portugal in the mid-19th century was based on the author's two years' residence in the north of the country. The first volume consists mainly of tours in the northern provinces from the Minho to the Mondego and aims to illustrate the political, social and religious structure of the country. The second volume gives an account of the wine country and in particular of the production of port wine.

89   **Travels in Portugal.**
John Latouche [pseudonym of Oswald Crawfurd].   London: Ward,
Lock & Tyler, no date [ca. 1874]. 354p.

A portrayal of the author's extensive travels in Portugal in the mid-19th century.
In addition to providing details of most of the important towns and places of
interest, it includes numerous ancedotes relating to the people, their customs, and
their beliefs. It was first published in consecutive numbers of *The New Quarterly
Magazine* under the title of *Notes of travel in Portugal.*

90   **Iberian sketches: travels in Portugal and the north-west of Spain.**
Jane Leck.   Glasgow: Wilson & McCormick, 1884. 166p.

In this late 19th-century travelogue Portugal is described in Chapters Five to Seven
where details are given of Oporto, Coimbra, Lisbon, Belém, Cintra, Mafra and
Batalha.

91   **Travels in Portugal, and through France and Spain, with a
dissertation on the literature of Portugal, and the Spanish and
Portuguese languages.**
Henry Frederick Link, translated from the German by John
Hinckley. London: T. N. Longman & O. Rees, 1801. 504p.

Link accompanied the Count of Hoffmansegg on his travels to Iberia, departing
from Hamburg in 1797 and returning in 1799. The purpose of their visit was to
collect materials for a volume on the flora and fauna of Portugal, but Link, who
returned before the Count, published this detailed account of their travels. The
first eleven chapters record their journey through France and Spain but from
p. 130, where they arrived at Elvas, the remainder of the book concentrates on
Portugal. From Elvas they went to Estremoz, Arrayolos, Montemor o Novo,
Lisbon, Queluz, Cintra, Alcacer do Sal, the Serra da Arrabida, Caldas da
Rainha, Alcobaça, Batalha, Coimbra, Aveiro, Oporto, Braga, Amarante, the
Serra de Maraõ, Estrella, back to Lisbon, and then on via the Serra de
Monchique to the Algarve, where they visited Cape St. Vincent, Lagos,
Villanova, Loule, and Tavira before returning through Mertola, Serpa and Évora
to Lisbon. Throughout the journey Link recorded details of the flora, agriculture,
economy and villages through which he travelled. The book ends with two short
dissertations on Portuguese literature and on a comparative view of the Spanish
and Portuguese languages. In Chapter Thirty-one there is a particularly
interesting account of the culture of the vine.

92   **They went to Portugal.**
Rose Macaulay.   Harmondsworth, England: Penguin, 1985. 443p.
bibliog.

This new edition of the author's unusual travel history of Portugal was first
published by Jonathan Cape in 1946. It provides accounts of visitors' experiences
in Portugal and is divided into sections on royalty, writers, clergymen, port wine,
tourists, the earthquake in Lisbon in 1755, the war of the two brothers Dom
Miguel and Dom Pedro, plotters, ambassadors, learned consul, prisoners of Dom
Miguel, the Earl of Essex and the bishop's books, and two captains and a major.
Each section has its own short bibliography.

93 **Travels in Portugal: through the provinces of Entre Douro & Minho, Beira, Estremadura and Alem-Tejo in the years 1789 and 1790. Consisting of observations on the manners, customs, trade, public buildings, arts, antiquities, &c., of that kingdom.**
James Murphy.   London: A. Strahan, T. Cadell Jun, W. Davies, 1795. 311p.

An account of the author's travels in Portugal, beginning in December 1788, and paying particular attention to the architecture and buildings he saw. Murphy was an architect himself and the book contains twenty-four plates, engraved from drawings, illustrating some of the buildings and inscriptions to which he refers. Specific details are provided of Oporto, Coimbra, Batalha, Leiria, Marinha Grande, Alcobaça, Lisbon, Cintra, Mafra, Setuval, Beja and Evora.

94 **Here and there in Portugal: notes of the present and past.**
Hugh Owen.   London: Bell & Daldy, 1856. 216p.

Sketches of different parts of Portugal based on a visit by the author to the country in the mid-19th century. The work provides a wide range of anecdotes relating to the history, culture and people of Portugal, and includes twelve illustrations drawn from the author's photographs.

95 **Traits and traditions of Portugal collected during a residence in that country.**
Julia H. S. Pardoe.   London: Saunders & Otley, 1833. 2 vols.

Provides a record of scenes and incidents observed by the author during her sojourn in Portugal following her arrival with the English troops in January 1827. As well as recounting a number of legends, the book describes her opinions of Lisbon and visits to Cintra, Rio Mayor, Batalha, Leiria, Alcobaça, the source of the River Alcoa, Pombal, Redinha, Coimbra, and the village of Sacavém ten miles from Lisbon. As a Catholic she pays particular attention to the activities of the monasteries and monastic orders she visited.

96 **Three pleasant springs in Portugal.**
Henry N. Shore.   London: Sampson Low, Marston & Company, 1899. 395p. map.

Presents an account of Portugal at the end of the 19th century. 'Spring the first' is mainly concerned with the region around Lisbon; 'Spring the second' with the north of Portugal; and 'Spring the third', the shortest section, with the Algarve. It provides some historical details, particularly of British military activities in the country, as well as giving general information concerning the people and places of Portugal.

97 **Letters written during a short residence in Spain and Portugal, with some account of Spanish and Portuguese poetry.**
Robert Southey.   Bristol, England: printed by Bulgin & Rosser, 1797. 551p.

A collection of Southey's letters from Iberia, the first dated 13 December 1795, which includes numerous anecdotes and descriptions of the areas through which he travelled, together with examples of Iberian poetry. Portugal is discussed mainly in letters XIII-XXX, which describe Elvas, Lisbon, Setuval and Cintra. These letters include discussions concerning the effects of the Lisbon earthquake in 1755, the activities of the Church and the treatment of Jews, and some Portuguese writers.

98 **Journals of a residence in Portugal 1800-1801 and a visit to France 1838, supplemented by extracts from his correspondence.**
Robert Southey, edited by Adolfo Cabral.   Oxford: Clarendon Press, 1960, 285p. 2 maps.

This edited volume containing Southey's journals and unpublished letters was written during his 1800-01 visit to Portugal and his 1838 visit to France. His Portuguese journal is divided into three sections covering his arrival in Lisbon and his excursions northward to Coimbra and southward to the Algarve. The journal and the fifty-five letters from Portugal provide numerous details of the country at the beginning of the 19th century.

99 **A journal of a three months' tour in Portugal, Spain, Africa, &c,**
Marchioness of Londonderry [Frances Anne Vane Stewart].
London: J. Mitchell, 1843. 134p.

These private notes of the Marchioness of Londonderry about her tour of Portugal, Spain and Africa in 1839 were published to provide money for the construction of an infirmary at Seaham Harbour in the county of Durham. While in Portugal she visited Lisbon, Cintra and Mafra, but did not greatly enjoy her stay. She described Lisbon in the following terms: 'I had always heard of Lisbon as a detestable residence, but the reality far surpassed my expectations; the smell, the noises, and discomforts of all sorts, the impossibility of walking, driving, moving, breathing, without having every sense offended, becomes very tiresome; and the noise day and night precludes all rest and sleep'.

100 **Lord Byron's Iberian pilgrimage.**
Gordon Kent Thomas.   Provo, Utah: Brigham Young University Press, 1983. 92p. map. bibliog.

Provides a narrative of Byron's 1809 visit to Iberia when he travelled from Lisbon to Cadiz, based on accounts by Byron himself, by his companions on the trip and on the author's own visit in 1981 over the same route.

101 **Travels through Portugal and Spain in 1772 and 1773.**
Richard Twiss. London: printed for the author and sold by G.
Robinson, T. Becket, J. Robson, 1775. 473p. map.

A general account in the form of a diary of the author's travels in Portugal and
Spain. While in Portugal he travelled from Lisbon to Cintra, Mafra, Castanhera,
Alcobaça, Batalha, Leyria, Pombal, Coimbra, Oporto, the valley of the Mondego
and Almeida.

102 **The visit to Portugal in 1779-1780 of William Julius Mickle,
translator of Os Lusíadas.**
S. George West. Lisbon: Junta de Investigações do Ultramar,
1972. 13p.

A description of Mickle's time spent in Portugal as a result of his appointment as
secretary to his cousin, Governor George Johnstone, who was commander of a
small squadron of ships operating off Portugal against France and the American
colonies. It is based mainly on Mickle's manuscript diary of the time he spent
ashore in his capacity as joint agent for the prizes taken by the squadron.

103 **Journal of a few months residence in Portugal, and glimpses of the
south of Spain.**
[Dorothy (Wordsworth) Quillinan]. London: Edward Moxon,
1847. 2 vols.

This diary, kept between 7 May 1845 and 20 May 1846, was published by the
author in order to remove the prejudices which she thought made Portugal an
avoided land by many British travellers. It provides a wide-ranging description of
the countryside and the people of Portugal in the mid-19th century, paying
particular attention to the Minho and Douro provinces, and the area around
Lisbon.

20th century

104 **A winter holiday in Portugal.**
B. Granville Baker. London: Stanley Paul, 1912. 324p. map.

Presents a touristic portrayal of Portugal at the beginning of the 20th century.
Particular attention is paid to the region around Lisbon, but there are descriptions
of most parts of the country. It is illustrated with forty drawings by the author.

105 **Portuguese panorama.**
Oswell Blakeston. London: Burke, 1955. 224p. map.

Presents an account of the author's experience in Portugal when he visited the
country with the painter Max Chapman. As well as details of the places they
visited, the book also provides sketches of a number of artists, painters and
novelists they met in Lisbon.

106 **Madeira: pearl of the Atlantic.**
Robin Bryans [Robert Harbinson].   London: Robert Hale, 1959,
191p. map.
Narrates the author's travels in the Madeira archipelago. As well as some
information on the archipelago's history it provides details of the life and customs
of the people, the scenery, wine production and the economy during the 1950s.

107 **The Azores.**
Robin Bryans [Robert Harbinson].   London: Faber & Faber,
1963. 203p. map.
This descriptive and partly historical account of the Azores was based on a visit to
the nine islands by the author. There is a chapter on each island, describing his
experiences there and some aspects of its history.

108 **Afoot in Portugal.**
John Gibbons, with a foreword by G. K. Chesterton.   London:
George Newnes, 1931. Reprinted, 1933. 207p.
Provides a travel account of the author's visit to southern Portugal. He arrived
from Spain across the River Guadiana at Vila Real São Antonio on the south
coast and travelled west from there to Lagos, Sagres, Monchique, a variety of
small places in the Alentejo region, Setúbal, Lisbon and Fatima before returning
to Spain by train. The account says more about the author's experiences with
people than it does actually about the Algarve.

109 **I gathered no moss.**
John Gibbons, with a foreword by Edgar Prestage.   London:
Robert Hale, 1939. 280p.
A portrayal of the four autumn and winter months spent by the author in Trás-os-
Montes, where he lived in a small village high above the Upper Douro. It
provides a very readable narrative of life in this poor part of Portugal during the
late 1930s and of the social interaction between the local population and the
English 'outsider'.

110 **To Portugal.**
Douglas Goldring.   London: Rich & Cowan, 1934. 295p. map.
bibliog.
Gives an account of the information gathered by the author in preparation for a
holiday tour made in the late summer of 1933. After an introductory chapter on
the Portuguese people and their history the book is divided into sections on the
regions and towns of the country.

111 **Portuguese somersault.**
Jan Gordon, Cora Gordon.   London: Harrap, 1934. 311p. map.
Describes the authors' visits to Portugal in 1926 and 1933. The first visit was to the
north of the country and the first part of the book relating to this visit describes
Oporto and a town in the Douro province. The second part of the book describes

the south of the country, visited during 1933, and is divided up into chapters on
the main towns that they visited.

112 Portuguese journey.
Garry Hogg. London: Museum Press, 1954. 208p. 2 maps.
Presents a description of the author's travels in Portugal. The first part of the
journey was a round trip from Lisbon to Sagres and Olhão in the south. He then
travelled north to Batalha, Alcobaça, Fatima, the Serra da Estrela, Coimbra,
Caminha and Chaves. It provides a general descriptive account of life in Portugal
at the beginning of the 1950s.

113 South of Lisbon: winter travels in southern Portugal.
Frank E. Huggett. London: Victor Gollancz, 1960. 224p.
Portrays the author's travels in southern Portugal from Lisbon to the Algarve. He
sees Portugal as a poor, backward and impoverished land, and in so doing
describes many aspects of the lifestyle of the people of south Portugal during
António de Oliveira Salazar's dictatorship.

114 Through Portugal.
Martin Hume. London: E. Grant Richards, 1907. 317p.
This account of Portugal at the beginning of the 20th century includes forty
contemporary photographs. It is divided into chapters on the towns of Oporto;
Braga and Bom Jesus, Citania and Guimarâes; Bussaco; Coimbra, Thomar and
Leiria; Batalha and Alcobaça; Cintra; Lisbon; Setúbal, Troya and Évora. A final
chapter gives hints for travellers in Portugal.

115 This delicious land Portugal.
Marie Noële Kelly. London: Hutchinson, 1956. 192p. map.
bibliog.
An attempt to describe what the author calls 'the quintessence of the spirit of
Lusitania'. It was based on a journey made by the author through Portugal and
provides information on the country's architecture, azulejos (decorative tiles), the
University of Coimbra, fish, food, shrines, houses and the regions of the Minho
and the Algarve.

116 Invitation to Portugal.
Mary Jean Kempner, with photographs by Russell Lynes, and an
introduction by Alan Pryce Jones. New York: Atheneum, 1969,
314p. map. bibliog.
Presents a personal appreciation of Portugal covering its history; bullfighting; fado
singing; the towns of Évora, Coimbra, Viseu and Braga; food and drink,
particularly port; the Convento dos Jerónimos de Belém, the abbeys at Alcobaça
and Batalha, and the Convento do Cristo at Tomar; and the royal palaces at
Sintra, Mafra, Queluz, Pena and Ajuda. It concludes with a journal recording the
author's journey through Portugal in just over a month travelling from Lisbon to
Sagres, Serpa, Castelo de Vide, back to Lisbon and then to Abrantes, the Serra

do Estrêla, Viseu, Miranda do Douro, the Serra do Marâo, Braga, Valença do Minho, Oporto, Coimbra and Sintra before returning to Lisbon.

117 **Moments in Portugal, or land of the laurel.**
Lady Lowther. London: Luzac, 1939. 132p.
Pages from the author's diary from 24 April to 11 May 1936 describing Lisbon, Cintra, Coimbra, Alcobaça, Batalha, Thomar and Buçaco as they were in the mid-1930s.

118 **Portuguese panorama.**
Iris Merle. London: Ouzel Press, 1958, 224p. 2 maps.
A travel book on Portugal and Madeira written in a narrative style. It covers all regions of the country and the way of life of its people from wine-making and bullfighting to fishing and industry. There are also individual chapters on the major towns and the book is illustrated with numerous black-and-white photographs.

119 **Portugal and Madeira.**
Sacheverell Sitwell. London: Batsford, 1954. 242p.
A wide-ranging account of Portugal based on the author's five visits to the country between 1926 and 1954. It is divided up on a regional basis with chapters on: Madeira; Lisbon; Belém, Sintra and Queluz; the abbeys; Setúbal and the Algarve; Trás-os-Montes; Minho; and Oporto, Aveiro and Coimbra. It includes seventy-one photographs and covers an extensive variety of subjects relating to the country, its people and their culture.

120 **Until tomorrow: Azores and Portugal.**
Karine R. Smith. USA: Karine R. Smith, no date [ca. late 1970s]. 152p. map. bibliog.
The recollections of the wife of a United States Air Force Commander of the American station at Lajes Field in the Azores, who first arrived there in 1952 and stayed for six years. It includes personal views of Portuguese culture, history, politics, American-Portuguese relationships and information on the Azores covering points of interest, climate and the customs of the people. It is written from a viewpoint in which the author 'can never forget the tranquility, the orderliness, the dignity, the aesthetics of Salazar's Portugal'.

121 **Sunshine and sentiment in Portugal.**
Gilbert Watson. London: Edward Arnold, 1904. 295p.
An account of the author's experiences in the Serra de Monchique in the Algarve while part of an archaeological expedition to the caves found there. It describes the relationships between an unusual group of Englishmen and the local population.

Tourism

Travel guides (pre-1980)

122 **In Portugal.**
Aubrey F. G. Bell.   London: John Lane, Bodley Head, 1912.
227p.

Presents an early 20th-century guidebook whose aim is to illustrate the individual character of Portugal. It is written on a regional basis, but concludes with a chapter on the Portuguese language and one on the poetry of Abilio Guerra Junqueira (1850-1923).

123 **Portugal and Madeira: a guide and gazetteer, where to stay, what to see, what to eat, what to buy.**
Sarah Bradford.   London, Sydney: Ward Lock, 1969, 160p. 2
maps.

Following an introduction covering ways of getting to Portugal, touring in the country, and other useful items of general information, this guidebook is divided into three sections. The first is on the country's history, architecture, azulejos, (decorative tiles), painting, the fado, bullfighting, port, food, wine, and shopping in Lisbon. The second section provides a comprehensive gazetteer and description of the country's towns, and the third section gives a short account of Madeira.

124 **The selective traveller in Portugal.**
Ann Bridge [pseudonym for Mary Dolling, Lady O'Malley], Susan
Lowndes [afterwards Marques].   London. Chatto & Windus,
1967. [3rd] new rev. ed. 292p. 2 maps. bibliog.

A thorough, if now slightly dated, guide to Portugal. After introductory chapters on the country's history, its land and people, each of the main regions is discussed in turn. Within each region historical and economic information is given concerning all the places the authors consider to be of importance.

125 **Brown's Madeira, Canary Islands and Azores: a practical and complete guide for the use of tourists and invalids.**
A. Samler Brown. London: Sampson Low, Marston & Company, 1905. 8th rev. ed. 11 maps. bibliog.

An early 20th-century tourist guide to the Madeira and Azores archipelagos and the Spanish Canary Islands, covering general information, social structure, industries and agriculture, flora and fauna, weather conditions, illness, geology and history. It also provides details of the places of interest on each island.

126 **Algarve, Portugal: the holiday land for all seasons.**
José Carrasco, with photographs by Asta and Luís de Almeida d'Eça. Loures, Portugal: Luís de Almeida d'Eça, 1971. 3rd ed. 75p.

A copiously-illustrated introduction to the tourist region of the Algarve. in English, French and German. It concludes with a short itinerary providing details of the more important places in the region.

127 **Madeira: a concise guide for the visitor. Plates, map and plans, and suggestions for those spending three hours ashore.**
A. Gordon-Brown. London: Union-Castle Mail Steamship Company, 1951. 56p. 3 maps.

A short guide to Madeira divided into four sections: a general introduction; the city of Funchal; suggestions for the Mail Ship visitor with three hours ashore; and excursions for those staying on the island.

128 **The tourist in Portugal.**
W. H. Harrison. London: Robert Jennings, 1839. 290p. (Landscape Annual Series).

This volume of Jennings' *Landscape Annual* for 1839 is illustrated with engravings of paintings by James Holland. After an introductory historical chapter it provides contemporary accounts of Oporto, Coimbra, Pombal, Leiria, Batalha and Porto de Moz for the 19th-century traveller. It also aims 'to beguile the tedium of the journey by many a quaint legend and strange tale'.

129 **Portugal and Madeira.**
John Hawkes, Moira Hawkes. London: Dickens Press, 1969. 48p. map. (Holiday Factbooks).

This short guide to Portugal was written in the late 1960s from a pro-Salazar background. It covers a broad range of information on such things as seasons. resorts, transport, accommodation, food, drink, clothing, entertainment, money, shopping and everyday words. It is now considerably out of date.

Tourism. Travel guides (pre-1980)

130 **Lisbon and Cintra, with some account of other cities and historical sites in Portugal.**
A. C. Inchbold, illustrated by Stanley Inchbold. London: Chatto & Windus, 1907. 248p.

Although mainly on Lisbon and Cintra, this early 20th-century guide gives details of the towns of Mafra, Thomar, Alcobaça, Batalha, Coimbra, Bussaco, Oporto, Braga and other places of interest. It concentrates on the monuments, history and legends of the places described.

131 **The islands of Madeira: a handbook for tourists.**
Newport, Isle of Wight: J. Arthur Dixon, no date [ca. 1958]. 33p. map.

A short, illustrated guide to Madeira, now somewhat out of date.

132 **A wayfarer in Portugal.**
Philip S. Marden. London: Methuen, 1927. 210p. map.

A guide to Portugal based on the author's own travels. After an historical introduction to the country, most of the chapters are concerned with the regions around specific towns. The work concludes with a short section of useful hints to the traveller in Portugal in the 1920s.

133 **A handbook for travellers in Portugal.**
John Mason Neale. London: John Murray; Paris: Galignani; Lisbon: Lewtas, 1887, 4th ed. 201p. 3 maps.

Provides a thorough 19th-century guide to Portugal. A section entitled 'preliminary remarks' covers the country's geography, geology, history and language, and includes a range of useful advice for the traveller. The remainder of the handbook is divided into eight sections of touring routes covering the main regions of the country including Madeira and the Azores. Each of these sections describes the places visited in terms of their economy and history.

134 **Madeira and the Canaries: a travellers note-book.**
Elizabeth Nicholas. London: Hamish Hamilton, 1953. 218p. 2 maps.

A mid-20th-century guidebook to Madeira and the Canaries describing the author's visits to the islands. The first part, on Madeira, has chapters on travel to the island, its history, the town of Funchal, industry and Madeira wine.

135 **Introducing Portugal.**
Cedric Salter. London: Methuen, 1956. 197p. map.

An introduction to Portugal for holiday makers in the 1950s. It provides a broad background to the country and describes the main places of tourist interest.

136 **A fortnight in Portugal.**
Cedric Salter. London: Percival Marshall, 1957. 106p. maps.
(The Fortnight Holiday Series).
This somewhat dated tourist guide to Portugal is divided into four main sections
describing places to visit on holidays of two weeks based around Lisbon, Figuiera
da Foz, Oporto and the Algarve. There are introductory chapters entitled 'Before
you leave home' and 'After your arrival', and the book concludes with chapters
on additional places to visit and key dates in Portuguese history.

137 **Algarve and southern Portugal.**
Cedric Salter. London: Batsford, 1974. 208p. map.
Provides an account for tourists of southern Portugal, concentrating on the
Algarve. It also provides broad descriptions of the countryside, main towns, and
places of tourist interest in the provinces of Estremadura, Ribatejo and Alentejo.

138 **Algarve.**
A. H. Stuart. Lisbon: SNI Books, no date [ca. 1940s]. 70p.
bibliog.
Provides a short account of the Algarve for tourists written in 1941 but updated
shortly after then. It has chapters on communications, place-names, excursions
from the village of Praia da Rocha, resources and industries, and tourism.
Appendixes cover money, postal communications, coasts and useful words and
phrases.

139 **Portugal.**
Franz Villier. London: Vista Books; New York: Viking Press,
1963. 192p. map.
This tourist guide to the Portugal of the early 1960s provides a general
introduction to the country's history, art, culture, religion and way of life. There
are also sections on each of the country's main provinces.

140 **Algarve.**
David Wright, Patrick Swift. London: Barrie & Rockliff, 1965.
279p.
This evocative account of the Algarve is intended for both the traveller requiring
a guide and handbook, and also for the 'armchair tripper'. Written in the 1960s it
illustrates the people of the Algarve and their way of life at a time when tourism
had only recently begun. Appendixes cover: 'The birds of the Algarve', by
Randolph Cary; 'Algarve cuisine', by Agnes Ryan; 'The wine of the Algarve,' by
Tim Motion; and general notes for tourists.

141 **Minho and north Portugal: a portrait and guide.**
David Wright, Patrick Swift. London: Barrie & Rockliff, 1968.
224p. map.
Gives an account of three different visits by the authors to the north of Portugal.
It provides a guide to the main towns and regions of the Minho and Trás-os-

Montes. Two concluding chapters give information on the language of the Minho and notes for tourists, which are now somewhat outdated.

142 Lisbon: a portrait and a guide.
David Wright, Patrick Swift. London: Barrie & Jenkins, 1971. 270p. map.

Presents a general introduction to Lisbon describing the experiences of the authors in the city in 1969. Following an introduction in the form of a diary by David Wright, there are chapters on the literature, songs, bullfights, restaurants and history of Lisbon by Patrick Swift. There is also a section on a journey they made to Abrantes, Castelo Branco, Nisa, Castelo de Vide, Marvão, Portalegre, Elvas and Estremoz.

143 The Algarve: province of Portugal, Europe's southwest corner.
Charles Wuerpel. Newton Abbott, England: David & Charles, 1974. 223p. 5 maps.

This regional survey of the Algarve covers its history, physical geography, flora and fauna, the government, development, cottage industry, larger industry and tourism. Appendixes provide lists of flowering plants and marine life to be found in the Algarve.

144 Blue moon in Portugal: travels; by . . .
William Younger, Elizabeth Younger. London: Eyre & Spottiswoode, 1956. 298p. bibliog.

A wide-ranging introduction to Portugal divided into twelve chapters, each on one of the country's provinces. It provides information on the country's history, economy and the lifestyles of the people in the 1950s. Five appendixes cover the subjects of: hotels, food and wine, port wine, Portuguese recipes and roads.

Portugal.
See item no. 25.

Let's visit Portugal.
See item no. 35.

Lisbon.
See item no. 45.

Portuguese panorama.
See item no. 105.

Current travel guides

145 Ballard's travel guide to the pousadas of Portugal: lodgings in state-owned castles, palaces, mansions, historic hotels.
Sam Ballard, Jane Ballard. Washington, DC: Ballard's Travel Guides, 1980. 160p. 33 maps.

Following a brief introduction to Portugal covering its history, geography and culture, and giving information on travel, this illustrated guide describes each of the thirty state-run *pousadas* and historic hotels of the country, and also provides some information on the main tourist towns.

146 Portugal.
Pat Brooks, Lester Brooks. Edited and annotated by Robert C. Fisher. New York: Fisher Travel Guides, 1981. 118p. 4 maps.

An American travel guide to Portugal divided into three broad sections. The first, on 'hard facts' covers the subjects of planning ahead, getting there, formalities on arrival, settling down, getting around and going home. This is followed by regional descriptions of Lisbon; the Algarve; north from Porto; central Portugal; and Évora and the Alentejo, each of which has sections on 'inside information' covering hotels, restaurants, entertainment, shopping, museums and galleries, historic buildings and sites, spectacles and displays, tours, parks, sports and getting around. A final short section gives information on food, drink and the cultural scene.

147 Portugal: a Rand McNally pocket guide.
R. A. N. Dixon. Chicago; New York; San Francisco: Rand McNally, 1984. 95p. 8 maps.

This pocket guide to Portugal is particularly notable for its good quality colour photographs. An introductory section provides information on paper-work, customs, currency, how to get there, internal travel, motoring, accommodation, food and drink, enjoying yourself, what you need to know, and the language. This is followed by maps and accounts of the country divided into six regions, each of which contains a decription of the major towns and places of interest.

148 The rough guide to Portugal.
Written and researched by Mark Ellingham, John Fisher, Graham Kenyon with an additional account by Sarah Peel. Edited by Mark Ellingham, John Fisher. London; Boston, Massachusetts; Melbourne: Routledge & Kegan Paul, 1984. rev. ed. 200p. 25 maps.

A guide to Portugal for those prepared to rough it. It is divided into three parts: basics, the guide and contents. The first provides basic information on living in the country, the second provides a guide to each of the main regions and the third gives information about the country's history, monumental chronology and language.

Tourism. Current travel guides

149 **Fodor's Lisbon 1985.**
London: Hodder & Soughton, 1985. 101p. 4 maps.
An abridged account of Lisbon derived from *Fodor's Portugal 1985* (q.v.). It provides a description of the city, its shopping facilities, food and drink, the environs of Lisbon and Estremadura, and concludes with a short English-Portuguese vocabulary.

150 **Fodor's Portugal 1985.**
Edited by: Susan Lowndes, Frances Howell, Ira Mayer, David Tennant, Richard Moore. London; Sydney; Auckland: Hodder & Stoughton, 1985. 312p. 12 maps.
A useful guide to Portugal divided into three main sections. The first entitled 'facts at your fingertips' gives a summary of basic travel information. The second section consists of essays on the cultural scene, history, art and gastronomy of the country. The third section provides a regional description covering all of the main places in the country, including Madeira and the Azores. It concludes with a short English-Portuguese vocabulary.

151 **Travellers Portugal.**
Anthony Hogg. London: Solo Mio Books, 1983, 278p. 11 maps.
A collection of fly/ and sea/drive holiday routes to and in Portugal, divided into five parts. The first section provides an introduction to the country covering its history, culture and visits for travellers. Part Two gives six routes to Oporto and Coimbra from Santander, Part Three is on fly/drive from Oporto, Part Four on fly/drive from Lisbon, and Part Five on fly/drive from Seville through the Algarve.

152 **The Portuguese travelmate.**
Lexus, with Mike Harland, Alberto Luis de Moura Rodrigues. Glasgow: Richard Drew Publishing, 1982. 128p. map.
A list of English words and phrases together with their Portuguese translations, covering most of the material a traveller is likely to need on a visit to the country. Included within the text are travel tips and Portuguese words to be found on signs and notices.

153 **Frommer's dollarwise guide to Portugal. Madeira and the Azores.**
Darwin Porter. New York: Frommer/Pastmantier, 1984. 300p. 2 maps.
A tourist guide to Portugal covering hotels and restaurants, with detailed information on sights, night-life, shopping, transport and tourist facilities.

154 **Frommer's guide to Lisbon, Madeira and the Costa del Sol.**
Darwin Porter. New York: Frommer/Pastmantier, 1985. 218p. 6 maps.
A guide mainly referring to Lisbon and Madrid. The chapters on Lisbon cover shopping, hotels, night-life, restaurants and sightseeing. There is also a short chapter on touring in Portugal.

155 **Portugal, Madeira: Michelin tourist guide.**
London: Michelin, 1980. 146p. 41 maps.

A useful short tourist guide to Portugal. In addition to a detailed gazetteer of towns, sights and tourist regions, it provides background material on the economy, food and wine, history, the arts, major writers and traditional and festive Portugal.

156 **Blue guide: Portugal.**
Ian Robertson. London: Ernest Benn; New York: W. W.
Norton, 1984. 2nd ed. 328p. 19 maps. bibliog.

A thorough and detailed guide to mainland Portugal. Three introductory chapters cover: 'The history of Portugal', by Richard Robinson; 'The art and architecture of Portugal', by J. B. Bury; and 'Port and the wines of Portugal', by David Francis. There is also a geographical and general introduction, and a section on practical information. The main part of the book describes thirty-seven routes, some of which cover the journeys between major towns, with the others focusing on walks around the towns themselves. A detailed index enables places to be identified other than through their location in a 'route'.

Landscapes of Madeira: a countryside guide for ramblers and picnickers.
See item no. 42.

Prehistory
and Archaeology

157 **Papers in Iberian archaeology.**
Edited by T. F. C. Blagg, R. F. J. Jones, S. J. Keay.   Oxford:
British Archaeological Reports, 1984, 2 vols. (BAR International
Series 193(i) and 193(ii)).

A collection of twenty-five papers on Iberian archaeology, the following of which
refer to Portugal: 'The Castro culture of the peninsular north-west: fact and
inference', by C. F. C. Hawkes; and 'Pliny and the gold-mines of north-west
Iberia', by D. G. Bird.

158 **The Bell Beaker cultures of Spain and Portugal.**
Richard J. Harrison.   Cambridge, Massachusetts: Peabody
Museum of Archaeology and Ethnology, Harvard University,
1977. 257p. 18 maps. bibliog. (American School of Prehistoric
Research, Peabody Museum, Harvard University, bulletin no. 35).

Provides an introduction to, and catalogue of, the Bell Beaker (late Neolithic)
cultures of Spain and Portugal. The main sites discussed in Portugal are in the
neighbourhood of Lisbon.

159 **The Iberian stones speak: archaeology in Spain and Portugal.**
Paul MacKendrick.   New York: Funk & Wagnalls, 1969. 238p. 21
maps. bibliog.

Presents a reconstruction of the cultural history of Iberia based on archaeological
evidence. It is divided into chapters on different archaeological periods from
12,000 BC to AD 350, and particular attention is paid to the following Portuguese
sites: Vila Nova de São Pedre (Azambuja); the hilltop *citânias* of the north such
as Briteiros and Sanfins; the Roman bridges at Chaves, Vila Formosa and
Portagem; the Roman temple at Évora; and the Roman towns at Miróbriga
(Santiago do Cacém), Cetóbriga (Troia) and Conimbriga.

160 **Unknown Portugal: archaeological itineraries illustrated with photographs by the author.**
Georges Pillement, translated by Arnold Rosin. London: Johnson Publications, 1967. 248p. 10 maps.

A book of nine tourist itineraries of Portugal for those particularly interested in the past. The archaeology of the title is very broadly defined and much of the book is concerned with Portugal's architectural heritage from the mediaeval and early modern periods. There is little material on the country's prehistoric remains.

161 **Spain and Portugal: the prehistory of the Iberian peninsula.**
H. N. Savory. London: Thames & Hudson, 1968. 324p. 23 maps. bibliog. (Ancient Peoples and Places, vol. 61).

A general introduction to prehistoric Iberia. Although most of the emphasis is on Spain, it provides a straightforward summary of Portugal's archaeological heritage from the Palaeolithic period to the Celtic Iron Age, and includes discussions of most of the major pre-Roman archaeological sites which were known in the late 1960s.

History

General

162 A history of Spain and Portugal.
William C. Atkinson.   London: Penguin Books, 1960. 382p. map.
bibliog. (The Pelican History of the World).

This short history of the Iberian peninsula from the Roman period to the 20th
century includes discussions on literature and the arts in Spain and Portugal and
concludes with a chronological table.

**163 Mary and misogyny: women in Iberian expansion overseas 1415-
1815, some facts, fancies and personalities.**
C. R. Boxer.   London: Duckworth, 1975. 142p.

An unusual account of Portuguese and Spanish colonialism divided into three
chapters on north and west Africa, America and Asia. The final chapter argues
that in all of these areas three elements went hand in hand: the exaltation of
female chastity; male denigration of women; and the claim that for men
fornication was no sin. It provides a general account of the role of women in
Iberian colonialism.

164 Eight centuries of Portuguese monarchy.
V. de Bragança-Cunha.   London: Stephen Swift, 1911. 265p.
bibliog.

A broad account of the Portuguese nation from the 11th century to the end of the
monarchy and the declaration of the Republic on 5 October 1910. Particular
attention is paid to the 18th and 19th centuries, and the debates over
Constitutionalism and Republicanism.

165 The natural and political history of Portugal. From its first erection
into a kingdom, by Alphonso son of Henry Duke of Burgundy, anno
1090, down to the present time. Shewing its extents, soil,
production, history, trade, manufactures, customs, and manners of
its inhabitants; with its revolutions and conquests. As also its
provinces, cities and noted towns, with their antiquity, building and
present state. To which is added, the history of Brazil and all other
dominions subject to the crown of Portugal in Asia, Africa and
America.
Charles Brockwell.   London: printed for the author and sold by
T. Warner at the Black-Boy in Pater-noster-Row, 1726. 426p.
map.

A detailed early 18th-century account of Portugal and its colonies based on the
author's four year sojourn in the country. It provides a wealth of information
about the country's history and the people and their lifestyles. After an
introduction there is an outline of political events in Portugal between 1090 and
the 18th century. This is followed by a detailed survey of the provinces, towns,
mountains and rivers of the country in the form of an early gazetteer. The last 125
pages describe Brazil and other Portuguese colonies.

166 The Portuguese in America 590 BC – 1974: a chronology & fact
book.
Compiled and edited by Manoel da Silveira Cardozo.   Dobbs
Ferry, New York: Oceana Publications, 1976. 154p. bibliog.
(Ethnic Chronology Series, no. 22).

A reference book on the Portuguese in the United States divided into two main
sections. The first part is a chronology, which, apart from three earlier references,
begins in 1415. The second part provides a series of texts and studies, the former
being transcriptions of illustrative documents, and the latter being brief historical
essays on themes and people. The volume concludes with a brief statistical section
which includes data on Portuguese migration to the United States between 1820
and 1972.

167 Historical account of Lisbon College.
Canon Croft.   London: St. Andrew's Press, 1902. 275p.

Presents an account of the English College founded on paper in 1622 and
established with students in 1628 in Lisbon for the education of Catholic priests
who were to devote their labours to the spread of the Catholic faith in England. It
concludes with an appendix listing the Alumni of the College compiled by Joseph
Gillow.

168 The Royal House of Portugal.
Francis Gribble.   London: Eveleigh Nash, 1915. 328p.

An anecdotal and unscholarly history of Portugal from the 12th century to the
collapse of the House of Braganza and the proclamation of the Republic in 1910.
It pays considerable attention to the lives and loves of members of the Portuguese
royal family, and concentrates mainly on the 19th century.

169 **History of Portugal.**
   Lisbon: Office of the Secretary of State for Information and
   Tourism, [1971-72]. 91p.

This general account of the history of Portugal is divided into sections on the
origins of the Portuguese nation, political independence, the discoveries, the
Restoration and national reorganization, the constitutional monarchy and the
Republic. It concludes with a chronological table of events up to 1971.

170 **A history of Portugal.**
   H. V. Livermore.   Cambridge, England: Cambridge University
   Press, 1947. 502p. 7 maps. bibliog.

Provides a thorough coverage of the history of Portugal from pre-Roman times to
the Republic and the rise of Salazar, ending with a short reference index
providing summary information on the country's geography and economy.

171 **A new history of Portugal.**
   H. V. Livermore.   London: Cambridge University Press, 1966;
   first paperback edition, 1969. 365p. 7 maps. bibliog.

A revised and shortened version of the author's *History of Portugal* (q.v.), first
published in 1947. The section on the Roman, Germanic and Muslim periods is
much abbreviated, and that on the mediaeval period has also been compressed.

172 **Portugal; a short history.**
   H. V. Livermore.   Edinburgh: Edinburgh University Press, 1973.
   218p. 4 maps.

Presents a relatively short, general history of Portugal from its origins through to
the Republic established in 1910 and Salazar's New State, the principles of which
were laid down in 1933. Most attention is paid to the period since the Restoration
in the mid-17th century.

173 **The history of Portugal.**
   Edward McMurdo.   London: Sampson Low, Marston, Searle &
   Rivington, 1888-89. 2 vols.

The author found himself in Lisbon having been granted a concession to operate
the Lourenço Marques and Transvaal Railway (Delagoa Bay) and was unable to
find a history of Portugal in English. Consequently, he made a collection of
Portuguese historical works which were then translated by Mariana Monteiro and
formed the basis of these volumes. The first volume is subtitled 'From the
commencement of the monarchy to the reign of Alfonso III' and the second
'From the reign of D. Diniz to the reign of D. Alfonso V'.

174 **History of Portugal.**
   A. H. de Oliveira Marques.   New York: Columbia University
   Press, 1976. 2nd ed. 2 vols. 11 maps. bibliog.

The most important book on Portuguese history in English. The first volume
traces the emergence of Portugal from Roman times, through the voyages of

discovery in the 15th and 16th centuries, to its union with Spain and the empire in Brazil prior to the 19th century. The second volume concentrates on the 19th and 20th centuries, covering the constitutional monarchy, Portugal's African colonies, the First Republic and Salazar's New State. A short epilogue discusses the events leading up to, and immediately following the events of 25 April 1974. It concludes with a good and partially annotated bibliography.

175   A history of Iberian civilization.

J. P. de Oliveira Martins, translated by Aubrey F. G. Bell.

London: Oxford University Press; Humphrey Milford, 1930. 292p.

The first English translation of this classic book on Iberian history which was published originally as *Historia da Civilisação Iberica* in 1879. After an introduction, the volume is divided into five 'books': the constitution of society; the decay of ancient Spain; the growth of nationality; the Spanish empire; and the ruins. The whole volume presents a clear impression of the author's intensely patriotic view of Portugal's importance in the history of Iberia.

176   A history of Portugal.

Charles E. Nowell.   Princeton, New Jersey: D. van Nostrand, 1952. Reprinted, 1958. 259p. 5 maps. bibliog.

A general history of Portugal directed at an American audience. Although concentrating on the period prior to the 18th century, it does bring the account up to the beginnings of Salazar's régime in the 1930s.

177   Portugal.

Charles E. Nowell.   Englewood Cliffs, New Jersey: Prentice Hall, 1973. 178p. 2 maps. bibliog. (Modern Nations in Historical Perspective Series).

A general survey of Portugal, which is in part contemporary and in part historical, intended for the non-specialist. It concentrates on the last two centuries and provides a broad introduction to the history and political structure of the country prior to the events of 1974.

178   Outline of Portuguese history.

Lisbon: SNJ Books, [no date]. 32p.

A short, eulogistic account of Portuguese history from the 12th century to the 1930s.

179   A history of Spain and Portugal.

Stanley G. Payne.   Madison, Wisconsin: University of Wisconsin Press, 1973, 2 vols. 6 maps. bibliog.

A comprehensive general history of the Iberian peninsula. It provides an analytical account of the significant political, social, economic and cultural events and trends which have shaped the character of Spain and Portugal. The first volume covers the period up to the 17th century and the second volume continues the account to include the régimes of General Franciso Franco and António de Oliveira Salazar.

180 **Chapters in Anglo-Portuguese relations.**
Edited by Edgar Prestage. Watford, England: Voss & Michael, 1935. 198p. map.

A series of lectures, the majority of which were delivered in the Portuguese Department at King's College, London in 1934 and 1935. It consists of the following chapters: 'English crusaders in Portugal', by H. A. R. Gibb; 'The expedition of John of Gaunt to the peninsula', by C. H. Williams; 'Anglo-Portuguese rivalry in the Persian Gulf, 1615-1635', by C. R. Boxer; 'The treaties of 1642, 1654 and 1661', by Edgar Prestage; 'The treaties of 1703', by Richard Lodge; and 'Portuguese expansion overseas, its causes and results', by Edgar Prestage.

181 **Portugal and its people: a history.**
W. A. Salisbury. London, Edinburgh, New York: T. Nelson & Sons, 1893. 334p.

This broad history traces the emergence of the kingdom of Portugal, the union with Spain (1580-1640), the Peninsular War (1808-14), and events later in the 19th century. Three interesting chapters towards the end provide a 19th-century interpretation of Portuguese activities in Africa, Asia and America.

182 **The commercial relations of England and Portugal.**
V. M. Shillington, A. B. Wallis Chapman. London: George Routledge; New York: E. P. Dutton, [1907]. 344p. map. bibliog.

Divided into two sections, the work analyses the commercial links between England and Portugal. The first part, by V. M. Shillington, is on the mediaeval period and traces the alliance between the two countries from the assistance given to early Portuguese kings by English crusaders, through the Treaty of Windsor in 1386, to trading conditions in the mid-15th century. The second part, by A. B. Wallis Chapman, on the modern period, begins with the colonial rivalry between England and Portugal in the 16th century. It goes on to study the Treaty of 1654 in which England assumed a position of superiority; the Methuen Treaty of 1703 concentrating on the trading of wool and wine; the Brazil trade; and wine production in the Alto-Douro. Appendixes provide transcripts of documents pertaining to the commercial links between Portugal and England.

183 **The history of Portugal from the first ages of the world, to the late great revolution, under King John IV in the year MDCXL.**
Emanuel de Faria y Sousa, translated, and continued down to this present year, 1698, by Capt. John Stevens. London: printed for W. Rogers & Abel Roper; J. Harris & J. Nicholson; T. Newborough; T. Cockerill, 1698. 572p.

This translation claims to be the first history of Portugal in the English tongue. Emanuel de Faria y Sousa's original history was finished in 1640 and Stevens continues the history to 1698 concentrating on the period of war following the Portuguese declaration of independence from Spain in 1668. The first four chapters trace the emergence of the kingdom of Portugal from the time of the grandson of Noah to the reconquest from the Moors by Ferdinand the Great in the eleventh century, and the remaining five chapters of Faria y Sousa's history trace the reigns of the Portuguese and Spanish monarchs prior to 1640.

184 **Portugal.**
H. Morse Stephens. London: T. Fisher Unwin, 1891. 448p. map.
(The Story of the Nations).

A chronological history of Portugal from the earliest times to the end of the 19th century. Although mainly a political history, it also devotes some space to Portuguese literature.

185 **The present and ancient state of Portugal. Containing a particular description of that kingdom, its present and former divisions, the antiquity of it, the manner of the cortes or Parliament, its several names, rivers, forts, lakes, baths, minerals, plants, and all other product, the religious and military orders of the nobility, prelates, prime families, great officers, courts and councils, the coins, language, famous writers, and other great men. With a curious account of the Inquisition, and of all the towns and rivers in that kingdom. Also an account of the towns of the frontiers of Spain. To which is added, an alphabetical index to the whole; and a map of Portugal and Spain. Written by a gentleman who lived several years in that country.**
John Stevens. London: printed and sold by J. King, 1711. 317p.

An early 18th-century account of the geography and history of Portugal, which also covers its literature and language. The first part is taken from *Europa Portuguesa* by Emanuel de Faria y Sousa, the account of the Inquisition is a translation of a work by Dr Carena, the description of the towns of Portugal and the Spanish frontiers is based on that of Rodrigo Mendez Sylva, and the account of Lisbon is by Stevens himself.

186 **Portugal.**
J. B. Trend. London: Ernest Benn, 1957. 218p. map. (Nations of the Modern World).

This general examination of the history of Portugal explains the reasons for its strongly individual character. It concludes with a short chapter on the Portuguese language.

187 **Portugal, old and young: an historical study.**
George Young. Oxford: Clarendon Press, 1917. 342p. 3 maps.

This book was designed to explain why Portugal was an ally of Britain during the First World War. It provides an account of Portugal's role in past European history, of the position of Portugal in the European polity of the early 20th century and of the potential moral and intellectual power of the Portuguese people.

Portugal.
See item no. 5.

Portugal.
See item no. 31.

Spain and Portugal. Volume II: Portugal.
See item no. 37.

The individuality of Portugal: a study in historical-political geography.
See item no. 58.

Unknown Portugal: archaeological itineraries illustrated with photographs by the author.
See item no. 160.

The Factory House at Oporto.
See item no. 528.

The British Factory Oporto.
See item no. 546.

Subsídios para a bibliografia da história local Portuguesa. (Material for a bibliography of Portuguese local history.)
See item no. 784.

Mediaeval

188 **Portuguese portraits.**
Aubrey F. G. Bell. Oxford: Blackwell, 1917. 144p.

An account of the lives of seven famous Portuguese men from the 13th to the 16th centuries: King Dinis (1261-1325), Nun' Alvarez (1360-1431); Prince Henry the Navigator (1394-1460), Vasco da Gama (1460?-1524); Duarte Pacheco Pereira (1465?-1533?), Affonso de Albuquerque (1462?-1515), and Dom João de Castro (1500-48).

189 **Fernam Lopez.**
Aubrey F. G. Bell. Oxford: Oxford University Press; London: Humphrey Milford, for the Hispanic Society of America, 1921. 62p. (Hispanic Notes and Monographs, Portuguese Series 2).

Surveys the life and works of the Portuguese chronicler Fernam Lopez who was born ca. 1380 and died ca. 1460. Only his chronicles of Dom Pedro I, Dom Fernando, and Dom Joam survive in their original form, but the rest may be found in the work of later authors who revised them. Bell argues that Lopez was not only a good historian but also a poet, a dramatist, a critic and a philosopher. For Bell he was the greatest of all the chroniclers.

190 **Portuguese pioneers in India: spotlight on medicine.**
P. D. Gaitonde. London: Sangam Books, 1983. 188p. bibliog.
Studies the interaction of European and Indian medicine in the 16th century
following the arrival of the Portuguese in India in 1498. It argues that Europe was
more influenced by India in the field of medical science at this time than was India
by Europe.

191 **The patrimonial state and patron-client relations in Iberia and Latin**
America: sources of 'the system' in the fifteenth century writings of
the Infante D. Pedro of Portugal.
Sidney M. Greenfield. Amherst, Massachusetts: University of
Massachusetts at Amherst, 1976. 40p. (Program in Latin American
Studies Occasional Papers Series no. 1).
Discusses the life and thought of the Infante Dom Pedro of Portugal (1392-1449),
the son of King Dom João I, and in particular the recommendations for the
reduction and elimination of poverty in human society made by the Infante in a
book entitled the *Livro da virtuosa bemfeitoria* in which he wrote about the
corporate patrimonial state and systems of patronage and heritage prior to the
discovery of the New World.

192 **The origins of Spain and Portugal.**
Harold V. Livermore. London: Allen & Unwin, 1971. 438p. 12
maps. bibliog.
A thorough survey of the emergence of the independent countries of Spain and
Portugal. It is divided into three sections on the later Roman empire, the
Hispano-Gothic kingdom of Toledo and the Muslim invasions. The north of
Portugal lay in the Roman province of Gallaecia, but most of the later country lay
in Lusitania. By about 411 the central European Suevi had established themselves
in northern Portugal, and the author notes that as a result of this, the proportion
of Germanic toponyms is higher between the rivers Douro and Minho than
anywhere else in Iberia. The volume relates how the Muslim conquest of the 8th
century led to the emergence of an Islamic core in al-Andalus in what had been
the most Romanized part of Spain. It then traces the reconquest which spread
from the north in the 11th century and in which Portugal played a considerable
role.

193 **Daily life in Portugal in the late Middle Ages.**
A. H. de Oliveira Marques, translated by S. S. Wyatt. Madison,
Wisconsin; London: University of Wisconsin Press, 1971. 355p. 2
maps. bibliog.
Presents an account of Portuguese mediaeval society in its daily actions. A wealth
of information is provided on food, dress, the house, hygiene and health,
affection, work, faith, culture, amusements and death in late mediaeval Portugal.
The work was originally published in Portuguese as *A sociedade medieval*
Portuguesa: aspectos de vide quotidiana, Lisbon: Livraria Sá da Costa Editora.
1964.

194 **The chivalry of Portugal.**
Edgar Prestage. In: *Chivalry: a series of studies to illustrate its historical significance and civilizing influence.* Edited by Edgar Prestage. London: Kegan Paul, Trench, Trubner & Company; New York: Alfred A. Knopf, 1928. p. 141-66.

An account of chivalry and knighthood in Portugal. It traces the origins of chivalry in the country, the role of knights, the effects of the Crusades, the activities of the Military Orders and the importance of religion in impelling the Portuguese overseas.

195 **The royal power and the cortes in Portugal.**
Edgar Prestage. Watford, England: Voss & Michael, 1927. 32p. bibliog.

A short account of the institutions of the monarchy and the cortes (legislative assembly) in mediaeval Portugal.

196 **The chronicles of Fernão Lopes and Gomes Eannes de Zurara.**
Translated by Edgar Prestage. Watford, England: Voss & Michael, 1928. 99p.

An account of the life and works of historians Fernão Lopes (ca. 1380-ca. 1460) and Gomes Eannes de Zurara (ca. 1410-74) set against a background of the times in which they lived. It includes extended extracts from the chronicles of King Pedro I, King Fernando and King João I by Lopes, and the chronicles of Ceuta and Guinea by Zurara.

197 **The Moors in Spain and Portugal.**
Jan Read. London: Faber & Faber. 1974. 268p. 4 maps. bibliog.

A broadly chronological survey of the Moorish occupancy of Iberia. Until the 12th century southern Portugal formed the most distant and provincial part of al-Andalus and as such it is generally not treated separately in this account. However, the emergence of Portugal as an independent kingdom and her subsequent role in the reconquest is described in much greater detail in the second half of the book, with the reconquest finally being completed in 1249 with the capture of Silves in the south by Afonso III.

198 **Philippa: Dona Filipa of Portugal.**
T. W. E. Roche. Chichester, England: Phillimore, 1971. 129p. 2 maps. bibliog.

An account of the life of Philippa of Lancaster, daughter of John of Gaunt and wife of King João I of Portugal, which highlights the Anglo-Portuguese alliance based on the Treaty of Windsor (1386). It traces her life from her birth in England in 1359 to her death from plague in the summer of 1415 and also includes a brief chapter on the early lives of her children.

199   The obedience of a King of Portugal.
       Translated and with a commentary by Francis M. Rogers.
       Minneapolis, Minnesota: University of Minnesota Press, 1958.
       120p. map.
A facsimile and translation of the 15th-century Vasco Fernandes oration, together
with a commentary. It is a rendering of the obedience of King John II of Portugal
to Pope Innocent VIII and recounts the merits of the Lusitanian Royal House as
well as the deeds and character of John II.

200   The English intervention in Spain and Portugal in the time of
       Edward III and Richard II.
       P. E. Russell.   Oxford: Clarendon Press, 1955. 611p. 11 maps.
       bibliog.
A reassessment of English policy and action in Iberia during the 14th century,
based mainly on Spanish archive material. With reference to Portugal it includes
chapters on the rivalry between the Black Prince and Fernando of Portugal for
the throne of Castile; the activities of Edmund of Cambridge in Portugal; the
Battle of Aljubarrota in 1385, in which the Portuguese defeated the Castilians and
established independence; the Anglo-Portuguese invasion of Leon in 1387; and
the Anglo-Portuguese alliance associated with the marriage of Philippa of
Lancaster to João I. An appendix provides the texts of twelve documents
pertaining to English intervention in Iberia during the 14th century.

201   The perfect Prince: a biography of the King Dom João II (who
       continued the work of Henry the Navigator).
       Elaine Sanceau.   Oporto, Portugal: Livraria Civilização-Editora,
       1959. 446p. map. bibliog.
A thorough biography of Dom João II (1455-95) who, the author argues, unified
Portugal around him to fulfil the work of the navigator Infante Dom Henrique.
She suggests that had Dom João II not lived it is doubtful whether Portugal would
have played the part she did in the 16th century.

202   A social history of black slaves and freedmen in Portugal, 1441-
       1555.
       A. C. de C. M. Saunders.   Cambridge, England: Cambridge
       University Press, 1982. 283p. 4 maps. bibliog.
A detailed study of black slavery in Portugal during the 15th and 16th centuries. It
begins with a general investigation of the slave trade together with an account of
its legal and philosophical justifications. The bulk of the book then surveys the
demography, occupations, lifestyles, legal positions, possibilities of freedom, and
religion of the black slaves in Portugal.

History of the origin and establishment of the Inquisition in Portugal.
See item no. 388.

St. Elizabeth of Portugal.
See item no. 391.

A history of the Marranos.
See item no. 396.

Bibliografia geral Portuguesa: seculo XV. (General Portuguese bibliography: 15th century.)
See item no. 744.

Discoveries and exploration

203 **Conquests and discoveries of Henry the Navigator, being the chronicles of Azurara, Portuguese navigators and colonizers of the fifteenth and sixteenth centuries.**
Edited by Virginia de Castro e Almeida, translated by Bernard Miall. London: Allen & Unwin, 1936. 253p. map.
An abridged translation of the chronicles of Gomes Eannes de Azurara, recording the siege and capture of Ceuta in 1415 by the Portuguese, and the discovery of Guinea, Senegal and Sierra Leone. It begins with a short chapter providing notes on the history of Portugal prior to the 16th century.

204 **Congo to Cape: early Portuguese explorers.**
Eric Axelson. London: Faber & Faber, 1973. 224p. 3 maps. bibliog.
An account of the explorations of Diogo Cão (1482-86) in the Congo and southwest Africa, and of Bartolomeu Dias (1487-88) when he rounded the Cape of Good Hope and opened the sea route into the Indian Ocean. It includes a discussion of the discoveries of the inscribed stone pillars raised by Cão and Dias as landmarks, assertions of Portuguese sovereignty, and symbols of Christianity.

205 **Prince Henry the Navigator: the hero of Portugal and of modern discovery 1394-1460 AD, with an account of geographical progress throughout the Middle Ages as the preparation for his work.**
C. Raymond Beazley. New York, London: G. P. Putnam's Sons, 1895. 336p. 17 maps. (Heroes of the Nations).
Provides an account of European exploration and discovery from the times of the early Christian pilgrims to the 15th century, culminating in the Portuguese discoveries undertaken under the direction of Prince Henry the Navigator (1394-1460). It provides an heroic view of Prince Henry's activities.

206 **Gaspar Corrêa.**
Aubrey F. G. Bell. Oxford: Oxford University Press; London:
Humphrey Milford, for the Hispanic Society of America, 1924.
93p. (Hispanic Notes and Monographs, Portuguese Series 5).
A study of the life and works of Gaspar Corrêa, the early 16th-century historian
of Portuguese India.

207 **Diogo do Couto.**
Aubrey F. G. Bell. Oxford: Oxford University Press; London:
Humphrey Milford, for the Hispanic Society of America, 1924.
82p. (Hispanic Notes and Monographs, Portuguese Series 4).
Studies the life and works of Diogo Couto (1542-1616) whose *Decadas* provided a
history of the Portuguese in India to 1600.

208 **Portugal and the quest for the Indies.**
Christopher Bell. London: Constable, 1974. 247p. 3 maps.
bibliog.
A study of Portuguese overseas expansion during the late 14th and 15th centuries
from the marriage of King João I and Philippa of Lancaster in 1387 to Vasco da
Gama's arrival in India in 1498. It provides an historical assessment of internal
changes in Portugal at a time when the country was at the forefront of overseas
exploration.

209 **The tragic history of the sea 1598-1622: narratives of the shipwrecks
of the Portuguese East Indiamen *São Thomé* (1589), *Santo Alberto*
(1593), *São João Baptista* (1622), and the journeys of the survivors
in south east Africa.**
Edited by C. R. Boxer. Cambridge, England: University Press
for the Hakluyt Society, 1959; Hakluyt Society, 2nd series no.
CXII, issued for 1957. 297p. 6 maps. bibliog.
Three shipwreck narratives edited and translated from the Portuguese *História
Trágico Marítima* (Tragic history of the sea) edited by Bernardo Gomes de Brito
at Lisbon in 1735-36.

210 **Further selections from the tragic history of the sea 1559-1565:
narratives of the shipwrecks of the Portuguese East Indiamen *Aguia*
and *Garça* (1559), *São Paulo* (1561), and the misadventures of the
Brazil ship *Santo António* (1565).**
Edited by C. R. Boxer. Cambridge, England: University Press
for the Hakluyt Society, 1968; Hakluyt Society, 2nd series no.
CXXXII, issued for 1967. 170p. 2 maps. bibliog.
A companion volume to the previous entry, illustrating what the editor calls the
characteristic improvidence of the Portuguese and their equally characteristic
tenacity.

211 **João de Barros; Portuguese humanist and historian of Asia.**
C. R. Boxer. New Delhi: Ashok Kumar, Concept Publishing,
1981. 159p. bibliog. (Xavier Centre of Historical Research Studies
Series, no. 1).

A biography of João de Barros (ca. 1496-1570), whose fame is primarily due to
his work as the semi-official chronicler of Portuguese expansion in his *Decades of
Asia.* The emphasis of the book is on Barros as a historian, but some attention is
devoted to him as a humanist, a moralist and a pedagogue. Particular attention is
paid to three works by Barros: *The first part of the Chronicle of the Emperor
Clarimundo, from whom the Kings of Portugal are descended*; the *Ropica pnefma
or Spiritual merchandise* of 1532; and his *Decades of Asia.*

212 **The discovery of the Atlantic.**
Costa Brochado. Lisbon: Comissão Executiva das
Comemorações do Quinto Centenário da Morte do Infante D.
Henrique, 1960. 126p. 5 maps.

An historical synthesis of Portuguese discoveries in the Atlantic, concentrating on
the Azores, the Caribbean and Brazil. It concludes with an account of the 1922
air-crossing from Lisbon to Rio de Janeiro by Carlos Viegas Gago Coutinho and
Artur de Sacadura Freire Cabral.

213 **Dom Henrique the Navigator.**
Costa Brochado, Vitorino Nemésio, Maurício S. J. Joaquim
Bensaúde, Damião Peres, Teixeira da Mota, Frederico Marjay.
Translated by George F. W. Dykes. Lisbon: Executive
Committee of the Quincentenary Commemorations of the Death
of the Infante Dom Henrique, 1960. 96p. bibliog.

An illustrated account of the life and times of Dom Henrique (1394-1460), paying
particular attention to the Portuguese discoveries in the 15th century.

214 **The mystery of Vasco da Gama.**
Armando Cortesão. Lisbon; Coimbra, Portugal: Junta de
Investigações do Ultramar, 1973. 195p. 10 maps.

Investigates why Vasco da Gama was chosen as the Commander-in-Chief of the
famous maritime expedition which he led in 1497-99 to discover the sea route to
India. It argues that a few years before this Pêro de Covilhã, probably together
with Vasco da Gama, had already secretly discovered this route, and it was for
this reason that Vasco da Gama was chosen to lead the expedition in the light of
the services he had already rendered to the Portuguese King, João II.

215　**Maps and their makers: an introduction to the history of**
　　cartography.
　　G. R. Crone.　London: Hutchinson University Library, 1968. 4th
　　rev. ed. 184p. 8 maps. bibliog.

A short, but fairly comprehensive history of cartography, which notes the great
contribution to the revival of cartography made by Portuguese and other
European seamen in the 15th and 16th centuries.

216　**Prelude to empire: Portugal overseas before Henry the Navigator.**
　　Bailey W. Diffie.　Nebraska City: University of Nebraska Press,
　　1960. 127p. bibliog. (A Bison Book).

Examines the events and developments in European history which prepared the
way for Henry the Navigator's activities and the age of the Great Discoveries. It
illustrates the importance of Portuguese overseas experience prior to 1415, and its
thesis is that without a Henry the Navigator, there would have been no Atlantic
discoveries, but that without the preceding centuries of commerce and fishing
there would have been no Navigator.

217　**Foundations of the Portuguese empire, 1415-1580.**
　　Bailey W. Diffie, George D. Winius.　Minneapolis, Minnesota:
　　University of Minnesota; Oxford: Oxford University Press, 1977.
　　533p. 6 maps. bibliog. (Europe and the World in the Age of
　　Expansion, vol. 1).

Provides a thorough and detailed account of the history of Portuguese overseas
discovery. It begins with a preliminary, brief description of geographical
discoveries from ancient times to 1415. This is followed by accounts of Portuguese
expansion into the Madeiras (1418-25), the Azores (1427), Guinea (1446), the
Congo (1482), the Cape of Good Hope (1488), India (1498), Brazil (1500),
Malacca (1509), China (1513) and Japan (1543). It includes a discussion of how
Portuguese power differed in its various colonies, and an analysis of the empire's
failure as a business enterprise.

218　**Sea road to the Indies: an account of the voyages and exploits of the**
　　Portuguese navigators, together with the life and times of Dom
　　Vasco da Gama, Capitão Mór, Viceroy of India and Count of
　　Vidiqueira.
　　Henry H. Hart.　London, Edinburgh, Glasgow: William Hodge,
　　1952. 296p. map. bibliog.

Although mainly concerned with the activities of Vasco da Gama in discovering
the sea route to India, this volume also discusses the discoveries of Bartolomeu
Dias, Pêro de Covilhã and Pedro Alvarez Cabral.

219 **Humanism and the voyages of discovery in 16th century Portuguese science and letters.**
R. Hooykaas. Amsterdam, The Netherlands; Oxford; New York: North Holland Publishing Company, 1979. 67p. (Medelingen der Koninklijke Nederlandse Akadeimie van Wetenschappen, Afd. Letterkunde, Nieuwe Reeks Deel 42, no. 4).

Studies the religious, economic, social and scientific conflicts engendered by the Portuguese discoveries in the 16th century.

220 **Vasco da Gama and his successors.**
K. G. Jayne. London: Methuen, 1910. 325p. map. bibliog.

A collection of biographies of Portuguese people of the 15th and 16th centuries, including Prince Henry the Navigator, Diogo Cão, Bartolomeu Dias and Affonso de Albuquerque, King Manoel (1469-1521), D. João de Castro (1500-48), King Sebastian (1554-78) and Luís de Camões (1524-80). It is divided into sections on: the early discoveries, 1415-97; Vasco da Gama, 1495-1524; from sea-power to empire, 1505-48; Judaism, humanism and the Church; art and literature; and the decline of Portugal, 1548-80.

221 **Portuguese voyages 1498-1663.**
Edited by Charles David Ley. London: J. M. Dent & Sons; New York: E. P. Dutton, 1947. 360p. (Everyman's Library, no. 986).

A collection of translations of seven Portuguese tales of exploration: the route to India 1497-98, from *Vasco da Gama's first voyage*; the discovery of Brazil 1500; the lands of Prester John 1520-26, from the *Narrative of the Portuguese Embassy to Abyssinia*; the Furthest East 1537-58, from the *Voyages and adventures of Fernand Mendes Pinto*; the tragic history of the sea 1552-85; the Jesuits in Abyssinia 1625-34, from *A voyage to Abyssinia*; and overland return from India 1663.

222 **The life of Prince Henry of Portugal, surnamed the Navigator; and its results: comprising the discovery, within one century, of half the world. With new facts on the discovery of the Atlantic Islands; a refutation of French claims to priority in discovery; Portuguese knowledge (subsequently lost) of the Nile lakes; and the history of the naming of America. From authentic cotemporary [sic] documents.**
Richard Henry Major. London, Berlin: A. Asher, 1868. 487p. 3 maps. bibliog.

A 19th-century survey of the life and times of Prince Henry the Navigator, paying particular attention to the voyages of discovery in the 15th and 16th centuries.

223 **The secret discovery of Australia: Portuguese ventures 250 years before Captain Cook.**
Kenneth Gordon McIntyre. London, Sydney: Souvenir Press, 1977. 427p. Sydney: Pan, rev. and abridged ed., 1982. 236p. 30 maps. bibliog.

This controversial book arguing that Australia was first 'discovered' by the Portuguese in the 16th century is based largely on an interpretation of the 16th-century Portuguese or Franco-Portuguese Dieppe maps, the most important of which, the so-called Dauphin map of 1536, can be found in the British Museum.

224 **The golden age of Prince Henry the Navigator.**
J. P. de Oliveira Martins, translated with additions and annotations by J. Johnston Abraham, W. Edward Reynolds. London: Chapman & Hall, 1914, 324p.

Provides an account of the lives, discoveries and fates of the sons of John of Aviz and Philippa of Lancaster in the 15th century based on the last edition published during the author's lifetime of *Os filhos de D. João I* (The sons of King John I) Lisbon, 1901. It provides an assessment of Henry the Navigator which is very different from that given by the Prince's early biographers Richard Henry Major and C. Raymond Beazley, and suggests that he was stubborn, ruled by his passions, and 'capable of combining, equally, cunning and violence' in order to bring his plans to a successful issue. It also describes the lives of John of Aviz's other sons, Duarte, Peter, John, Fernando and Barcellos. An appendix gives a synopsis of the autoscript of Prince Peter, written by Gomes de Santo Estevam, and first published in 1544.

225 **Portuguese voyages to America in the fifteenth century.**
Samuel Eliot Morison. Cambridge, Massachusetts: Harvard University Press, 1940, 151p. 6 maps. (Harvard Historical Monographs, 14).

An account of Portugese voyages of discovery across the Atlantic Ocean during the 15th century. It concentrates on the Teive-Velasco voyages of 1452, the alleged voyage of João Vaz Corte-Real to Newfoundland, the Dulmo-Estreito attempt to find Antilla, the adventures of João Fernandes, the voyages of the Cortes-Reais between 1499 and 1502, and Pedro Álvares Cabral's voyage to Brazil. It suggests that the first Portuguese discoveries in the New World were made in 1500 by Pedro Alvares Cabral in Brazil and by Gaspar Real in Newfoundland.

226 **So noble a captain: the life and times of Ferdinand Magellan.**
Charles McKew Parr. New York: Thomas Y. Crowell, 1953. 423p. bibliog.

A biography of the Portuguese explorer Ferdinand Magellan, whose two voyages from Lisbon eastwards to the Philippines in 1505-12 and from San Lucar westward to the Philippines in 1519-21 opened up the Far East sea trade to Europe.

227 **The Portugal story: three centuries of exploration and discovery.**
John Dos Passos. London: Robert Hale, 1969. 402p. 2 maps.
bibliog.
An historical account of Portugal's rise to power in the 15th century. It is
particularly concerned with the development of Portugal's empire, and is divided
into five main parts: how Portugal began; heirs to the adventurers; the enterprise
of the Indies; peak of empire; and Portugal and America.

228 **A history of the Portuguese discoveries.**
Damião Peres. Lisbon: Comissão Executiva das Comemorações
do Quinto Centenário da Morte do Infante D. Henrique, 1960.
128p.
A short historical account of the Portuguese discoveries in Africa, Asia, America,
and the Atlantic, Indian and Pacific Oceans.

229 **The Portuguese pioneers.**
Edgar Prestage. London: Adam & Charles Black, 1933.
Reprinted 1966. 352p. 4 maps. (The Pioneer Histories).
This comprehensive account of Portuguese exploration recounts the discoveries of
Madeira, the Azores, the Cape Verde islands, the coasts of Africa, Brazil and the
sea passages to India and the Far East. It includes some discussion of the reasons
why the Portuguese undertook their overseas expansion and of the role played by
Prince Henry the Navigator.

230 **Prince Henry the Navigator and Portuguese maritime enterprise:
catalogue of an exhibition at the British Museum September-
October 1960.**
Compiled by R. A. Skelton with the collaboration of H. G.
Whitehead and P. D. A. Harvey. London: British Museum,
1960. 166p.
A catalogue of 326 items displayed in a British Museum exhibition. In addition to
providing details of the exhibits it includes introductions on each of the major
themes, covering subjects such as the discoveries themselves, settlement,
commerce, missionary enterprises, nautical science, cartography and relations
with England.

231 **A journal of the first voyage of Vasco da Gama 1497-1499.**
Translated and edited, with notes, an introduction and appendixes
by E. G. Ravenstein. London: The Hakluyt Society, 1898 (no.
99). 250p. 8 maps.
Following an introduction on the life of Vasco da Gama (1469?-1524) and on the
manuscript of the *Roteiro* (log-book), this volume provides a translation of this
journal of Vasco da Gama's journey from Lisbon to Calecut in India and back
starting in 1497 and ending in 1499. Eight appendixes provide details of other
accounts of the voyage, the ships, early maps, relevant letters, honours and
rewards bestowed upon Vasco da Gama, and aspects of the voyage itself.

232 **Magellan of the Pacific.**
Edouard Roditi. London: Faber & Faber, 1972. 271p. map.
bibliog.

A biography of Fernando de Magalhães, known in most languages as Magellan,
who was the first person to circumnavigate the earth, setting sail in 1519. He
described himself as a citizen of Oporto and the first part of the book traces his
life from childhood to his departure on his final expedition. The second part of
the book follows his major voyage of discovery and exploration, his death in
battle in 1521, and the final return of the remains of his crew.

233 **Prince Henry the Navigator.**
P. E. Russell. London: The Hispanic and Luso-Brazilian
Councils, 1960. 30p. 2 maps.

A published lecture on Prince Henry the Navigator, delivered at Canning House
in May 1960. It provides a succinct account of Prince Henry's life and
experiences.

234 **Henry the Navigator.**
Elaine Sanceau. London: Hutchinson, no date [ca. 1946]. 144p.
map. bibliog.

As well as being a biography of the Infante Dom Henrique, this work also
provides a survey of Portuguese history in the 15th century.

235 **Knight of the Renaissance: D. João de Castro, soldier, sailor,**
scientist, and viceroy of India 1500-1548.
Elaine Sanceau. London, New York, Melbourne, Sydney, Cape
Town: Hutchinson, no date [ca. 1949]. 235p. map. bibliog.

Surveys the life and times of Dom João de Castro, who was born in 1500 and was
made Governor of India in 1545. On each of his main voyages, he kept a log-book
covering details of coastal waters and ocean phenomena, and much of this volume
is based on the surviving three of these *Roteiros* from his journeys from Lisbon to
Goa, Goa to Diu and Goa to Suez.

236 **Prince Henry the Navigator.**
John Ure. London: Constable, 1977. 207p. 2 maps. bibliog.

A biography of Prince Henry, who the author reveals to be a far more complex
character than that presented by the heroic view of many early writers. He
suggests that Prince Henry was 'a man torn between the conflicting influences of a
mediaeval background and upbringing on the one hand, and a pragmatic and
forward-looking personality on the other'.

Portugal
See item no. 44.

Mary and misogyny: women in Iberian expansion overseas 1415-1815, some facts, fancies and personalities.
See item no. 163.

The perfect Prince: a biography of the King Dom João II (who continued the work of Henry the Navigator).
See item no. 201.

Four centuries of Portuguese expansion, 1415-1825: a succinct survey.
See item no. 316.

The discovery of the East.
See item no. 321.

Letters of John III King of Portugal 1521-1557: the Portuguese text edited with an introduction.
See item no. 323.

Letters of the court of John III, King of Portugal.
See item no. 324.

Portuguese rule on the Gold Coast, 1469-1682.
See item no. 337.

The rise of Portuguese power in India 1497-1550.
See item no. 338.

The Church militant and Iberian expansion 1440-1770.
See item no. 384.

Portugal: a pioneer of Christianity.
See item no. 395.

The romance of the Portuguese in Abyssinnia: an account of the adventurous journeys of the Portuguese to the empire of Prester John; their assistance of Ethiopia in its struggle against Islam and their subsequent efforts to impose their own influence and religions, 1490-1633.
See item no. 447.

From Lisbon to Goa 1500-1750: studies in Portuguese maritime enterprise.
See item no. 490.

Early Portuguese books 1489-1600 in the library of His Majesty the King of Portugal.
See item no. 772.

1575-1800

237　The battle of Alcazar: an account of the defeat of Don Sebastian of
Portugal at El-Ksar el-Kebir.
E. W. Bovill.　London: Batchworth Press, 1952. 198p. 3 maps.
bibliog.

A detailed description of the Battle of Alcazar in 1578 and the circumstances
surrounding it. The short introduction is by the Rev. R. Trevor Davies and sets
the wider European scene for the events described in the book. Dom Sebastian,
King of Portugal (1557-78) invaded Morocco in July with a badly-trained and
disorganized army and was met and defeated by Abd el-Malek at El-Ksar on 4
August. Dom Sebastian was killed during the battle and Abd el-Malek died from
poison which he had been given several days before, while encouraging his
troops. With the flower of Portuguese nobility dead on the field of battle, the
Portuguese crown passed to Philip II of Spain and Portugal became an appendage
of the Spanish crown.

238　Commentaries of Ruy Freyre de Andrada, in which are related his
exploits from the year 1619, in which he left this Kingdom of
Portugal as General of the Sea of Ormuz, and Coast of Persia, and
Arabia until his death.
Edited and with an introduction by C. R. Boxer.　London:
George Routledge & Sons, 1930. 328p. map. bibliog. (The
Broadway Travellers).

An English edition of the *Commentarios do Grande Capitão Ruy Freyre de
Andrade* first published in Lisbon in 1647. The work describes the operations
leading up to the capture of Ormuz by an Anglo-Persian force from the
Portuguese in 1622.

239　On a Portuguese carrack's bill of lading in 1625.
C. R. Boxer.　Coimbra, Portugal: Coimbra Editora, 1938. 32p.

Discusses the *Conhecimento* or bill of lading from the carrack *Conceição* signed in
Goa in February 1625. It provides a range of information on Portuguese shipping
to India in the 17th century and is reprinted from *Biblios*, (1938) vol. 14.

240　Some contemporary reactions to the Lisbon earthquake of 1755.
C. R. Boxer.　Lisbon: Faculdade de Letras, Universidade de
Lisboa, 1956. 21p.

A short survey of contemporary responses to the 1755 earthquake in Lisbon, in
which tens of thousands lost their lives and which destroyed the city, including
eyewitness descriptions of the devastation, first attempts at reconstruction and the
aid given by the countries of England, Ireland and Spain.

241   **Portuguese bankers at the court of Spain 1626-1650.**
      James C. Boyajian.   New Brunswick, New Jersey: Rutgers
      University Press, 1983. 289p. bibliog.

Analyses Lisbon's merchants and the shift of fortunes that transformed a few of
them into the foremost financiers of the Spanish Habsburgs, and thus of Europe,
between 1627 and 1647.

242   **A King for Portugal: the Madrigal conspiracy, 1594-95.**
      Mary Elizabeth Brooks.   Madison; Milwaukee, Wisconsin:
      University of Wisconsin Press, 1964. 192p. bibliog.

A detailed account of the story in history and literature of Gabriel de Espinosa,
the pastry-maker of Madrigal, who was executed by the Spanish authorities in
1595 for impersonating the deceased King of Portugal, Sebastian I. It also
provides a summary chapter on Sebastianism and the other false Sebastians who
tried to claim the Portuguese throne.

243   **The Marquis of Pombal.**
      Conde da Carnota.   London: Longmans, Green, Reader & Dyer,
      1871. 2nd ed. 387p.

A 19th-century biography of the Marquis of Pombal (1699-1782), under whose
direction Lisbon was rebuilt after the earthquake of 1755 and Portugal's economy
revitalized.

244   **Dictator of Portugal: a life of the Marquis of Pombal, 1699-1782.**
      Marcus Cheke.   London: Sidgwick & Jackson, 1938. 315p.
      bibliog.

A biography of Sebastian Joseph de Carvalho e Mello, the Marquis of Pombal,
who became the effective dictator of Portugal during the reign of King Joseph I.
Pombal was made Minister of Foreign Affairs and War on the accession of King
Joseph in 1750, and in his subsequent career he oversaw the rebuilding of Lisbon,
the expulsion of the Jesuits and the development of Portugal's economy, before
his fall from grace on the accession of Queen Maria in 1777.

245   **An account of the court of Portugal under the reign of the present
      King Dom Pedro II with some discourses on the interests of
      Portugal, with regard to other sovereigns; containing a relation of
      the most considerable transactions that have pass'd of late between
      that court, and those of Rome, Spain, France, Vienna, England,
      etc.**
      [John Colbatch].   London: printed for Thomas Bennet at the
      Half-Moon in St. Paul's Churchyard, 1700. 352p.

The first part of this volume is a detailed account of the Portuguese court
referring to the royal family and ministers at the end of the 17th century. The
second part concerns Portuguese foreign relations with the other European
powers.

246 **Espingarda perfeyta or the perfect gun.**
Edited and translated by Rainer Daehnhardt, W. Keith Neal.
London; New York: Sotheby Parke Bernet; Cascais, Portugal:
Sociedade Portuguesa de Armas Antigas, 1974. 466p.

A treatise on gun-making written in Lisbon in the latter part of the 17th century by three brothers, José Francisco, João Rodrigues and Manoel António. It was published in Lisbon in 1718 with the names of the authors given as César Fiosconi and Jordam Guserio and provides details of all facets of gun-making at this time. It has been reprinted to 'throw more light on the subject of gun-making in the 17th and 18th centuries than any other known book'. A concluding selection of photographs illustrates various locks from the 16th to the 18th century, and the volume includes the Portuguese text as well as an English translation.

247 **Catherine of Bragança, infanta of Portugal & queen-consort of England.**
Lillias Campbell Davidson.   London: John Murray, 1908. 517p.

A eulogizing account of the life of Catherine Bragança. Although the majority of the book is devoted to her life as the queen of King Charles II of England, introductory chapters comment on her early life in Portugal and on the details of the treaty associated with her marriage in 1662. Final chapters also cover her return to Portugal in 1692 following the death of King Charles II and her appointment as Queen Regent of Portugal in 1705.

248 **Atlantic islands: Madeira, the Azores and the Cape Verdes in seventeenth century commerce and navigation.**
T. Bentley Duncan.   Chicago; London: University of Chicago
Press, 1972. 291p. 9 maps. bibliog. (Studies in the History of
Discoveries).

A thorough historical account of the economic and political importance of the Atlantic islands of the Azores, Madeira and the Cape Verdes in the 17th century. Specific chapters cover the wine and slave trades, and appendixes give information on the geography and historical demography of the islands, Portuguese weights and measures, and Portuguese money.

249 **Catherine of Braganza – Charles II's queen.**
Hebe Elsna.   London: Robert Hale, 1967. 192p. bibliog.

A biography of Catherine of Braganza (1640-1705), queen of Charles II of England, from her days as a princess in Portugal, through her time in England, to the final period of her life when she was Queen Regent of Portugal.

250 **The Baron de Fagel's account of the campagne in Portugal of 1705. In several letters from the late King of Portugal, Queen Dowager, Baron de Fagel, the Dutch Pleniopotentiary Schoonberg, and others. With the reasons of the ill success of the siege of Badajoz; and an exact plan of that city and country adjacent. Lately published in Holland, by order of General Fagel, and done out of French into English.**
Baron de Fagel.   London: printed for John Morphew near Stationers-Hall, 1708. 30p. map.

Presents an account of events in Portugal in 1705 based largely on contemporary correspondence to the author, Baron de Fagel. It includes an account of the failure of the siege of Badajoz which was attempted, against Fagel's advice, in order to penetrate Andalusia as part of the war of the Spanish Succession.

251 **The Methuens and Portugal 1691-1708.**
A. D. Francis.   London: Cambridge University Press, 1966. 397p. map. bibliog.

Analyses Anglo-Portuguese commercial and diplomatic relations beteen 1691, when John Methuen was appointed English Minister in Lisbon, and 1708, when his son Paul who succeeded his father as Ambassador in Lisbon in 1706, departed. Considerable attention is paid to the Commercial Treaty of 1703, which cemented the Triple and Quadruple offensive alliance of the same year.

252 **The married life of Anne of Austria, Queen of France, Mother of Louis XIV. And Don Sebastian, King of Portugal: historical studies from numerous unpublished sources.**
Martha Walker Freer.   London: Tinsley Brothers, 1865. 2 vols.

The biography of Dom Sebastian (1554-1578) is included in the second volume, and attention is paid specifically to his birth and education, his interview with Philip II of Spain and his crusade against the Moors, his death at the Battle of Alcazar, and a final chapter on the pretenders to his name and crown.

253 **The Jesuit António Vieira and his plans for the economic rehabilitation of seventeenth century Portugal.**
Richard Graham.   São Paulo, Brazil: Seção de Publicações da Divisão de Arquivo do Estado, 1978. 216p. bibliog.

A Brazilian edition of the author's 1957 MA thesis. It presents an analysis of the influence of the preacher and missionary António Vieira (1608-97) on the economy of Portugal in the 17th century, paying particular attention to his background, his campaign for the creation of a mercantile company, the influence of his ideas and the failure of his later proposals.

254 **Economy and society in baroque Portugal, 1668-1703.**
Carl A. Hanson. London: Macmillan, 1981. 354p. 2 maps.
bibliog.

Provides an account of Portuguese history in the reign of Pedro II. It argues that behind the façade of baroque calm there were dramatic shifts in the socio-economic foundations of the age. Despite the efforts of the government to develop a mercantilist approach to the economy and to curb the inquisitional persecution of New Christian merchants, the established social order was able to reassert itself and eventually find security under an increasingly absolutist government.

255 **The Lisbon earthquake.**
T. D. Kendrick. London: Methuen, 1956. 170p. 2 maps. bibliog.

Describes the events in Portugal surrounding the Lisbon earthquake of 1755, and the universal heart-searching which followed it, particularly in London. Its influence on literature and religious thought is also discussed.

256 **Never a Saint.**
F. W. Kenyan. London: Hutchinson, 1958. 319p.

An historical novel about the life of Queen Carlota Joaquina (1775-1830) who was married at the age of ten to Dom João VI in 1786, and of her love affair with Manuel de Sabatini.

257 **The private correspondence of Sir Benjamin Keene, K. B.**
Edited by Sir Richard Lodge. Cambridge, England: Cambridge University Press, 1933, 548p.

Following a career in which he became Consul General and then Minister Plenipotentiary at Madrid, Keene became Envoy Extraordinary and Plenipotentiary to the Court of Portugal in 1745 where he remained for two years before returning to Spain. His favourite correspondent was Abraham Castres who had succeeded to Keene's post at Lisbon in 1749. Many of the letters printed in this book refer to Portugal and in particular to Lisbon and its environs in the mid-18th century. Several of these are related to the Lisbon earthquake of 1755.

258 **Catherine of Braganza.**
Janet Mackay. London: John Long, 1937. 320p. bibliog.

Presents a biography of Catherine of Braganza, the daughter of Duke João of Portugal, born in 1640. She married Charles II of England, and then after his death in 1685 she returned to her own country and was appointed Regent of Portugal. She died in 1705.

259   A general view of the state of Portugal: containing a topographical
      description thereof. In which are included, an account of the
      physical and moral state of the kingdom; together with observations
      on the animal, vegetable and mineral productions of its colonies.
      James Murphy.   London: T. Cadell Jun. & W. Davies, 1798.
      272p. map.

A general survey of the topography, economy and society of Portugal in the late
18th century based on the author's experiences and also on a variety of
Portuguese sources. It begins with chapters on the geography and geology of the
country. These are followed by various chapters on agriculture, commerce and
industry, with further sections on antiquities, ceremonies, customs and language.
It concludes with a short account of the history of Portugal. Two chapters, on the
relationship between agriculture and manufacturing, and on some of the natural
productions of the Portuguese colonies, are written by Dominick Vandelli. There
are fifteen plates engraved from sketches made by the author.

260   Memoirs of the Marquis of Pombal; with extracts from his writings,
      and from despatches in the State Paper Office, never before
      published.
      John A. Smith.   London: Longman, Brown, Green & Longmans,
      1843. 2 vols.

Presents a biography of Joseph Sebastian de Carvalho e Mello, the Marquis of
Pombal, designed primarily to vindicate his character. It provides a wide range of
material and comment on Portuguese history in the 18th century, and pays
particular attention to Pombal's conflicts with the Jesuits, his early rise to power
and fame, and his subsequent ignominy and retreat from public affairs.

261   The history of the revolutions of Portugal, from the foundation of
      that kingdom to the year MDCLXVII with letters of Robert
      Southwell, during his embassy there to the Duke of Ormand; giving
      a particular account of the deposing [sic] Alfonso, and placing Don
      Pedro on the throne.
      Robert Southwell.   London: printed for John Osborn at the
      Golden Ball in Pater-noster Row, 1740. 374p.

An account of the revolution in Portugal in 1667 (led by Pedro, brother of Afonso
VI) together with the letters of Robert Southwell to the Duke of Ormond when
the author was envoy extraordinary from King Charles II to the Court of Lisbon.
It also considers the revolutions of 1640 and 1580 when the crown of Portugal was
subjected to that of Castile.

262   The revolutions of Portugal.
      Abbot de Vertot. [Aubert de Vertot d'Aubeuf]   London: printed
      for William Chetwood, 1721. 138p.

An English translation of the author's original French history of Portugal
extracted from the writings of French, Spanish, Portuguese and Italian authors. It
traces the end of Dom Sebastian's reign, the accession of Portugal by Spain in
1580, and Portugal's eventual independence in 1640.

The journal of William Beckford in Portugal and Spain 1787-1788.
See item no. 65.

Italy, with sketches of Spain and Portugal.
See item no. 73.

Letters from Portugal on the late and present state of that kingdom.
See item no. 75.

Sketches of society and manners in Portugal. In a series of letters from Arthur William Costigan, Esq., late a Captain of the Irish Brigade in the service of Spain, to his brother in London.
See item no. 79.

An account of Portugal as it appeared in 1766.
See item no. 83.

Letters written during a short residence in Spain and Portugal, with some account of Spanish and Portuguese poetry.
See item no. 97.

A Portuguese embassy to Japan (1644-1647) translated from an unpublished Portuguese ms. and other contemporary sources, with commentary and appendices.
See item no. 314.

The affair of the 'Madre de Deus' (A chapter in the history of the Portuguese in Japan.)
See item no. 315.

Conflicts and conspiracies: Brazil and Portugal 1750-1808.
See item no. 331.

Portugal and Rome c.1748-1830: an aspect of Catholic enlightenment.
See item no. 393.

The relations between Portugal and Japan.
See item no. 442.

The diplomatic and commercial relations of Sweden and Portugal from 1641 to 1670.
See item no. 443.

Malabar and the Portuguese being a history of the relations of the Portuguese and Malabar from 1500 to 1663.
See item no. 444.

Diplomatic relations of Portugal with France, England and Holland from 1646 to 1668.
See item no. 445.

A short survey of Luso-Siamese relations – 1511-1900.
See item no. 446.

From Lisbon to Goa 1500-1750; studies in Portuguese maritime enterprise.
See item no. 490.

Portugal and the War of the Spanish Succession: a bibliography with some diplomatic documents.
See item no. 777.

19th century

263 **The wars of succession of Portugal and Spain, from 1826 to 1840, with résumé of the political history of Portugal and Spain to the present time.**
William Bollaert. London: Edward Standford, 1870. 2 vols. 3 maps.

The war for the Portuguese throne between Dom Pedro and Dom Miguel following Wellington's defeat of the French in Iberia is described in detail in Volume One and the beginning of Volume Two, the remainder of which is concerned with the events in Spain. The author, having failed to obtain a chemical assistantship at King's College London, met Sir John Milly Doyle and volunteered for the forces of Donna Maria II (daughter of Dom Pedro to whom, while he governed Brazil, he handed the Portuguese throne.) Much of the book is based on Bollaert's own experiences and traces events following Dom Miguel's taking of the throne in 1824, and Dom Pedro's landing at Oporto in 1832, with chapters being devoted to each month between January and February 1833. Eventually, on 16 May 1834, the Pedroites won the final battle at Aceiceira and Dom Miguel left for Italy. The last four chapters of Volume One trace the political history of Portugal from the reign of Donna Maria II following the death of her father Dom Pedro in 1834, through the reigns of Dom Pedro V (1853-1861) and Dom Luiz I (1861-1889) to 1869.

264 **An historical view of the revolutions of Portugal, since the close of the Peninsular War: exhibiting a full account of the events which have led to the present state of that country.**
An eye-witness [J. M. Browne]. London: John Murray, 1827. 392p.

Gives details of the background to the war between Dom Miguel and Dom Pedro for the Portuguese crown following the Peninsular War, based largely upon the author's seventeen years personal knowledge of the country as an army officer. It concentrates on the 1820 revolution in Oporto, stimulated by the revolution in Spain and the 1823 counter-revolution, led by Dom Miguel, after which event the author spent some time at the Court of John VI. This experience enabled him to comment with much insight on the political manoeuverings of the various sides between 1814 and 1827. An appendix provides a translation of the 1826 Constitutional Charter of Portugal.

265   **Memoirs of Field-Marshal the Duke de Saldanha, with selections**
       from his Correspondence.
       Conde da Carnota.   London: John Murray, 1880. 2 vols. 2 maps.
A biography of the Duke of Saldanha, soldier and statesman, with whom the
author maintained a friendship from 1827 to 1876. It is an account of Saldanha's
role in the events surrounding the conflict between Dom Pedro and Dom Miguel
over the Portuguese throne and the consequent battle between the absolutist and
liberal movements. It also provides a contemporary account of events in Portugal
between his birth in 1790 and his death in 1876.

266   **Bussaco.**
       G. L. Chambers   London: Swan Sonnenschein & Company, 1910.
       260p. 7 maps. (Wellington's Battlefields Illustrated).
Describes the Battle of Bussaco fought on 27 September 1810 in which
Wellington, commanding the British-Portuguese army, defeated the French under
Marshal André Masséna. Numerous appendixes provide extracts from des-
patches and letters, and give details of casualties.

267   **Carlota Joaquina, Queen of Portugal.**
       Marcus Cheke.   London: Sidgwick & Jackson, 1947. 212p.
A history of the half-century in Portugal following the death of the Marquis of
Pombal in 1782, and based around the central theme of Queen Carlota Joquina
(1775-1830). The author sees this as a period of national calamity, civil discord
and of economic distress, which exhausted Portugal's vitality and led to her
stagnation in the 19th century.

268   **A question of slavery: labour policies in Portuguese Africa and the**
       British protest, 1850-1920.
       James Duffy.   Oxford: Clarendon Press, 1967. 240p. 2 maps.
Studies the labour policies of the Portuguese in Africa which resulted in a form of
legislation perpetuating a land of slavery in Angola and Moçambique lasting well
into the 20th century. The issue of slavery engendered a bitter controversy
between Portugal and the British governments and this, together with the reaction
in Lisbon to it, forms the core of the book.

269   **A treatise on the defence of Portugal, with a military map of the**
       country; to which is added, a sketch of the manners and customs of
       the inhabitants, and principal events of the campaigns under Lord
       Wellington.
       William Granville Elliot.   London: T. Egerton, Military Library,
       1811. 2nd ed. 304p. 6 maps.
A wide-ranging early 19th-century account of Portugal by a captain in the Royal
Regiment of Artillery. After chapters on the geography and topography of
various parts of the country, the author pays particular attention to the
implications of these for defence. There are then four chapters on the lifestyle of
the Portuguese, the problems of travelling, the economy, and the environs of
Lisbon. These are followed by chapters on the campaigns of the Duke of

Wellington in Portugal, and the book concludes with details of weights and measures, exchange rates and lists of principal routes giving distances between places.

270   **A guide to the grand national and historical diorama of the campaigns of Wellington.**
Richard Ford.   London: Thomas Grieve, William Telbin & John Absolon, 1852. 64p.

A short guide to the diorama of Wellington's campaigns painted by Grieve, Telbin and Absolon. It includes comments on, and line-drawings of, the dioramas of his landing at Lisbon on 22 April 1809, the passage of the Duero near Oporto on 12 May 1809, the Battle of Bussaco on 27 September 1810 and the Lines of Torres Vedras.

271   **Britannia sickens: Sir Arthur Wellesley and the convention of Cintra.**
Michael Glover.   London: Leo Cooper, 1970. 208p. 3 maps. bibliog.

Describes the 1808 Portuguese campaign of Sir Arthur Wellesley, later the Duke of Wellington, paying particular attention to the way in which Wellesley managed to overcome the obstacles to success caused by an ossified British tradition of waging war. Considerable detail is given of the events leading up to, and the action involved in the Battle of Vimeiro to the north-west of Torres Vedras in which Wellesley beat Andoche Junot but was prevented from marching on Lisbon by Sir Harry Burrard. The subsequent convention permitting the French army to leave Portugal is also analysed in detail.

272   **The Peninsular War, 1807-1814, a concise military history.**
Michael Glover.   Newton Abbot, England: David & Charles; Hamden, Connecticut: Archon Books, 1974. 431p. 24 maps. bibliog.

This thorough volume provides a basic skeleton of facts surrounding the Peninsular War together with first-hand accounts of military life at the time. Particular stress is laid on the technological limitations of warfare early in the 19th century. Portugal was the scene of battles in the early stages of the War and there is detailed discussion of the battles of Vimeiro and Bussaco, the forcing of the Douro, and the defensive network of the Lines of Torres Vedras. Wherever possible, the author describes events in the words of those who took part in them. Appendixes provide biographical notes about participants in the war; details of regiments and British Army staff in the Peninsular War; commanders of the French armies; battle orders of the British Army at the principal battles; and outlines of the organization of the French army at various periods during the war.

273 **Observations on the present state of the Portuguese army as**
   organised by Lieutenant-General Sir William Carr Beresford, K. B.
   Field Marshal and Commander in Chief of that army. With an
   account of the different military establishments and laws of
   Portugal, and a sketch of the campaigns of the last and present
   year, during which the Portuguese army was brought into the field
   against the enemy, for the first time as a regular force.
   Andrew Halliday.   London: John Murray; Edinburgh: William
   Blackwood; Dublin: John Cumming, 1811. 149p. 5 maps.

A portrayal of the activities of the Portuguese army between 1809 and 1811 based
upon the author's experiences while serving in it. Particular attention is paid to its
activities around Rio Maior while Masséna was at Santarem, and to the Battle of
Fuentas de Onoro (5 May 1810) which saw the defeat of Masséna.

274 **Siege lady: the adventures of Mrs. Dorothy Proctor of Entre**
   Quintas and of divers other notable persons during the siege of
   Oporto and the war of the two brothers in Portugal 1832-1834,
   extracted from her unpublished letters and other contemporary
   sources.
   C. P. Hawkes, Marion Smithes.   London: Peter Davies, 1938.
   288p. map. bibliog.

Provides an account of the siege of Oporto in 1832 and the war between Dom
Pedro and Dom Miguel, based on the letters and reports of Dorothy Proctor, wife
of John Proctor of Knowles, Proctor and Bold, shippers and merchants of
Liverpool and Oporto, whose villa stood outside the western walls of Oporto at
Entre Quintas.

275 **Uniforms of the Peninsular War in colour 1807-1814.**
   Philip J. Haythornthwaite, illustrated by Michael Chappell. Poole,
   England: Blandford Press, 1978. 180p. map. bibliog.

Following a brief historical introduction this book provides a survey of the armies
and uniforms of the countries involved in the Peninsular War. Coloured
illustrations provide pictures of sixteen different officers and troops in the
Portuguese army.

276 **Memoranda relative to the Lines thrown up to cover Lisbon in**
   1810.
   John T. Jones.   London: printed by G. Roworth for private
   circulation, 1829. 188p. map.

Memoranda written by the aide-de-camp to the King and Colonel in the Corps of
Royal Engineers, describing the nature and extent of the defences constructed to
protect Lisbon in 1810, known as the Lines of Torres Vedras. It concludes with an
appendix of letters from Lieut. Colonel Fletcher and the then Captain Jones
during the period when the latter was charged with completing the Lines. There
are twenty-seven figures showing plans of the fortification.

277 **The British battalion at Oporto: with adventures, anecdotes, and exploits in Holland; at Waterloo; and in the expedition to Portugal.**
Corporal [Thomas] Knight.   London: Effingham Wilson, 1834. 126p. map.

An account of Corporal Knight's soldiering in the first third of the 19th century. Chapters Six to Sixteen provide a description of the activities of the British battalion recruited to fight for Dom Pedro in his war against Dom Miguel and in particular of their actions around Oporto in 1832.

278 **Narrative of the expedition to Portugal in 1832, under the orders of his Imperial Majesty Dom Pedro, Duke of Braganza.**
G. Lloyd Hodges.   London: James Fraser, 1833. 2 vols. map.

Describes the expedition undertaken by the author, who had been a Colonel in the service of Queen Maria II of Portugal, with ships and troops from England to the north of Portugal in support of Dom Pedro, the Queen's father, in 1832. It provides an insight into the political intrigues and military conflict between Dom Pedro and Dom Miguel at that time. Thirty-three appendixes provide translations and copies of letters, documents and orders of the day, pertaining to the activities of the British battalions fighting for Dom Pedro.

279 **An account of the war in Portugal between Dom Pedro and Dom Miguel.**
Admiral Charles Napier.   London: T. & W. Boone, 1836. 2 vols.

A wide-ranging contemporary account of the war between Dom Pedro and Dom Miguel for the crown of Portugal. In addition to military details it pays considerable attention to broader issues concerning the feelings of the people and the nature of the administration of both sides. The author participated in the war as Admiral on the side of Dom Pedro, and much information is provided concerning his naval engagements. Sixty-one appendixes give the texts of numerous letters and documents mainly concerning the author's participation in the war.

280 **A history of the Peninsular War.**
Charles Oman.   Oxford: Clarendon Press, 1902-30. 7 vols. maps.

The definitive and detailed history of the Peninsular War. Portugal featured mainly in the early campaigns, with the combat of Rolica, the Battle of Vimeiro (in which the French under Junot were defeated by Wellington) and the convention of Cintra in 1808, being discussed in Volume One; Marshal Nicolas Soult's invasion of Portugal and the capture and recapture of Oporto in 1809 being described in Volume Two; the Portuguese campaign of 1810 including the Battle of Bussaco and the Lines of Torres Vedras being described in Volume Three, and Masséna's retreat from Portugal in 1811 being discussed in Volume Four.

281 **The Peninsular War.**
Roger Parkinson. London: Hart-Davis MacGibbon, 1973. 208p.
7 maps. bibliog. (Series: The British at War).

A short examination of the Peninsular War (1807-14) during which the Duke of
Wellington swept the French, under Napoleon, out of Iberia. There are frequent
mentions of Portugal, which formed the final bastion and also point of departure
for many of the campaigns of the War. The work includes specific discussions of
the battles of Vimiero (1808), Oporto (1809) and Bussaco (1810), and of the
Torres Vedras defensive system.

282 **The French campaign in Portugal, 1810-1811.**
Jean Jacques Pelet-Clozeau, edited, annotated and translated by
Donald D. Horward. Minneapolis, Minnesota: University of
Minnesota Press, 1973. 570p. 9 maps. bibliog.

A translation of the 1,178 page handwritten manuscript entitled *Campagne de
Portugal* by Jean Jacques Germain Pelet-Clozeau, who had been first aide-de-
camp to Marshal André Masséna during the French invasion of Portugal in 1810-
11. It is important for its accurate description of the campaign from the view of
the French staff.

283 **The Portuguese army of the Napoleonic Wars.**
Otto von Pivka, with colour plates by Michael Roffe. London:
Osprey Publishing, 1977. 40p. (Men-at-Arms Series).

Presents an illustrated account of the Portuguese army at the time of the
Napoleonic Wars, which includes an interesting assessment of its capabilities
based on French sources. It is divided into four main sections: a chronology
(1806-13); the army's organization in 1809, covering its division into Infantry of
the Lines, Caçadores, Cavalry, Artillery, the Loyal Lusitanian Legion, Engineers
and Militia; uniforms; and a section describing the colour plates.

284 **Unjust Proclamation of His Serene Highness Don Miguel as King of
Portugal, or an analysis and juridical refutation of the Act passed
by the denominated Three Estates of the Kingdom of Portugal on
the 11th of July, 1828. Dedicated to the most high and powerful
Dona Maria II, Queen Regent of Portugal.**
Antonio da Silva Lopes Rocha. London: printed by R.
Greenlaw, 1829. 226p.

Written by an advocate at the Court of Appeal in Lisbon, this work refutes the
Act of 11 July 1828 which proclaimed the Infante Dom Miguel, rather than his
brother Dom Pedro, as King of Portugal.

285 **An ensign in the Peninsular War: the letters of John Aitchison.**
Edited by W. F. K. Thompson. London: Michael Joseph, 1981.
349p. 19 maps. bibliog.

Coverage of the Duke of Wellington's campaigns in Spain and Portugal between
1809 and 1814, based around the letters and diaries of General Sir John Aitchison

who had served during the campaigns as a junior officer in the 3rd Regiment of Guards.

286 **The Azores: or Western Islands. A political, commercial and geographical account, containing what is historically known of these islands, and descriptive of their scenery, inhabitants, and natural productions; having special reference to the eastern group consisting of St. Michael and St. Mary, the Formigas and Dollabaret Rocks; including suggestions to travellers and invalids who may resort to the archipelago in search of health.**
Walter Frederick Walker. London: Trübner & Company, 1886. 335p. 2 maps.

Although the author claims that this work is 'devoid of any scientific or literary merit', it provides a fascinating account of the Azores in the 19th century, including details of the archipelago's history, geography and economy. It concludes with a short collection of island melodies.

287 **A century of Spain and Portugal (1788-1898).**
George Frederick White. London: Methuen, 1909. 415p. bibliog.

A history of Portugal and Spain from the French Revolution to the Spanish-American War. Particular attention is paid to the relationships between Portugal and Brazil, the war between Dom Pedro and Dom Miguel, and the rising unrest in the country culminating in the assassination of King Carlos in 1908.

Impressions of Madeira in the past.
See item no. 23.

Sketches in Portugal during the civil war of 1845, with observations on the present state and future prospects of Portugal.
See item no. 68.

Lisbon in the years 1821, 1822, and 1823.
See item no. 71.

Portugal and Gallicia with a review of the social and political state of the Basque provinces; and a few remarks on recent events in Spain.
See item no. 85.

Travels in Portugal.
See item no. 89.

Here and there in Portugal: notes of the present and past.
See item no. 94.

Journals of a residence in Portugal 1800-1801 and a visit to France 1838, supplemented by extracts from his correspondence.
See item no. 98.

Journal of a few months residence in Portugal, and glimpses of the south of Spain.
See item no. 103.

Anglicans abroad: the history of the chaplaincy and Church of St. James at Oporto.
See item no. 386.

William Wordsworth's Convention of Cintra: a facsimile of the 1809 tract.
See item no. 455.

The British Factory in Lisbon and its closing stages ensuing upon the Treaty of 1810.
See item no. 457.

20th century

288   **The downfall of a King: Dom Manuel II of Portugal.**
     Russel E. Benton.   Washington, DC: University Press of
     America, 1977. 238p. bibliog.
A biography of the last King of Portugal, Dom Manuel II, who was overthrown by the Republican revolution in 1910 and who died in 1932. It concentrates mainly on the 1910 revolution and on his life in exile which was largely occupied with the collection of an extensive library of early Portuguese literature.

289   **J. P. Hornung: a family portrait.**
     Bertha M. Collin.   Orpington, England: Orpington Press, [1970].
     188p.
An account of an Anglo-Portuguese family in the late 19th and early 20th centuries based on the author's memories of her father.

290   **The Portugal of Salazar.**
     Michael Derrick.   London: Sands: The Paladin Press, 1938. 159p.
This reasonably balanced early account of Salazar's Portugal traces Salazar's rise to power, the principles and practices of the Corporate State, its political structure and its foreign relations, arguing that Portugal was not at that time a Fascist state.

291   **Salazar, rebuilder of Portugal.**
     F. C. C. Egerton.   London: Hodder & Stoughton, 1943. 336p.
Presents an account of what the author sees as Salazar's rebuilding of Portugal, which argues that in 1943 no country had a nobler and a greater outlook. It covers Salazar's principles and activities as a statesman, the constitution of the New

Portuguese State, the colonial empire, and Portugal's foreign policy in a eulogistic manner.

292 **Professor Oliveira Salazar's record.**
Tomaz Wylie Fernandes.   Lisbon: Editions SPN, 1936. 48p.

A study of the early stages of Portugal's reconstruction under Salazar, concerned mainly with fiscal and budgetary matters.

293 **Salazar: Portugal and her leader.**
António Ferro, translated by H. de Barros Gomes, John Gibbons, with a preface by Sir Austen Chamberlain, and foreword by Dr. Oliveira Salazar.   London: Faber & Faber, 1939, 364p.

This eulogistic account of Salazar is based on interviews between himself and the author between 1926 and 1932. It includes a lengthy introduction by Salazar on Portugal and its government.

294 **Portugal: fifty years of dictatorship.**
Antonio de Figueiredo.   Harmondsworth, England: Penguin, 1975. 261p. bibliog.

An account of Salazar's rule in Portugal from the high tide of Fascism to the colonial wars that led to the fall of Dr. Marcello Caetano in 1974. In particular it analyses the economic, social, religious and class interests involved, and shows how Salazar used several obscure currents in Portuguese history to bring about his police state. Salazar's absolute authority over the state is demonstrated in 'Salazar's Portugal: the "Black Book" on Fascism' by Tom Gallagher in *European History Quarterly* vol. 14, no. 4 (1984), p. 479-87. This article reviews ten recently published books of documents on the dictatorship.

295 **Oldest ally: a portrait of Salazar's Portugal.**
Peter Fryer, Patricia McGowan Pinheiro.   London: Dennis Dobson, 1961. 280p. 2 maps. bibliog.

This highly critical account of Salazar's régime in Portugal is divided into three parts. The first provides a general historical and geographical account of the country, which also includes chapters on how the people live, and on food and drink. The second covers the political, social and economic structure of the country with chapters on Salazar, the colonies, the police state and the resistance movement, while the final part is on language, culture and the uniqueness of Portugal including a section on contemporary literature.

296 **Portugal: a twentieth century interpretation.**
Tom Gallagher.   Manchester, England: Manchester University Press, 1983. 278p. 2 maps. bibliog.

Provides a thorough exploration of Portugal under the régime created by Salazar between 1926 and 1974. It analyses Salazar's political philosophy, power structure, economic policies, the nature of his repression and the role of the colonies. A concluding chapter analyses the shortcomings and achievements of Portuguese democracy following the 1974 revolution.

297   **Portugal: the decline and collapse of authoritarian order.**
      Lawrence S. Graham.   Beverly Hills, California; London: Sage
      Publications, 1975. 67p. bibliog. (Comparative Politics Series, no.
      01-053 vol 5).

Analyses the Portuguese experience with authoritarian rule under the Corporative
State established by Salazar in the early 1930s and which culminated in the
revolution of 25 April 1974.

298   **H. R. H. the Duke of Oporto (Crown Prince of Portugal, Dom**
      Affonso Henriques, Prince Royal of Bragança). Memories.
      By permission of H. R. H. the Duchess of Oporto.   London:
      George Routledge & Sons, 1921. 188p.

A biography of the last Prince Royal of Portugal, from his birth in 1865 to his
death in 1920 in Naples. It provides details of the personal relationships and
lifestyles of the Portuguese royal family, particularly at the time prior to the
assassination of King Carlos in 1908 and the subsequent revolution. The work also
includes numerous photographs of the Portuguese royal family.

299   **Salazar and modern Portugal.**
      Hugh Kay.   London: Eyre & Spottiswoode, 1970. 478p. 3 maps.
      bibliog.

A detailed biography of Dr. António de Oliveira Salazar, Prime Minister of
Portugal from 1932 to 1968. While being generally favourable to Salazar, it
presents a balanced account, clearly illustrating the problems of his régime as well
as pointing out its successes. It suggests that the poverty, degradation and internal
confusion in Portugal in 1928 was so bad that had not Salazar assumed office,
Portugal might well have become a province of Spain. The book attempts to
dispense with passion and over-simplified judgements, and to see beyond them to
the multiple complexities in the life of Salazar's elusive public personality.

300   **Politics, a Portuguese statesman.**
      Arthur Ribeiro Lopes.   London: Methuen, 1938. 136p.

Presents a series of essays by a lawyer on the changes introduced into Portugal
following the rise to power of Oliveira Salazar. It argues that he was a sagacious
leader who gave Portugal a well-ordered financial and economic structure.

301   **Portugal.**
      Herminio Martins.   In: *European fascism*. Edited by S. J.
      Woolf.   London: Weidenfeld & Nicolson, 1968. 302-36. (Reading
      University Studies on Contemporary Europe, I).

A detailed investigation of the emergence of the extreme right in Portugal from
its birth in the journal *Integralismo Lusitano* in 1914, to the development of
Salazar's New State and the rise of National Syndicalism. Forming the only
political movement allowed to define its own historical identity under the 'New
State', the strength of the extreme right always lay with the country's youth.

302 **Political constitution of the Portuguese Republic approved by the National Plebiscite of the 19th March 1933. Entered into force on 11th April of same year, and was modified by Laws No. 1885, 1910, 1945, 1963, 1966 and 2009, of 23rd March and 23rd May 1935, 21st December 1936, 18th December 1937, 23rd April 1938 and 17th September 1945 respectively. Colonial Act with alterations contained in Laws No. 1900 and 2009 of 21st May 1935 and 17th September 1945 respectively.**
Lisbon: SNI Books, 1948. 2nd ed. 78p.

Translates the Portuguese Constitution and Colonial Act which emerged under Salazar's régime. Part One on fundamental guarantees is divided into sections on the Portuguese nation; citizens; the family, corporative organizations and autonomous bodies as political units; public opinion; the administrative order; the economic and social order; education, instruction and national culture; the relations of the State with the Catholic Church and the régime of worship; the public and private domains of the State; national defence; administration of undertakings of collective interest; and state finances. Part Two on the political organization of the state is divided into sections on sovereignty; the head of state; the National Assembly; the government; the courts; political and administrative divisions and local autonomous authorities; and the Portuguese Colonial Empire. The volume concludes with the Colonial Act organized into sections on general guarantees; the natives; the political and administrative system; and economic and financial guarantees.

303 **Contemporary Portugal: a history.**
Richard A. H. Robinson. London: Allen & Unwin, 1979. 297p. 2 maps. bibliog.

A comprehensive general survey of the political, economic and social evolution of Portugal during the half-century prior to its publication. It provides a thorough survey of the country during Salazar's régime and a detailed appraisal of the factors leading up to the revolution of 1974. It concludes with a glossary of political terms.

304 **Doctrine and action: internal and foreign policy of the New Portugal, 1928-1939.**
António de Oliveira Salazar, translated by Robert Edgar Broughton. London: Faber & Faber, 1939. 399p.

A collection of Salazar's speeches dating from his acceptance of the Ministry of Finance in 1928 to his views on the political crisis in Europe in 1939. It begins with a detailed introduction in which he gives a background to his opinions and the actions he undertook during the period in which he created what he called the New Portuguese State.

305 **Salazar Prime Minister of Portugal says. . . .**
António de Oliveira Salazar. Lisbon: SPN Books, [1938]. 85p.

A collection of two hundred thoughts selected from the writings of Salazar, chosen to 'prove the activity of the Leader of the Portuguese Recovery'. It is divided into sections on principles and action, state and régimes, order and government, men and nation, production and work, our nationalism, the Portuguese empire, and Portugal in the world. It provides considerable insights into the background to Salazar's policies and actions.

306   **The road for the future.**
       António de Oliveira Salazar.   Lisbon: SNI, 1963. 244p.

A systematic exposition of a number of Salazar's political statements dating from the period 1928-62. The editors have divided it into five broad parts: realities and trends of the Portuguese polity; the hostile nature and activity of international communism; shortcomings favourable to the expansion of international communism; the bullwarks of the homeland; and the road for the future. Considerable attention is paid to Salazar's comments on communism, but attention is also concentrated on his views on national identity, financial and economic autonomy, social harmony and political stability.

307   **Corporatism and public policy in authoritarian Portugal.**
       Philippe C. Schmitter.   London; Beverly Hills, California: Sage
       Publications, 1975. 72p. bibliog. (Contemporary Political Sociology
       Series).

Investigates the nature of the Corporate State in Portugal, and in particular its relations with public policy formulation. It provides a short account of the political evolution of Salazar's New State from its beginning in 1933 to its overthrow in 1974. The author argues that four aspects of the practice of state corporatism are crucial to understanding its relation to social structure and to public decision-making in an authoritarian political context: the extent to which sponsored or state corporatism is pre-emptive; the extent to which the corporative experience is preventive; the extent to which such a mode of interest representation is defensive; and the extent to which it is compartmental.

308   **Portugal: the price of opposition.**
       H. Ward.   London: British Committee for Portuguese Amnesty,
       1963. 16p.

Examines the system of repression operated by Salazar in Portugal in the early 1960s. It analyses the activities of the various police forces; imprisonment; torture; the courts; and prison conditions.

309   **The New Corporative State of Portugal. An inaugural lecture
       delivered at King's College, London, the 15th of February, 1937.**
       S. George West.   London: New Temple Press; Lisbon; SPN
       Books, 1937. 32p. bibliog.

An account of the New Corporative State introduced following the 1926 revolt against President Bernardino Machado by General da Costa Gomes which led to General Oscar Carmona becoming President and in 1928 to Dr Oliveira Salazar becoming Minister of Finance.

310 Republican Portugal: a political history 1910-1926.

Douglas L. Wheeler. Madison, Wisconsin; London: University of Wisconsin Press, 1978. 340p. 2 maps. bibliog.

A definitive account of Portugal's First Republic, which provided the interim between the Constitutional Monarchy (1834-1910) and the Dictatorship (1926-74). It argues that the failure of the Republic was as much due to its extremist enemies as to internal political behaviour and the flaws of the political system. Considerable attention is paid to the role of the military in Portuguese politics and to the reasons why they intervened directly in 1926.

311 Corporatism and development: the Portuguese experience.

Howard J. Wiarda. Amherst, Massachusetts: University of Massachusetts Press, 1977. 447p. bibliog.

Provides a comprehensive investigation of the emergence of corporatism and economic change under the Salazar régime in Portugal. The book is organized around the subject area of the theory and practice of Portuguese Corporatism, and it seeks to strike a balance between conflicting interpretations of the Portuguese régime. It argues that the corporative system of Salazar and Caetano was far more oriented towards social justice than is often portrayed, and that the use of the 'Fascist' label serves more to perpetrate myths about the régime than to illuminate its actual assumptions and workings. Nevertheless, it is clear that the corporative system failed to work in accord with the original theory.

Portugal: twenty years of change.
See item no. 413.

Overseas Territories

312 **Portugal and the scramble for Africa 1875-1891.**
Eric Axelson. Johannesburg: Witwatersrand University Press,
1967. 318p. 11 maps. bibliog.

This detailed account of Portugal's interests in the partition of Africa pays
particular reference to the resolution of boundaries. It traces the emergence of
individual political entities in southern Africa, and discusses the Lourenço
Marques Treaty of 1879, the Berlin Conference (1884-85), the boundaries of
Moçambique, Gazaland, Manica, Zambezia and Nyasaland, and the treaties of 20
August 1890 and 11 June 1891 by which Portugal lost the high ground and gold-
producing areas of Mashonaland but was confirmed in her possession of 481,351
square miles in Angola and 302,328 square miles in Moçambique.

313 **Angola under the Portuguese: the myth and the reality.**
Gerald J. Bender. London: Heinemann, 1978. 287p. 2 maps.
bibliog.

This volume is divided into three main sections on Lusotropicalism, white
settlement and racial domination, and argues that the relationships between the
Portuguese and non-Europeans in Africa were neither appreciably better nor
worse than those in other colonies. It describes the background, economic
activities and settlement patterns of the Portuguese in Angola and the mechanics
of white domination, together with details of Portuguese counter-insurgency
measures during the war of independence in the 1960s.

314 **A Portuguese embassy to Japan (1644-1647) translated from an unpublished Portuguese ms, and other contemporary sources, with commentary and appendices.**
C. R. Boxer.   London: Kegan Paul, Trench, Trubner & Company, 1928. 64p. bibliog.

A translation of the narrative of the events surrounding the journey made by Gonçalo de Siqueira de Sousa to Japan as the Ambassador of King Dom João IV in 1664. It also includes translations of a number of related documents.

315 **The affair of the 'Madre de Deus' (A chapter in the history of the Portuguese in Japan.)**
C. R. Boxer.   London: Kegan Paul, Trench, Trubner & Company, 1929. 94p. 5 maps. bibliog.

Although the purpose of this volume is to provide an account of the loss of the Portuguese ship the *Madre de Deus* following its attack by the Japanese in 1610, it nevertheless also provides much information on Portugal's wider contacts with the Japanese in the late 15th and early 16th centuries.

316 **Four centuries of Portuguese expansion, 1415-1825: a succinct survey.**
C. R. Boxer.   Johannesburg: Witwatersrand University Press, 1961. 102p. map. bibliog.

The text of four public lectures delivered at the University of Witwatersrand, Johannesburg in 1960. It provides a succinct account of the various forms of conquest, commercial penetration and settlement which the Portuguese adopted and adapted in three continents from the time of their capture of Ceuta to their recognition of Brazilian independence.

317 **Race relations in the Portuguese empire, 1415-1825.**
C. R. Boxer.   Oxford: Clarendon Press, 1963. 136p.

This volume on Portuguese race-relations between the capture of Ceuta in North Africa in 1415 and the recognition of Brazilian independence in 1825 is divided into three sections on Morocco and West Africa; Moçambique and India; and Brazil and the Maranhão. It argues that although in theory the Portuguese never tolerated a colour-bar in their overseas possessions the truth was somewhat more complex.

318 **The Portuguese seaborne empire 1415-1825.**
C. R. Boxer.   Harmondsworth, England: Pelican, 1973. 438p. 7 maps. bibliog. (First published London: Hutchinson, 1969. 426p). (The History of Human Society Series).

A detailed historical account of the varying features of Portugal's overseas empire from the 15th to the 19th centuries, the volume is divided into two parts on the vicissitudes and the characteristics of empire. The first part is presented in historical sections tracing the emergence of the empire, its stagnation and eastern contraction, followed by its western revival. The second part is thematic describing the fleets, crown patronage and religious influences, soldiers and sailors, merchants and smugglers, and finally the nature of Portuguese nationalism and its relationship with Sebastianism and Messianism. Six appendixes give information on ships involved in the trade with Africa and India, and the values of exports and imports at various periods.

319 **Colonizing traditions, principles and methods of the Portuguese.**
Marcello Caetano. Lisbon: Agência Geral do Ultramar, 1951. 54p. map.

Caetano's account of Portuguese colonization, discussing its geography, history, principles and methods. In it he outlines the four fundamental principles which he saw as underlying Portugal's colonial administration: political unity; spiritual assimilation; administrative differentiation; and economic solidarity.

320 **Portuguese Africa.**
Ronald H. Chilcote. Englewood Cliffs, New Jersey: Prentice Hall, 1967. 149p. 4 maps. bibliog.

Presents a synthesis of developments in the Portuguese possessions of Africa. The first three chapters trace the emergence of a colonial policy in Portugal and Portuguese nationalism. These are followed by three detailed chapters studying the social, political and economic conditions of Portugal's African colonies.

321 **The discovery of the East.**
G. R. Crone. London: Hamish Hamilton, 1972. 178p. 3 maps. bibliog.

Studies the circumstances and motives behind Portugal's expansion overseas, the capture of the spice trade, the activities of the Jesuits in Japan and China, and the collapse of Portuguese domination in the face of the English and Dutch.

322 **Portuguese colonialism from South Africa to Europe.**
Eduardo de Sousa Ferreira. Freiburg, GFR: Aktion Dritte Welt, 1972. 232p. 4 maps. bibliog.

This critique of Portuguese colonialism in southern Africa is divided into seven main sections: the government of Marcello Caetano (1968-74) and the role of the colonies in the Portuguese economy; the development of the Portuguese economy and international capital in Portugal and the colonies; Namibia and the Cunene Project in Angola; the liberation movements in the Portuguese colonies; the new strategy of imperialism for 'Portuguese Africa'; revision of the Portuguese constitution and the colonial question; and the 'dialogue' or South Africa as secondary metropolis. Appendixes provide lists of medicines and requirements of the liberation movements in southern Africa during the early 1970s.

323 **Letters of John III King of Portugal 1521-1557: the Portuguese text edited with an introduction.**
J. D. M. Ford.   Cambridge, Massachusetts: Harvard University Press, 1931. 408p.

This volume presents the Portuguese texts of 372 letters written by King John III of Portugal in the 16th century, which were given to Harvard University following the death in 1897 of Senhor Fernando Palha who had created an extensive private library. Most of the letters are addressed to Dom Antonio de Ataide, John III's Chancellor of the Exchequer from 1530 to 1557, and provide important information concerning the King's policy in Africa, India and Brazil.

324 **Letters of the court of John III, King of Portugal.**
J. D. M. Ford, L. G. Moffatt.   Cambridge, Massachusetts: Harvard University Press, 1933. 169p.

A companion volume to the authors' *Letters of John III, King of Portugal* (q.v.). It contains material found in the Palha collection now in Harvard College Library, and comprises one letter by the King and 173 letters by exalted personages of his family and court ranging in date from 1524 to 1562. An English introduction is followed by the letters, which are in Portuguese.

325 **The masters and the slaves: a study in the development of Brazilian civilization.**
Gilberto Freyre, translated by Samuel Putnam.   London: Weidenfeld & Nicolson, 1946. 2nd rev. ed., 1956. 537p. bibliog.

This first volume of Freyre's monumental social history deals with the period from the 16th to the 19th centuries. It argues that the intermixing of races and cultures which occurred between the Portuguese masters and the slaves was a prime factor in the formation of the unique civilization of present Brazil. The volume also provides a wealth of information on the Portuguese colonization of Brazil and the subsequent social and cultural evolution of the country.

326 **The Portuguese and the tropics.**
Gilberto Freyre.   Lisbon: Executive Committee for the Commemoration of the Vth Centenary of the Death of Prince Henry the Navigator, 1961. 297p.

A collection of essays on the Portuguese and the tropics, including discussions of what the author terms Luso-Tropical culture, the arts, language, religion and social policy.

327 **Portugal's African Wars: Angola, Guinea Bissau, Mozambique.**
Arslan Humbaraci, Nicole Muchnik.   New York: Third Press, 1974. 250p. 4 maps.

Following an introductory section, which includes some 'basic facts' on Angola, Guinea Bissau and Mozambique at the end of the 1960s, this book provides an account of Portugal's history of colonization in Africa, of the birth of the three countries in question and of the relationships between Portugal and other countries concerning Portugal's colonialism. It argues that the power behind Portugal in her colonial wars was South Africa, supported by the North Atlantic Treaty Organization (NATO).

328 **Portuguese African territories: reply to Dr Livingstone's accusations and misrepresentations.**

D. José de Lacerda [Almeida e Araujo Correa de Lacerda]. London: Edward Stanford, 1865. 40p.

A translation of the author's comments first published in the *Diario de Lisboa* of 15, 17 and 19 December 1864 in reply to Dr. Livingstone's report on Portugal's African territories. The author argues that some of Livingstone's claims to 'discovery' in Africa were not valid because the Portuguese had been there before, and also that Livingstone seriously misrepresented Portuguese activities in Africa, particularly concerning slavery.

329 **Portuguese Brazil: the King's plantation.**

James Lang. New York, London, Toronto, Sydney, San Fransico: Academic Press, 1979. 266p. 2 maps. bibliog.

Examines the development of Brazil from its initial settlement by the Portuguese to the country's independence, studied within the context of Portuguese expansion in the Atlantic islands, Africa and Asia. It argues that the Crown was able to profit from Brazil's development, without establishing an elaborate overseas bureaucracy, by creating strict taxation systems on the colony's sugar when it was unloaded in Lisbon as well as through the taxation of slaves, gold and tobacco.

330 **The Angolan revolution: volume 1, the anatomy of an explosion (1950-1962); volume 2, exile politics and guerilla warfare (1962-1976).**

John Marcum. Cambridge, Massachusetts; London: Massachusetts Institute of Technology Press. Vol. 1, 1969; Vol. 2, 1978.

These two volumes provide a very detailed survey of the emergence of an independent Angola, tracing the rise of Angolan nationalism between 1950 and 1960, the rebellion of 1961, the beginnings of the revolution, the pan-African phase 1962-65 and the tripartite phase 1966-76, when UNITA (União Nacional para a Independência Total de Angola), the MPLA (Movimento Popular de Libertação de Angola) and the FNLA (Frente Nacional de Libertação de Angola) struggled for independence and power.

331 **Conflicts and conspiracies: Brazil and Portugal 1750-1808.**

Kenneth R. Maxwell. Cambridge, England: Cambridge University Press, 1973. 289p. 5 maps. bibliog. (Cambridge Latin American Studies, no. 16).

An analysis of social, political and economic compulsions and their interaction with policy and events in the historical development of Brazil between 1750 and

1808. It seeks to explain how and why Portuguese colonial policy changed in this period, and the actions of the Marquis of Pombal form an important thread in the argument. Portugal's relationships with the rest of Europe, and particularly with Great Britain, are also seen to be of specific significance. The volume concludes with a number of statistical tables concerning the economy and trade of Portugal and Brazil in the late 18th century.

332 Portugal in Africa: the last hundred years.
Malyn Newitt. London: C. Hurst, 1981. 278p. 4 maps. bibliog.

Presents an account of how the Portuguese obtained their African empire, pacified, occupied and attempted to develop it, and then eventually lost it. In so doing, the volume considers Portugal's colonial ideology, native policy, administration, contract labour, international relations and economic links with Africa. It argues that the changes which took place in the empire after 1875 were largely the result of the spread of international capital. A final chapter surveys the role of the political and economic events in Portugal in the 1960s and early 1970s which contributed to the overthrow of the colonial régime.

333 The United Nations and Portugal: a study of anti-colonialism.
Franco Nogueira. London: Sidgwick & Jackson, 1963. 188p. bibliog.

A defence of Portugal's colonial policy in the early 1960s by the Foreign Minister of Portugal who took office in 1961. It pays particular attention to the activities of the United Nations concerning the colonialism debate and Portugal's role therein.

334 African star in Spain and Portugal, 300 BC to 1800 AD.
Gabriel K. Osei. London: Gabriel K. Osei Press, 1963. 18p. bibliog.

A short account of the activities of Spain and Portugal in Africa, and the role of Africans in Iberian culture.

335 Portuguese rule in Goa.
R. P. Rao. London: Asia Publishing House, 1963. 242p. 2 maps.

An account of Goa's struggle for independence from Portuguese rule, set against its all-India background. It argues that the repressive measures resorted to by the Portuguese did not succeed in isolating the Goan people from the main body of Indian people, their way of life and their struggle for freedom.

336 Portugal and Africa: the people and the war.
John Sykes. London: Hutchinson, 1971. 199p. map.

Presents an interpretation of Portugal and her African colonies through the author's interactions with members of a single family, that of Dom Alcides a nobleman of the Alentejo. Dom Alcides himself is a Social Democrat, his brother is a general with dreams of Portuguese expansion, and his nephew, the general's son, is a Marxist driven to exile. The work provides interesting insights on the debates within Portugal, Moçambique and Angola in the 1960s concerning Portugal's empire and colonial presence in Africa.

337 **Portuguese rule on the Gold Coast, 1469-1682.**
John Vogt. Athens, Georgia: University of Georgia Press, 1979.
266p. map. bibliog.
Studies the rule of the Portuguese on the Gold Coast and their conflicts with the
Dutch. Between 1470 and 1520 Portuguese Mina provided the greatest source of
gold specie of all Europe's possessions overseas, and it was the prime source of
royal revenue for the Portuguese monarchs until the opening of eastern commerce
in 1499. Appendixes provide details of the sale of metal hardware at São Jorge da
Mina and Axem 1504-31, the governors and factors of São Jorge da Mina, the
annual gold receipts of São Jorge and Axem 1482-1560, and gold weights and
measures used in Mina.

338 **The rise of Portuguese power in India 1497-1550.**
R. S. Whiteway. London: Archibald Constable, 1899. 357p. map.
bibliog.
A history of the rise of Portuguese power in India in the 15th and 16th centuries,
giving not merely a record of military expeditions and of changes of government,
but also an account of social life and the idiosyncrasies of the chief men of the
time. Particular attention is paid to the following governors and viceroys: Dom
Franciso d'Almeida (1505-09), Afonso d'Albuquerque (1509-15), Lopo Soares,
Diogo Lopes de Sequiera (1515-21), Dom Duarte de Menezes, Vasco da Gama,
Dom Henrique de Menezes, and Lopo Vaz de Sampayo (1515-29), Nuno da
Cunha (1529-38), Dom Garcia de Noronha, Dom Estavão da Gama (1538-42),
Martin Afonso de Sousa (1542-45), Dom João de Castro, Garcia de Sa and Jorge
Cabral (1545-50).

339 **Password 'Anguimo': reports from Angola, Guinea Bissau and
Mozambique.**
Pyotr Yevsyukov, Oleg Ignatyev, Pavel Mikhalev, Anatoli
Nikanorov. Moscow: Novosti Press Agency Publishing House,
1974. 152p.
An account of the armed struggle for decolonization in what was Portuguese
Africa, written from a Soviet viewpoint. It includes the following four papers:
'Fighting for freedom', by Pyotr Yevsyukov; 'On the path of struggle (reports
from Guinea-Bissau)', by Oleg Ignatyev; 'With guerrillas in Angola', by Pavel
Mikhalev, and 'Mozambique, pages from a diary', by Anotoli Nikanorov.

**From Lisbon to Goa 1500-1750; studies in Portuguese maritime
enterprise.**
See item no. 490.

**Emerging nationalism in Portuguese Africa: a bibliography of docu-
mentary ephemera through 1965.**
See item no. 759.

Overseas Territories

Portuguese-speaking Africa 1900-1979: a select bibliography. Volume I: Angola.
See item no. 766.

Manuscritos Portugueses ou referentes a Portugal da Biblioteca Nacional de Paris. (Portuguese manuscripts or those referring to Portugal in the National Library of Paris.)
See item no. 780.

Population

General

340 **A century of Portuguese fertility.**
Massimo Livi Bacci.   Princeton, New Jersey: Princeton University
Press, 1971. 149p. 17 maps. bibliog.
Studies recent Portuguese demographic change, based largely on census statistics
and concentrating on fertility changes. It notes that Portugal had relatively low
levels of fertility prior to the start of the modern decline and that fertility in the
south of the country was considerably lower than that in the north.

341 **Death in Portugal: studies in Portuguese anthropology and modern
history.**
Edited by Rui Feijó, Herminio Martins, João de Pina-Cabral.
Oxford: Journal of the Anthropological Society of Oxford, 1983.
124p. bibliog. (JASO Occasional Papers, no. 2).
A collection of papers delivered at a conference on Death in Modern Portugal
held at St. Antony's College, Oxford, in June 1982. It includes the following:
'Introduction: *tristes durées*', by Herminio Martins; 'The good death: personal
salvation and community identity', by Patricia Goldey; 'Conflicting attitudes to
death in modern Portugal: the question of cemeteries', by João de Pina-Cabral
and Rui Feijó; 'Dying and inheriting in rural Trás-os-Montes', by Brian Juan
O'Neill; 'Death and the survival of the rural household in a north-western
municipality', by M. F. Brandão; 'Testamentary practices in Venade (Minho),
1755-1815', by Margarida Durães; 'Oliveira Martins: death in history', by
Augusto Santos Silva; and 'Death and the imagination in Alexandre Herculano's
Eurico', by T. F. Earle.

342 **The Portugal fertility survey, 1979-80: a summary of findings.**
World Fertility Survey. Voorburg, The Netherlands:
Inter-national Statistical Institute, 1983. 23p.

A summary report of the findings of the 1979-80 Portugal Fertility Survey
undertaken for the World Fertility Survey by the Centre for Demographic Studies
of the National Statistical Institute. It provides an account of nuptiality and
exposure to risk of pregnancy; fertility; preferences for family size and sex of
children; and contraceptive knowledge and use in Portugal.

Migration

343 **Portugal in development: emigration, industrialization, the
European Community.**
Edited by Thomas C. Bruneau, Victor M. P. da Rosa, Alex
MacLeod. Ottawa: University of Ottawa Press, 1984. 254p.
bibliog.

This volume is the outcome of a conference held at the Centre for Developing
Area Studies of McGill University, Montreal in October 1981. It includes the
following papers on emigration and industrialization in Portugal: 'Salazar's
"modelo económico": the consequences of planned constraint', by Elizabeth
Leeds; 'Regional distribution of Portuguese emigration according to socio-
economic context', by Mário Bacalhau; 'Emigration and underdevelopment: the
causes and consequences of Portuguese emigration to France in historical and
cross-cultural perspective', by Caroline B. Brettell; 'Immigration and the
Portuguese family: a comparison between two receiving societies', by Caroline B.
Brettell and Victor M. Pereira; 'Portuguese immigration to the east coast of the
United States and California: contrasting patterns', by Eduardo Mayone Dias; 'A
contribution to the study of the economics of reintegration of immigrants: the
case of Portugal', by E. de Sousa Ferreira, J. Leite Pereira and Amadeu Ferreira
de Paiva; 'Portuguese emigration to the EEC and the utilization of emigrants'
remittances', by Guy Clausse; 'The paradox of Portugal's industrialization:
emigrant labour, immigrant capital and foreign markets', by Christian Deubner;
'Structural adjustment in Portugal in the face of entry to the EEC', by João
Gravinho; and 'Portugal and Europe: the dilemmas of integration', by Jorge
Braga de Macedo. There is also an introduction and a conclusion.

344 **Population mobility: emigration, return migration and internal
migration.**
Russell King. In: *Southern Europe transformed: political and
economic change in Greece, Italy, Portugal and Spain.* Edited by
Allan Williams. London: Harper & Row, 1984. p. 145-78.

An account of the social and economic influence of emigration, return migration
and internal migration in southern Europe. It notes that Portuguese migrations
have their origin in mass emigrations to Brazil in the 19th century, and that
Portuguese emigration peaked between 1969 and 1971, with most emigrants going
to France, the USA, West Germany and Canada.

345 **The emigrants return.**
Jim Lewis. *Geographical Magazine*, vol. 57, no. 1 (January 1985), p. 30-34.
A short, illustrated account of the social and economic influences of migrant workers on their return to Portugal and Spain.

346 **Emigrating peasants and returning emigrants: emigration with return in a Portuguese village.**
Manuela Reis, Joaquim Gil Nave. *Sociologia Ruralis*, vol. 26, no. 1 (1986), p. 20-35.
Evaluates the elements of a peasant strategy of emigration based on a study of the village of Meimão in the northern interior of Portugal. It suggests that the household practice of pluri-activity, based on two quite distinct and distant socio-geographical contexts, makes viable a rural area which would otherwise have long ago been compromised through the process of social and demographic bleeding to which it was subjected.

347 **Portuguese rural migrants in industrialised Europe.**
Maria Beatrice Rocha Trinidade. *Iberian Studies*, vol. 4, no. 1 (spring 1975), p. 9-14.
A short analysis of Portuguese emigration to the more heavily industrialized countries of Europe.

348 **And yet they came: Portuguese immigration from the Azores to the United States.**
Jerry R. Williams. New York: Center for Migration Studies, 1982. 150p. 11 maps. bibliog.
Describes the network of factors leading to the migration of people from the Azores to the United States.

Atlantic islanders of the Azores and Madeiras.
See item no. 32.

Demographic patterns and rural society in Portugal: implications of some recent research.
See item no. 403.

Urbanization; growth, problems and policies.
See item no. 406.

Demographic Yearbook
See item no. 572.

Bibliografia analítica de etnografia Portuguesa. (Analytical bibliography of Portuguese ethnography.)
See item 775.

Language

General

349 Portuguese in three months.
Maria Fernanda S. Allen. London: Hugo's Language Books,
1983. 152p. (Hugo's Simplified Systems).

Provides an introduction to the Portuguese language for those wanting to learn it
from a practical angle. It is divided into ten main lessons with exercises and it
concludes with sections on reading, practice, letters, idiomatic expressions, useful
phrases and words, and an appendix of verbs.

350 Passive sentences in English and Portuguese.
Milton M. Azevedo. Washington, DC: Georgetown University
Press, 1980. 124p. bibliog.

A description of passivization in Portuguese and English and a contrastive
analysis of the main types of passive constructions in the two languages.

351 Portuguese.
Centre for Information on Language Teaching and Research.
London: Centre for Information on Language Teaching and
Research, 1982. 60p. (Language and Culture Guide, 20).

Presents a useful guide to Portugal and Portuguese for those concerned with the
provision and use of resources for learning Portuguese. It is divided into sections
on the Portuguese language, embassies and national tourist offices, organizations
and centres, teaching, learning and resource materials, libraries and special
collections, radio broadcasts, specialist booksellers and subscription agents, film
distributors, opportunities for learning Portuguese and examinations.

352   *Palavras amigas da Onça:* **a vocabulary of false friends in English and Portuguese.**
Leonard S. Downes.   Portsmouth, England: School of Languages and Area Studies, Portsmouth Polytechnic, 1980. 3rd ed. 159p.

This useful volume includes references to over 500 entries of words in English and Portuguese which appear to be similar, but which differ, often widely, in meaning and usage.

353   **The Spanish language (together with Portuguese, Catalan and Basque).**
William J. Entwistle, revised by W. D. Elcock, L. R. Palmer.
London: Faber & Faber, 1962. 2nd ed. 367p. 8 maps. bibliog. (The Great Languages).

Examines in detail the languages of the Iberian peninsula from the pre-Roman period to the 20th century. The Portuguese language, both in Portugal and overseas, is discussed in the last two chapters, the former of which traces the emergence of Gallaeco-Portuguese, the divergence of Portuguese from Galician, modern Portuguese and Portuguese dialects.

354   **Portuguese phrasebook.**
Antonio de Figueiredo, Jillian Norman.   Harmondsworth, England: Penguin Books, 1971. 198p.

A useful short English-Portuguese phrase-book divided into broad sections on 'first things': signs and public notices; money; travel; directions; motoring; accommodation; restaurants; the menu; shopping; barbers and hairdressers; the post office; sightseeing; entertainment; sports and games; on the beach; camping and walking; at the doctors; at the dentists; problems and accidents; times and dates; public holidays; numbers; and weights and measures. There are short sections on pronunciation and grammar, and it concludes with an extensive practical vocabulary.

355   **Portuguese office and occupational surnames.**
Joseph G. Fucilla.   *Onoma,* Vol. 23, no. 1 (1979), 33-51.

Investigates those Portuguese surnames which are derived from official positions and occupations, based mainly on an analysis of names in the Lisbon telephone directory for 1974-75. The names are studied under broad headings: noblemen and their attendants and servants; military names; churchmen and church related names; civil administrators and their subordinates; the learned professions; music and musical entertainers; farm and field occupations; tradesmen and craftsmen; and miscellaneous occupational names.

356 **Basic Portuguese palaeography.**
The Genealogical Department of the Church of Jesus Christ of
Latter-day Saints. Salt Lake City, Utah: Corporation of the
President of the Church of Jesus Christ of Latter-day Saints, 1978.
41p. bibliog.

This thorough account of Portuguese palaeography covers its history, the
alphabet, variations in spelling, unfamiliar and Latin terms, special concerns,
abbreviations, names and naming customs, and the transcription of characters.

357 **Portuguese at sight.**
Alexander Gode, illustrated by Edgard Cirlin. New York:
Thomas Y. Crowell, 1943. 100p.

This early introduction to the Portuguese language presents Portuguese words in
association with pictures illustrating their meaning. There is a concluding note on
grammar and a short vocabulary.

358 **A grammar of the Portuguese language compiled from the best
sources, and chiefly for the use of Englishmen studying that tongue
without the help of a master. In three parts, to which is added a
copious mercantile vocabulary, together with sundry commercial
letters.**
John Laycock. Leeds, England: printed for the author by T.
Inchbold, 1825. 456p.

An early 19th-century grammar of the Portuguese language. It pays particular
attention to words and phrases of use to those involved in commerce in Portugal.

359 **Palatable Portuguese for self study.**
T. J. Mammatt. London: Bailey Bros. & Swinfen, 1948. 72p.

A simple introduction to the Portuguese language based on a course of twelve
lessons given by the author to members of the Anglo-Brazilian Society in London.

360 **Colloquial Portuguese.**
Maria Emília de Alvelos Naar. London: Routledge & Kegan
Paul; New York: Dover Publications, 1974. 3rd ed. 184p.

Provides a useful and easy to follow introduction to the Portuguese language
designed for those on holiday, those with business dealings, or those choosing to
retire there. It is divided into twelve lessons each with some grammar, vocabulary
and conversational matter or translation. Appendixes provide lists of idiomatic
expressions, revision exercises and tables of regular and irregular verbs. A short
vocabulary is included at the end.

361 **Say it in Portuguese (European usage).**
Alexander da Prista. Special editorial consultant João G. Bastos.
New York: Dover Publications, 1979. 203p.

A phrase-book, designed for Americans, with over 2,000 practical entries, each of which has a pronunciation transcription. There is also a short introduction and a guide to pronunciation. It concludes with an index.

362 **Portuguese phrase book.**
Edmund Swinglehurst, with Portuguese translation and phonetic transcription by Teresa de Paiva-Raposo. London, New York, Sydney, Toronto: Hamlyn, 1981. 224p.

A useful phrase-book designed for the user with no previous knowledge of Portuguese. There is a guide to pronunciation and a useful short grammar. Each entry has a phonetic transcription and the volume includes an index.

363 **The ancient language of Spain and Portgual.**
Antonio Tovar. New York: S. F. Vanni, 1961. 138p.

An account of the ancient languages of the Iberian peninsula divided into chapters on ancient epigraphic remains, the Iberian inscriptions and language, the Celtiberian language, the western linguistic remains, pre-Roman onomastics in Iberia and the Basque language. The ancient script of Iberia is seen as representing a unique episode in the history of writing since it preserved syllabic signs created in very remote times when syllabic writing was used in the whole of the 'Near East'.

364 **A Portuguese grammar, with the Portuguese words properly accented.**
Anthony Vieyra. London: J. Collingwood, 1827. 10th ed. 391p.

A 19th-century Portuguese grammar which also has sections on proverbs, dialogues, commercial letters and literary extracts.

365 **Remains of Arabic in the Spanish and Portuguese languages, with a sketch by way of introduction of the history of Spain, from the invasion to the expulsion of the Moors. Also extracts from the original letters in Arabic to and from Don Manoueel and his governors in India and Africa. Appendix containing a specimen of the introduction to the Hitopadesa translated into three languages, the principal metre of which is that of the Sanscrit.**
Stephen Weston. Spa Fields, [London]: printed by S. Rousseau, 1810. 186p.

Following an introduction to the history of the Moors in Iberia this work provides alphabetical lists of the remains of Arabic in Spanish and then in Portuguese. The Portuguese list is prefaced by extracts of Arabic letters to and from Dom Manuel, King of Portugal (1495-1521), copied by João de Sousa in 1790 from the royal archives. The extracts date from between 1502 and 1517, although the remaining letters in the collection are mainly to Dom João III prior to 1530. The extract from the 'Hitopadesa', or 'Amicable instruction', is taken from Wilkins's *Sanscrita grammar*, but it is not concerned with Portuguese.

366　**From Latin to Portuguese: historical phonology and morphology of the Portuguese language.**
　　　Edwin B[ucher] Williams.　Philadelphia: University of Pennsylvania Press, 1962. 2nd ed. 317p. bibliog.

A detailed survey of the emergence of the Portuguese language from vulgar Latin, concentrating only on historical phonology and morphology. This is the second edition of a work published first in 1938 and it includes some revisions as well as an updated bibliography.

367　**An essential course in modern Portuguese.**
　　　R. Clive Willis.　London: Harrap, 1968. Rev. ed., 1971. 523p.

This basic and clear teaching-grammar is intended for first-year university students with no previous knowledge of the language, but is of use for anyone wishing to learn Portuguese. It is divided into forty lessons and includes appendixes of regular verb tables and the Portuguese of Brazil. It concludes with a Portuguese-English and English-Portuguese vocabulary.

Travels in Portugal, and through France and Spain, with a dissertation on the literature of Portugal, and the Spanish and Portuguese languages.
See item no. 91.

In Portugal.
See item no. 122.

Modern Iberian language and literature: a bibliography of homage studies.
See item no. 765.

Dictionaries

368　**Dicionário Inglês-Português para economistas.** (English-Portuguese dictionary for economists.)
　　　José Cândido Marques Cavalcante.　Rio de Janeiro; São Paulo, Brazil: Livraria Freitas Bastos, 1960. 458p.

An English-Portuguese dictionary for economists, initially intended to help staff members of the Banco do Nordeste do Brasil in South America. It includes an extended list of abbreviations, noting common usage mainly in America.

369 **International Bee Research Association dictionary of beekeeping
terms with allied scientific terms, volume 8, giving translations from
and into English-French-Italian-Spanish-Portuguese-Romanian with
Latin index.**
General editor Eva Crane. Bucharest: Apimoridia in
collaboration with International Bee Research Association, 1979.
252p.

A practical, technical dictionary of beekeeping terms, providing translations from
Portuguese into the other languages mentioned in the title.

370 **Dicionário de têrmos médicos: Inglês-Português.**
(English-Portuguese dictionary of medical terms.)
Hugo Fortes. Rio de Janeiro: Editôra Científica, 1958. 2nd ed.
702p. bibliog.

An English-Portuguese medical-term dictionary.

371 **The multilingual computer dictionary.**
Edited by Alan Isaacs. London: Frederick Muller, 1981. 332p.

Provides a dictionary covering 1,600 computer terms in English, French, German,
Spanish, Italian and Portuguese.

372 **Dicionário Inglês-Português, de termos militares.**
(English-Portuguese dictionary of military terms.)
Homero de Castro Jobim. Pôrto Alegre, Brazil: Edição da
Livraria do Globo, 1944. 162p.

An English-Portuguese dictionary of military terms produced towards the end of
the Second World War and now somewhat out of date.

373 **Dicionário de Inglês-Português** (English-Portuguese dictionary.)
Armando de Morais. Oporto, Portugal: Porto Editora, Lda.,
1966. 2nd. ed. 1492p.

Presents a thorough and comprehensive single-volume English-Portuguese
dictionary. Pronunciation guides are only given for English words.

374 **The New Michaelis illustrated dictionary: volume 1 English-
Portuguese; volume 2 Portuguese-English.**
Sao Paulo, Brazil: Edições Melhoramentos; Wiesbaden, GFR: F.
A. Brockhaus, rev. eds. 1958, 1961, 2 vols.

A comprehensive English-Portuguese and Portuguese-English dictionary with
over 4,000 illustrations. Guides to pronunciation are only given for English words.

375   **A technical dictionary in English, Spanish and Portuguese.**
Thomas F. Palmer.   London: E. Marlborough & Company, 1923.
72p.

A short and out-of-date dictionary covering technical terms in the following fields:
aeroplanes, agriculture, automobiles, building, electricity, machine tools, mining,
shipping, textiles and wood-working.

376   **A Portuguese-English dictionary.**
James L. Taylor.   Stanford, California: Stanford University Press,
1958. 662p. bibliog.

A comprehensive Portuguese-English dictionary with over 60,000 entries. An
introduction provides some background information on Portuguese and an
appendix by James S. Holton gives details of verb models.

377   **Dicionário escolar Inglês-Português e Português-Inglês.** (English-
Portuguese and Portuguese-English student's dictionary.)
Leonel Vallandro.   Pôrto Alegre, Brazil: Editôra Globo, (1965),
1967. 982p.

This two-way dictionary is primarily intended for students. Pronunciation
guidance is only given for English words.

378   **Elsevier's dictionary of personal and office computing: English,
German, French, Italian, Portuguese.**
Otto Vollnhals.   Amsterdam, The Netherlands; Oxford; New
York; Tokyo: Elsevier, 1984. 504p.

A dictionary of 5,106 entries covering the essential terminology of personal and
office computing. It contains a main section in the five languages arranged in
English alphabetical order, and four alphabetical indexes in German, French,
Italian and Portuguese.

Religion

379 The secret of Fatima: fact and legend.
Joaquin Maria Alonso, translated by the Dominican nuns of the
Perpetual Rosary. Cambridge, Massachusetts: Ravengate Press,
1979. Reprinted 1982. 122p. map.

An English translation of *La verdad sobre el secreto de Fatima*, first published by
Centro Mariano, Madrid, in 1976. It is a study of the sealed letter written by
Lucia dos Santos, one of the three people to whom the Mother of God appeared
at Fatima in central Portugal in 1917.

380 Fátima: pilgrimage to peace.
April Oursler Armstrong, Martin F. Armstrong, Jr. Kingswood,
Surrey, England: World's Work, 1955. 217p.

The personal and informal account of the pilgrimage of two young Americans to
the shrine of Our Lady of Fatima. It includes details of the visions, the prophecies
and the history of the three children who saw the visions in 1917.

381 Spanish and Portuguese monastic history, 600-1300.
Charles Julian Bishko. London: Variorum Reprints, 1984. 336p.
bibliog. (Collected Studies Series, no. 188).

A collection of thirteen papers on Iberian monastic history between the years 600
and 1300, which cast a revealing light upon the history, institutions, lines of
cultural innovation and circulation, and factors of growth in secular no less than in
religious life. Eleven of the studies are reprints from other publications. The first
four studies examine the indigenous traditional Iberian pactual cenobitism, and
the last six treat major issues in the Europeanizing penetration of the ideas of St.
Hugo of Cluny (1024-1109) into Iberia. The studies specifically on Portugal
include: 'Portuguese pactual monasticism in the 11th century – the case of São
Salvador de Vacariça'; 'Count Henrique of Portugal, Cluny, and the antecedents

of the Pacto Sucessório'; and 'The Cluniac priories of Galicia and Portugal: their acquisition and administration, 1075-ca.1230'.

382 Freedom and Catholic power in Spain and Portugal: an American interpretation.

Paul Blanshard. Boston, Massachusetts: Beacon Press, 1962. 300p.

Presents an indignant indictment of the Fascist régimes of Spain and Portugal which are seen as anachronisms in the modern Western World. It provides a critique of the influence of the Catholic religion on a wide range of social, economic and political issues in Iberia in the 1940s and 1950s.

383 Our Lady at Fatima: prophecies of tragedy or hope for America and the world?

Antonio A. Borelli, John R. Spann, with a special contribution by Plinio Corrêa de Oliveira. USA: The American Society for the Defense of Tradition, Family and Property, 1985. 121p. map. bibliog.

Presents an account of the apparitions at Fatima in 1917 and their relevance to the United States of America in the 1980s. It begins with a chapter on the relevance of the Fatima message to the dilemma presented by communism, written by Plinio Corrêa de Oliveira. This is followed by a detailed account of the apparitions themselves and of Sister Lucia's mission, by Antonio Borelli, and an interpretation of Fatima as an explanation and cure for contemporary crisis by John Spann. A short concluding section by Plinio Corrêa de Oliveira discusses the weeping statue of Our Lady of Fatima in New Orleans in 1972. It is written from a strictly anti-communist viewpoint.

384 The Church militant and Iberian expansion 1440-1770.

C. R. Boxer. Baltimore, Maryland; London: Johns Hopkins University Press, 1978. 148p. bibliog.

An analytical survey of the role of Portuguese and Spanish missionaries in the overseas expansion of the Iberian powers. The first three chapters investigate race relations, cultural interactions and organizational problems before a concluding chapter establishes a tentative balance sheet.

385 Hugo Gurgeny, prisoner of the Lisbon Inquisition.

Mary Brearley. London: Jonathan Cape, 1947. 176p. bibliog.

Reconstructs the arrest in 1606 and the subsequent trial of the Englishman Hugo Gurgeny by the Inquisition in Lisbon. The work provides an interesting case of the methods used by the Inquisition to undermine a prisoner both physically and psychologically.

386   **Anglicans abroad: the history of the chaplaincy and Church of St. James at Oporto.**
John Delaforce.   London: SPCK, 1982, 141p. bibliog.
An account of the establishment of the first Anglican Church in Portugal, whose first chaplain was appointed in 1671. Among the subjects discussed are the difficulties experienced by the chaplains of the British Factory (collection of British businessmen and merchants) in the 17th and 18th centuries, the advent of religious freedom and tolerance in Portugal in the early 19th century, the establishment of the bishopric of Gibraltar in 1842 and the termination in 1875 of the British Government grants to Anglican Churches abroad.

387   **Early Portuguese missionaries in East Africa.**
John [Milner] Gray.   London: Macmillan, 1958. 53p. bibliog.
This account of 16th- and 17th-century contacts between Portugal and East Africa concentrates mainly on Portuguese missionary activity in Malindi, Mombasa, Kilwa and Zanzibar. An appendix provides a list of Christian remains of the 16th and 17th centuries which have been found in East Africa.

388   **History of the origin and establishment of the Inquisition in Portugal.**
Alexandre Herculano, translated by John C. Branner.   Stanford, California: Stanford University Press, 1962. 447p. map. (History, Economics and Political Science, Vol. 1, no. 2).
A translation of Herculano's *Historia da origem e estabelecimento da Inquisação em Portgual* first published at Lisbon in 1852. Following a short chapter on the Inquisition in Europe prior to the end of the 15th century, it traces the emergence and establishment of the Inquisition in Portugal prior to 1561 noting the frequent conflicts between Dom João III and the Pope over the role of the Inquisition.

389   **Fatima: the great sign.**
Francis Johnston.   Chulmleigh, England: Augustine Publishing, 1980. 148p.
An account of the Fatima apparitions of 1916-29 and the subsequent development of the cult based on Our Lady's message. It includes an analysis of the theology of Fatima, especially that concerning devotion and reparation to the Immaculate Heart of Mary, together with a synthesis of declarations by popes, cardinals, bishops and theologians concerning the message of Fatima.

390   **Fatima in Lucia's own words: Sister Lucia's memoirs.**
Edited by Fr. Louis Kondor with an introduction by Dr. Joaquin M. Alonso, translated by the Dominican Nuns of the Perpetual Rosary.   Fatima, Portugal: Postulation Centre, 1976. 206p.
The memoirs of Sister Lucia, who together with her cousins Jacinta and Francisco Marto saw a vision of the Blessed Virgin Mary in 1917 at Cova da Iria, Fatima. There is a short general introduction which includes a biographical sketch of Lucia, and there is also a brief introduction to each of the four memoirs.

Religion

391 St. Elizabeth of Portugal.
Vincent McNabb.   London: Sheed & Ward, 1937. 62p.

A short biography of Saint Isabel (Elizabeth) the Patroness of Peace, born in 1271 at Saragossa, Spain, and married to King Diniz of Portugal. She died in 1336 and was buried at the convent church of Santa Clara at Coimbra.

392 Portuguese pilgrimage July 1st-September 4th 1947.
C. C. Martindale.   London: Sheed & Ward, 1949. 165p.

This account of the author's sojourn in Portugal is mainly concerned with the regions around Lisbon, Fatima, the Serra da Arrabida, Colares and Sintra, but includes some comments on the history of the country. It pays particular attention to religion and the reasons for the pilgrimages to Fatima.

393 Portugal and Rome c.1748-1830: an aspect of Catholic Enlightenment.
Samuel J. Miller.   Rome: Universita Gregoriana Editrice, 1978.
412p. bibliog. (Pontifica Universitas Gregoriana Miscellanea
Historiae Pontificiae 44).

An analysis of how a series of 18th-century ideological elements, including Portuguese regalism, Gallicanism, Jansenism and episcopal jurisdictionalism, together commonly known as Reform or Enlightened Catholicism, were combined under the aegis of the Marquis of Pombal, and the extent to which they became constituent elements of Portuguese life in the period 1748 to 1830.

394 The English Church in Madeira now the Church of the Holy and Undivided Trinity: a history.
H. A. Newell.   Oxford: printed at the University Press by John
Johnson, 1931. 48p. map.

Presents a history of the English Church in Madeira which was consecrated in 1860, covering its origins, its building and endowments, events during the 19th century and a list of its clergy.

395 Portugal: a pioneer of Christianity.
Edgar Prestage.   Lisbon: Empresa Nacional de Publicidade, 1945.
2nd rev. ed., 31p.

A short account of Portugal's role in spreading Christianity to Asia, Africa and Latin America.

396 A history of the Marranos.
Cecil Roth.   Philadelphia: The Jewish Publication Society of
America, 1932. 422p. bibliog.

An historical survey of crypto-Judaism in Iberia. Marranism began during the reconquest of Spain from the Moors when large bodies of Jews accepted Christian baptism en masse to escape death. The author traces the rise of the Inquisition and the mass emigration of Jews to Portugal after their expulsion from Spain in

1492. This was followed by their forced general conversion by the Portuguese. Considerable attention is then paid to the activities and procedures of the Inquisition. The remainder of the book covers the Marrano Diaspora, and their subsequent dispersal to England and the New World. There are also chapters on the literature of the Marranos, and on the lives of some Marrano worthies.

397   **Fatima, hope of the World.**
      J. R. Whitaker.   Glasgow: John S. Burns, no date [ca. mid-1950s]. 24p.

Provides a short introduction to the story of Fatima, recounting the apparitions seen in 1917 and giving a summary of the message given to those who saw the visions.

Historical account of Lisbon College.
See item no. 167.

Humanism and the voyages of discovery in 16th century Portuguese science and letters.
See item no. 219.

Society

Social Conditions

398 **Etat et paysannerie: politiques agricoles et stratégies paysannes au Portugal depuis la Seconde Guerre Mondiale.** (State and peasantry: agricultural policies and peasant strategies in Portugal since the Second World War.)
Manuel Vilaverde Cabral. *Sociologia Ruralis*, vol. 26, no. 1 (1986), p. 6-19.

This paper argues that the agricultural policies of the Portuguese state appear to be increasingly powerless to control peasant behaviour, and that paradoxically the peasantry seem to have gained in autonomy. It asserts that this autonomy of rural social groups, strengthened by the advent of democracy since 1974, is leading to a serious food crisis which the democratic state has not yet been able to control.

399 **A Portuguese rural society.**
José Cutileiro. Oxford: Clarendon Press, 1971. 314p. map. bibliog.

Presents a social-anthropological study of a small area in south-east Portugal. It provides one of the best academic introductions to the people and the character of rural Portugal, and is based on detailed field-work undertaken by the author. It covers the whole range of life as it affects the rural population of the country and is divided into five main sections: land-tenure and social stratification; family, kinship and neighbourhood; political structure; patronage; and religion.

400 **Portuguese contribution to cultural anthropology.**
A. Jorge Dias. Johannesburg: Witwatersrand University Press,
1961. 112p. map. (Publications of the Ernest Oppenheimer
Institute of Portuguese Studies of the University of Witwatersrand,
Johannesburg, II).

This book comprises the six public lectures given by the author at the University
of Witwatersrand in 1959. The first of these is an historical introduction to
Portuguese anthropology. This is followed by two studies of the Makonde people
of Cape Delgado in Moçambique, and two studies of Portugal concentrating on its
land and people and on community studies. It concludes with an essay on the
Portuguese abroad.

401 **On household composition in north western Portugal: some critical
remarks and a case study.**
João Arriscado Nunes. *Sociologia Ruralis*, vol. 26, no. 1 (1986),
p. 49-69.

Studies household composition within the Minho, based on census data from 1960
at the scale of the municipality. It illustrates that substantial regional differences
exist in household composition within the region, and that ecotypal variation may
be a significant factor underlying both differences in residential pattern and
attitudes towards generalized images of the ideal type of social organization.

402 **Power and pawn: the female in Iberian families, societies and
cultures.**
Ann M. Pescatello. Westpoint, Connecticut: Greenwood Press,
1976. 281p. bibliog. (Contributions in Intercultural and
Comparative Studies, no. 1).

Analyses the historical experience of women in Iberia. The title refers to the
contradictory image of the female: on the one hand that of the fount of power and
wielder of influence, and on the other, that of the pawn in a world dominated by
men.

403 **Demographic patterns and rural society in Portugal: implications of
some recent research.**
Robert Rowland. *Sociologia Ruralis*, vol. 26, no. 1 (1986), p. 36-
47.

This paper presents a summary of demographic trends in Portugal since the 16th
century, and describes regional patterns in mortality, fertility and nuptiality within
the country.

404 **A outra face da emigração: estudo sobre a situação das mulheres
que ficam no país de origem.** (The other side of emigration: a study
on the position of women who remain in their country of origin.)
Karin Wall. Lisbon: Comissão da Condição Feminina, 1982. 43p.

An important study which focuses on the problems faced by women left behind in
a community when the men have emigrated in search of better employment

possibilities. It is largely based on a case study of the village of Moledo do Minho in the north-west of Portugal.

The road to Alto: an account of peasants, capitalists and the soil in the mountains of southern Portugal.
See item no. 15.

Area handbook for Portugal.
See item no. 16.

Portugal: a bird's eye view.
See item no. 28.

Portugal and Brazil in transition.
See item no. 34.

A social history of slaves and freedmen in Portugal, 1441-1555.
See item no. 202.

Portugal: fifty years of dictatorship.
See item no. 294.

Oldest ally: a portrait of Salazar's Portugal.
See item no. 295.

Portugal: a twentieth century interpretation.
See item no. 296.

Portugal: the decline and collapse of authoritarian order.
See item no. 297.

Contemporary Portugal: a history.
See item no. 303.

Race relations in the Portuguese empire, 1415-1825.
See item no. 317.

Death in Portugal: studies in Portuguese anthropology and modern history.
See item no. 341.

Portugal in development: emigration, industrialization, the European Community.
See item no. 343.

Portugal: women in prison.
See item no. 414.

Contemporary Portugal: the revolution and its antecedents.
See item no. 420.

In search of modern Portugal: the revolution and its consequences.
See item no. 421.

Portugal: birth of a democracy.
See item no. 423.

Portuguese agrarian reform and economic and social development.
See item no. 503.

The employment of women in Portugal.
See item no. 569.

Housing and urban development

405 **The illegal housing sector in Portugal – *Bairros clandestinos*.**
Abilio S. Cardoso.   Reading, England: Department of
Geography, Reading University, 1983. 41p. bibliog. (Geographical
Papers).
Analyses the general features of illegal housing in Portugal, and the evolution of
state policies towards illegal urbanization.

406 **Urbanization: growth, problems and policies.**
J. Gaspar. In: *Southern Europe transformed: political and
economic change in Greece, Italy, Portugal and Spain.* Edited by
Allan Williams.   London: Harper & Row, 1984, p. 208-35.
This paper notes that Portugal is probably exceptional because emigrants
normally return to their rural areas of origin rather than to towns. It also observes
that in the 1974-75 revolutionary period Portugal witnessed a climax of urban
struggles. The country's most rapid urban growth, though, occurred during the
period of dictatorial government.

407 **Urban development in southern Europe: Spain and Portugal.**
E. A. Gutkind.   New York: Free Press;   London:
Collier-Macmillan, 1967. 534p. 175 maps. bibliog. (International
History of City Development, vol. 3).
In this broad survey of urban development in Iberia the first 114 pages are
devoted to Portugal. After two introductory chapters on the land, history and
settlement, the forty-two main historic towns of the country are each described in
turn. This is a well-illustrated introduction to the towns of Portugal with maps and
photographs of most of the places described. An appendix also provides a
description of Lisbon translated from the 1567 chronicle of Damiania Goes,
Crónica do Felicíssimo Rei Dom Manuel.

408 **Portugal.**
J. R. Lewis, A. M. Williams.   In: *Housing in Europe*. Edited by
Martin Wynn. London: Croom Helm, 1984, p. 281-325.

A comprehensive account of housing issues in Portugal, which concentrates on
the housing crisis as a function of social, economic and political conditions within
the country. Particular attention is paid to housing provision, the control of
housing production, and housing developments since 1974.

409 **Conservation planning in Oporto: an integrated approach in the
Ribeira-Barredo.**
A. M. Williams.   *Town Planning Review*, vol. 51, no. 2 (1980),
p. 177-95.

Analyses urban planning in Oporto. It traces the historical development of the
town then investigates the integrated urban renewal scheme in its old historic
centre.

410 *Bairros clandestinos*: **illegal housing in Portugal.**
A. M. Williams.   *Geografisch Tijdschrift*, vol. 15, no. 1 (1981), p.
24-34.

Analyses the illegal housing sector in Portugal concentrating mainly on the Lisbon
region.

Politics

General

411   The *Santa Maria*: my crusade for Portugal.
Henrique Galvão, translated by William Longfellow.   London:
Weidenfeld & Nicolson, 1961. 212p.
On 22 January 1961, the Portuguese revolutionary Captain Henrique Galvão and twenty-four other men seized the Portuguese liner *Santa Maria* in Operation Dulcinea. The author explains his motives; the dramatic events of his life prior to the event, including his escape from prison in 1959; and the details of Operation Dulcinea which formed an important anti-Salazar revolutionary attempt.

412   **Political forces in Spain, Greece and Portugal.**
Beate Kohler, translated by Frank Carter, Ginnie Hole.   London:
Butterworth Scientific in association with the European Centre for
Political Studies, 1982. 281p. bibliog. (Butterworth's European
Studies).
Analyses the political parties of the three Mediterranean countries which applied for membership of the European Community after they had emerged from dictatorial political régimes during the mid-1970s. The political parties of each country in turn are discussed, giving an assessment of their historical development, current attitudes and future prospects. It provides a broad examination of the Partido Socialista (Socialist Party); the Partido Social Democrático (the Social Democratic Party) which was formerly the Partido Popular Democrático (the Popular Democratic Party); the Partido do Centro Democrático Social (the Central Social Democratic Party); and the Partido Comunista Portugues (the Portuguese Communist Party); as well as a survey of Portuguese trade unions and industrialists' associations.

413 **Portugal: twenty years of change.**
M. Porto. In: *Southern Europe transformed: political and economic change in Greece, Italy, Portugal and Spain.* Edited by Allan Williams. London: Harper & Row, 1984, p. 84-112.

Provides an account of political and economic change in Portugal since 1960. It argues that integration into the European Free Trade Association (EFTA), the colonial wars and emigration to the more industrialized countries of Europe led to important changes during the 1960s, and it provides an assessment of the impact of the coup of 1974.

414 **Portugal: women in prison.**
Helen Ward. London: British Committee for Portuguese Amnesty, no date [ca. mid/late 1960s]. 16p.

A short account of women in prison in Portugal in the 1960s. It includes selections from letters written by women in Caxias Prison and case histories of some women political prisoners.

415 **New international communism: the foreign and defense policies of the Latin European Communist Party.**
Lawrence L. Whetten. Lexington, Massachusetts; Toronto: Lexington Books (D. C. Heath), 1982. 262p.

This book is an attempt to refine insight into the field of comparative communism by focusing on specific aspects of the broader framework of the international workers' movement. Two chapters concentrate on the Portuguese Communist Party (PCP), with Chapter Six investigating its foreign and security policies, and Chapter Seven looking at the revolution of 1974. It suggests that the Portuguese revolution posed only a minimal threat to the security interests of the North Atlantic Treaty Organization (NATO).

Doctrine and action: internal and foreign policy of the New Portugal 1928-1939.
See item no. 304.

Salazar Prime Minister of Portugal says . . .
See item no. 305.

The road for the future.
See item no. 306.

Corporatism and public policy in authoritarian Portugal.
See item no. 307.

Portugal: the price of opposition.
See item no. 308.

The New Corporative State of Portugal. An inaugural lecture delivered at King's College, London, the 15th of February 1937.
See item no. 309.

Republican Portugal: a political history 1910-1926.
See item no. 310.

Corporatism and development: the Portuguese experience.
See item no. 311.

The Europa Yearbook: a World Survey.
See item no. 575.

I like it here.
See item no. 611.

Revolution (25 April 1974): origins, events, consequences

416 **Portugal: the last empire.**
Neil Bruce.   Newton Abbot, England; North Pomfret, Vermont; Vancouver, Canada: David & Charles, 1975. 160p. 6 maps. bibliog.

An account of the factors which precipitated the events of 25 April 1974 and their immediate aftermath. Particular attention is paid to Salazar's 'New State', the colonial wars in Africa and the role of General António de Spinola.

417 **Portugal's reasons for remaining in the overseas provinces.**
Marcello Caetano. Lisbon: Office of the Secretary of State for
Information & Tourism, General Direction for Information,
197[1]. 54p.

A collection of excerpts from speeches made by Caetano mainly during the time
when he was Prime Minister of Portugal between 1968 and 1971. They provide a
good coverage of his reasons for continuing to maintain Portugal's overseas
provinces in Africa.

418 **Portugal: the revolution in the labyrinth.**
Edited by Jean-Pierre Faye from the papers of the Russell
Committee for Portugal, translated by Sue Kortlandt, Micki
McCarthy. Nottingham, England: Spokesman Books, 1976. 231p.

Presents a report in the form of a chronicle of the Portuguese revolution,
describing the events that took place between April 1974 and June 1976. The
activities of the revolutionary leader Otelo Saraiva de Carvalho feature
prominently, and the report pays particular attention to the events of 25 and 26
November 1975, which, it asserts, saw the effective end of the revolution. It is
based on the investigations of the Russell Committee and consists mainly of
testimonies by those involved in the revolution and the reports by members of the
Committee.

419 **The Portuguese revolution and the Armed Forces Movement.**
Rona M. Fields. New York; Washington, DC; London: Praeger,
1975. 289p. map. (Praeger Special Studies in International Politics
and Government).

Analyses the background to the 1974 revolution by the MFA (Movimento das
Forças Armadas) and its processes, development and personality during the first
year of the provisional government. Ten appendixes provide details of various
aspects of the new government's policies ranging from the MFA programme, to
the Press Law and the agrarian reform programme.

420 **Contemporary Portugal: the revolution and its antecedents.**
Edited by Lawrence S. Graham, Harry M. Makler. Austin,
Texas; London: University of Texas Press, 1979. 357p.

An interdisciplinary study deriving from two conferences held by the International Conference Group on Modern Portugal in 1973 and 1976. It provides a
thorough collection of essays on the events leading up to the revolution, the
causes of the military coup, and the movement of a society on the brink of
revolutionary upheaval towards democratic parliamentary elections. It consists of
the following papers: 'The "régime d'exception" that became the rule: forty-eight
years of authoritarian domination in Portugal', by Philippe C. Schmitter; 'The
evolution of Portuguese corporatism under Salazar and Caetano', by Manuel de
Lucena; 'The corporatist tradition and the corporative system in Portugal:
structured, evolving, transcended, persistent', by Howard J. Wiarda; 'The
Portuguese industrial elite and its corporative relations: a study of compartment-
alization in an authoritarian regime', by Harry M. Makler; 'Peasants and politics

Politics. Revolution (25 April 1974): origins, events, consequences

in Salazar's Portugal: the corporate state and village "nonpolitics"', by Joyce Firstenberg Riegelhaupt; 'The military and the Portuguese dictatorship 1926-1974: "the honour of the army"', by Douglas L. Wheeler; 'The military in politics: the politicization of the Portuguese armed forces', by Lawrence S. Graham; 'Electoral behaviour and political militancy', by John L. Hammond; 'Emigration and its implications for the revolution in northern Portugal', by Caroline S. Brettel; 'Analysis and projection of macroeconomic conditions in Portugal', by Rudiger Dornbusch, Richard S. Eckaus and Lance Taylor; 'The present economic situation: its origins and prospects', by Mário Murteira; and an epilogue by Stanley G. Payne.

421 **In search of modern Portugal: the revolution and its consequences.**
Edited by Lawrence S. Graham, Douglas L. Wheeler. Madison, Wisconsin; London: University of Wisconsin Press, 1983, 380p.

Provides a comprehensive assessment of the political consequences of the Portuguese revolution in 1974. The volume includes sixteen papers resulting from the June 1979 meeting of the International Conference Group on Modern Portugal, held at Durham, New Hampshire: 'Popular support for democracy in post-revolutionary Portugal: results from a survey', by Thomas C. Bruneau; 'Political power and the Portuguese media', by Ben Pimlott and Jean Seaton; 'Populism and the Portuguese left: from Delgado to Otelo', by David L. Raby; 'From hegemony to opposition: the Ultra Right before and after 1974', by Tom Gallagher; 'Ideology and illusion in the Portuguese revolution: the role of the left', by Bill Lomax; 'Worker mobilization and party politics: revolutionary Portugal in perspective', by John R. Logan; 'Residents' Commissions and urban struggles in revolutionary Portugal', by Charles Downs; 'Worker management in industry: reconciling representative government and industrial democracy in a polarised society', by Nancy Bermeo; 'The continuing impact of the Old Regime on Portuguese political culture', by Walter C. Opello, Jr., 'Bureaucratic politics and the problem of the survival and revival of the industrial bourgeoisie', by Harry M. Makler; 'International ramifications of the Portuguese revolution', by José Madeiros Ferreira: 'The French and Italian Communist Parties and the Portuguese revolution', by Alex MacLeod; 'Portugal and the European Community', by Paulo de Pitta e Cunha; and 'The revolution in perspective: revolution and counter-revolution in modern Portuguese history', by Douglas L. Wheeler.

422 **Portugal in revolution.**
Michael Harsgor. Washington, DC: Centre for Strategic and International Studies, Georgetown University; Beverley Hills, California; London: Sage Publications, 1976. 90p. (The Washington Papers, no. 32).

This paper describes the emergence of new political forces in Portugal following the events of 1974, and their struggle in defence of the country's newly-won freedom. The author believes that despite the difficulties that lay ahead, democracy was then more deeply-rooted in Portugal than was generally perceived outside the country.

423 **Portugal: birth of a democracy.**
    Robert Harvey. London: Macmillan, 1978. 151p.
Analyses the events surrounding the Portuguese revolution of 25 April 1974. It traces the activities of the Armed Forces' Movement, their overthrow of Dr. Marcello Caetano's post-Salazar régime, and the establishment of a new democracy under the Presidency of Ramalho Eanes and the Prime Ministership of Mário Soares. A more recent study of the revolution and its consequences is provided by *Portugal's revolution: ten years on* by Hugo Gil Ferreira and Michael W. Marshall (Cambridge, England: Cambridge University Press, 1986). This presents a background, description and anlaysis of the 1974 revolution and offers a review of the political parties, social policies and economic conditions in Portugal since the end of the dictatorship.

424 **Portuguese revolution 1974-76.**
    Christ Hunt, edited by Lester A. Sobel. New York: Facts on
    File, 1976. 151p. map.
An account of the events leading up to the Portuguese revolution of 1974 and the following two years of turmoil in the country. After a short introduction, it is divided into five sections on the Caetano régime, mounting problems, the revolution of April 1974, the seeking of power by the left and the power struggle. The material included consists mainly of the records compiled by Facts on File in its weekly reports on world events.

425 **Insight on Portugal: the year of the captains.**
    The Insight Team of the Sunday Times: Simon Jenkins (Editor),
    Peter Kellner, Peter Pringle, Peter Watson. London: André
    Deutsch, 1975. 273p. 2 maps.
An account of the factors giving rise to, and the immediate aftermath of, the revolution of 25 April 1974. It provides a very readable account of the growing political and economic crisis, the role of the army Captains and the Movimento das Forças Armadas (MFA), the rise to power and subsequent demise of General Spinola, the awakening of the political parties and the state of uncertainty existing in early 1975.

426 **Portugal: revolution and backlash.**
    Hugh Kay. London: Institute for the Study of Conflict, 1975.
    35p. map. bibliog. (Conflict Studies, no. 61).
A report on political events in Portugal following the violent demonstrations of July 1975. The first part, by Hugh Kay, is entitled 'Quest for democracy', and it evaluates the activities of political parties in the period after April 1974 during which General António de Spinola was President. The second part by an un-named correspondent investigates the activities of the Communist Party and the way in which 250 agents trained in Czechoslovakia set up a country-wide communist network in Portugal.

427 **Portugal since the revolution: economic and political perspectives.**
Edited by Jorge Braga de Macedo, Simon Serfaty. Boulder,
Colorado: Westview Press, 1981. 217p.

Presents a collection of four substantive papers on the economic and political
consequences of the events of April 1974, each followed by comments. The four
papers are as follows: 'Patterns of politics in Portugal since the April revolution',
by Thomas C. Bruneau, with comments by Juan J. Linz and Eusebio Mujal-Leon;
'The economic consequences of the April 25th revolution', by Paul Krugman and
Jorge Braga de Macedo, with comments by T. Sriram Aiyer and Luis Miguel
Beleza; 'Portugal and the IMF: the political economy of stabilization', by Barbara
Stallings, with comments by Patrick de Fontenay and Pentti J. K. Kouri; and
'Portugal and Europe: the channels of structural interdependence', by Jorge
Braga de Macedo, with comments by Hans Schmitt and Juergen B. Donges.

428 **Portugal: the impossible revolution.**
Phil Mailer. London: Solidarity, 1977. 399p.

An account of what happened in Portugal between 25 April 1974 and 25
November 1975, written from the viewpoint of the people who were seeking, in
many contradictory ways, to write a chapter of their own history. Twenty-six
appendixes provide translations of the official statements of the MFA (Armed
Forces' Movement) and of the various political parties. It provides a committed
account of political, social and economic change during the events associated with
the Portuguese revolution and its aftermath.

429 **The Portuguese industrial elite and its corporative relations: a study
of compartmentalisation in an authoritarian regime.**
Harry M. Makler. *Economic Development and Cultural Change*,
vol. 24, no. 3 (1976), p. 495-526.

Explores the tendencies underlying the dissolution of the Salazar-Caetano régime
in 1974. It provides a detailed analysis of the nature of Portuguese Corporatism
and of the functioning of the patronal guilds known as *grémios*.

430 **Cartoons 1969-1975.**
João Abel Manta. Lisbon: Edições O Jornal, 1975. 175p.

A collection of mainly political cartoons by Manta from the years 1969 to 1975.
Many of them illustrate the events surrounding the revolution of 25 April 1974
and its immediate aftermath.

431 **Portugal: revolutionary change in an open economy.**
Rodney J. Morrison. Boston, Massachusetts: Auburn House,
1981. 184p. bibliog.

The main theme of this book is that the international sector was the most serious
limitation facing Portugal after the 1974 revolution as the government tried to
restructure society, reorganize the economy and raise the standard of living. It
concentrates on the interplay between economic and political factors in effecting
change, and it pays particular attention to Portugal's relationships with the
European Free Trade Association (EFTA) and the European Economic
Community (EEC).

432 **Portugal's political development: a comparative approach.**
Walter C. Opello, Jr. Boulder, Colorado; London: Westview
Press, 1985. 235p. bibliog. (Westview Special Studies in West
European Politics and Society).

An account of the constitutions, parties, voting behaviour and local government
of Portugal, paying particular attention to the period after 1974. It begins with a
broad sweep of Portuguese history up to the beginning of the New State
established by Salazar. This is followed by an analysis of the changes in régime
following 25 April 1974, and a discussion of the emerging political infrastructure
of parties and elections consequent to this event. The final chapters examine the
1976 constitution, discuss the policy-making process and relate the Portuguese
example to wider political theory.

433 **Social Democratic Parties in Western Europe.**
Edited by William E. Paterson, Alastair H. Thomas. London:
Croom Helm, 1977. 444p.

A collection of papers resulting from a conference on Social Democratic Parties
of the European Community held in 1974 at Birmingham University. The paper
by Jonathan Story on social revolution and democracy in Iberia traces the early
political turmoil in Portugal following the revolution of 1974 and the role of Mário
Soares as Prime Minister.

434 **The Portuguese armed forces and the revolution.**
Douglas Porch. London: Croom Helm; Stanford, California:
Hoover Institution Press, 1977. 273p. 3 maps. bibliog.

Analyses the role of the Portuguese armed forces in the politics of the country,
culminating in the revolution of April 1974. It traces the origins of this revolution
to the traditional political independence of the armed forces, their increasingly
strained relationships with the Salazar-Caetano régime, and to the colonial wars
which exacerbated professional discontent. A useful set of appendixes provides
information on the Armed Forces' Movement (MFA) and on the composition of
Portugal's governments between 1972 and 1975.

435 **Portuguese revolution and aftermath.**
Amsterdam, The Netherlands: Drijver & Koolemans NV, 1976.
[not paginated].

A collection of photographs of political posters concerning the Portuguese
revolution of 1974 and the emergence of political parties in its immediate
aftermath. It forms a catalogue for the collection of material held by the
antiquarian booksellers Drijver and Koolemans.

436 **The Portuguese revolution: selection of articles 1975-6.**
J. Posadas. London: Fourth International Publications, 1976.
32p. (A European Marxist Review Publication).

Presents a collection of three of the author's articles on the events surrounding
the revolution of April 1974: 'The military uprising of 25th November and the

114

process of revolution and counter-revolution in Portugal (30th November 1975)';
'The workers and peasant alliance with the armed forces to sustain and advance
the revolution in Portugal (25th January 1976)'; and 'Portugal votes for socialism
again (28th April 1976)'. It argues that the Portuguese revolution made its
advances without a leadership, and that its most striking aspect was the decision
and spirit of the masses.

437 **Socialism, democracy and self-management.**
Michel Raptis, translated by Marie-Jo Serrié, Richard Sissons.
London: Allison & Busby, 1980. 208p.

A collection of political essays, one of which, entitled 'The Portuguese revolution:
self-management and people's power' (p. 162-67) surveys the activities of
communist groups in Portugal at the time of the 1974 revolution.

438 **Portugal's struggle for liberty.**
Mário Soares, translated by Mary Gawsworth.   London: Allen &
Unwin, 1975. 313p.

A full account of Portuguese politics since 1945, written by the leader of the
Portuguese Socialist Party, who became President of Portugal in 1986. It was
begun on the island of São Tomé, where the author was sent without trial in 1968,
and was first published in France in 1972. It is the author's testimony, founded on
his personal experience and political commitment, and focuses especially on
Soares' own role in politics under the Salazar régime.

439 **Portugal and the future.**
António de Spinola.   Johannesburg: Perskor, 1974. 148p.

A translation of Spinola's book *Portugal e o futuro*. It presents his views
concerning Portugal's future at the time of the wars in Africa, and is divided into
five main sections entitled: 'The crisis'; 'Our position in the world'; 'Our
anomalies'; 'The basis for a national strategy'; and 'A hypothesis for the political
structure of the nation'.

440 **Eyewitness in revolutionary Portugal.**
Audrey Wise.   Nottingham, England: Spokesman Books, 1975.
72p.

An account of the effect of the revolution on what the author describes as the
ordinary working people of Portugal, based on a visit to the country in the
summer of 1975. There is an introductory preface by Judith Hart. Chapters
describe a farmworkers' occupation of a 1400 hectare farm in the Alentejo, a
Neighbourhood Committee assembly at Palmela, the Workers' Committee of the
SCC brewing concern, the changes at the offices of the *Republica* newspaper and
the Post Office Workers' Union, as well as a series of demonstrations and rallies.
An appendix gives details of the strategic programme of the MFA (Armed
Forces' Movement).

Politics. Revolution (25 April 1974): origins, events, consequences

Contemporary Portugal: a history.
See item no. 303.

Portugal: twenty years of change.
See item no. 413.

The political economy of Portugal's old regime: growth and change preceding the 1974 revolution.
See item no. 466.

The class struggle in Portugal: chronology and texts of 1976.
See item no. 566.

New life in Portugal: impressions and pictures of a newly born cooperative farm.
See item no. 567.

Thirteen days.
See item no. 624.

Revolution in Portugal: 1974-1976 a bibliography.
See item no. 770.

Foreign Relations

General

441 **Portugal and America: studies in honor of the bicentennial of American independence.**
Henry Hunt Keith, Maria José Lagos Trinidade, José Luís Sul Mendes, with an introduction by Joel Serrão. Lisbon: Luso-American Educational Commission and the Calouste Gulbenkian Foundation, 1976. 295p.

Following a short introduction on relations between Portugal and America by Joel Serrão, this volume consists of three papers: 'The "Gazeta de Lisboa" of London', by Henry Hunt Keith; 'Introductory notes to balance sheets for trade between Portugal and the United States, 1783-1831', by José Luís Sul Mendes; and 'Portuguese emigration from the Azores to the United States during the nineteenth century – a contribution to its study', by Maria José Lagos Trinidade.

442 **The relations between Portugal and Japan.**
Kiichi Matsuda. Lisbon: Junta de Investigações do Ultramar and Centro de Estudos Históricos Ultramarinos, 1965. 107p. bibliog.

This account of the relations between Japan and Portugal is divided into two parts. The first is an historical survey tracing Portuguese contact with Japan between the 16th and 20th centuries but concentrating mainly on the early 17th century. The second part surveys the influence of Portugal on Japanese civilization and is divided into sections on science, education, printing, fine arts and customs.

443 **The diplomatic and commercial relations of Sweden and Portugal from 1641 to 1670.**
Karl Mellander, Edgar Prestage. Watford, England: Voss & Michael, 1930. 123p.
An account of the diplomatic and commercial relations between Portugal and Sweden following Portugal's independence from Spain in 1640.

444 **Malabar and the Portuguese: being a history of the relations of the Portuguese with Malabar from 1500 to 1663.**
K. M. Panikkar. Bombay, India: D. B. Taraporevala, 1929. 221p. map.
An account of the relationships between the Portuguese and the Malabar coast of Western India over a 150-year span following Vasco da Gama's arrival in India in 1498.

445 **Diplomatic relations of Portugal with France, England and Holland from 1646 to 1668.**
Edgar Prestage. Watford, England: Voss & Michael, 1925. 237p.
Presents an account of Portugal's diplomatic relations during the Restoration period from the commencement of the revolution of 1 December 1640 (organized by João Robeiro and supported by the nobility who were disillusioned with Spanish rule) to Spain's final recognition of Portugal's independence in the peace treaty of 1668.

446 **A short survey of Luso-Siamese relations — 1511-1900.**
A. da Silva Rego. Macao: Imprensa Nacional, 1979. 28p.
A broad survey of the relations between Portugal and Siam, now Thailand, between 1511 and 1900.

447 **The romance of the Portuguese in Abyssinia: an account of the adventurous journeys of the Portuguese to the empire of Prester John; their assistance to Ethiopia in its struggle against Islam and their subsequent efforts to impose their own influence and religions, 1490-1633.**
Charles F. Rey. London: H. F. & G. Witherby, 1929. 319p. 2 maps. bibliog.
Provides an account of Portuguese relations with Abyssinia (now Ethiopia) in the 16th and 17th centuries. Particular attention is paid to the expeditions and activities of Pedro da Covilham, Dom Roderigo da Lima, and Dom Christovao da Gama, as well as the later activities of the Jesuit missionaries.

Area handbook for Portugal.
See item no. 16.

The Statesman's Year-book.
See item no. 27.

Background notes: Portugal.
See item no. 43.

Portuguese pioneers in India: spotlight on medicine.
See item no. 190.

Swedish-Portuguese cooperation in the field of scientific and technical information and documentation: project identification mission to Portugal, 2-14 February 1976.
See item no. 579.

Revised programme proposal for the Swedish-Portuguese cooperation in the field of scientific and technical information and documentation.
See item no. 580.

With Britain

448 **600 anos de aliança Anglo-Portuguesa; 600 years of Anglo-Portuguese alliance.**
London: Her Majesty's Government in association with the British Broadcasting Corporation and Canning House, no date [ca. 1973]. 48p.

This booklet, written in both Portuguese and English, describes the history of the oldest enduring alliance between any two countries, the 1373 treaty between King Fernando of Portugal and Edward III of England. It includes the following papers: 'The Anglo-Portuguese alliance: historical perspective', by H. V. Livermore; 'Prelude to the Anglo-Portuguese alliance', by P. E. Russell; 'The dawn of the Anglo-Portuguese alliance', by Virginia Rau; 'Vicissitudes of Anglo-Portuguese relations in the 17th century', by Charles Boxer; 'The Anglo-Portuguese alliance in the 18th century', by A. D. Francis; 'England and Portugal during the Peninsular War', by Michael Glover; '19th century: Anglo-Portuguese alliance and the scramble for Africa', by Douglas L. Wheeler; and 'The Anglo-Portuguese alliance in the 20th century', by Hugh Kay.

449 **British contributions to Portuguese and Brazilian studies.**
William C. Atkinson.   London: Longmans Green & Company 1945. 39p. 2nd ed. British Council, 1974. 47p. map.

The work is divided into sections on British contributions towards the study of the background of Anglo-Portuguese relations over the centuries; early contacts; Luis de Camoens; the Marquis of Pombal; Napoleon; and contemporary scholarship. There is also a section on British contributions to Brazilian studies.

450 **The Anglo-Portuguese alliance.**
Eduardo Brazão. London: Sylvan Press, 1957. 55p.
An account of the history of the political alliance between England and Portugal.
It includes extracts from the following treaties: the Commercial Treaty of 1353 (in
Portuguese); the Treaty of 1373 (extract translation); the Treaty of 1386 (extract
translation); the Treaty of 1642 (extract); the Treaty of 1654 (extract); the Treaty
of 1660 (extract); the Treaty of 1661 (extract); the Treaty of 1703 (extract); the
Commercial Treaty of 1703 (extract translation); the Treaty of 1810 (extract); the
Treaty of 1815 (extract); the Treaty of 1891 (extract); the secret declaration
between the United Kingdom and Portugal, 14 October 1899; the Arbitration
Agreement of 1904; and the agreement regarding the use of facilities in the
Azores, 17 August 1943.

451 **Souvenir brochure commemorating the 600th anniversary of the
Anglo-Portuguese treaty of alliance and friendship, 1373-1973.**
British Community Council of London. Lisbon: British
Community Council, 1973. 56p.
A celebration of the 600th anniversary of the Anglo-Portuguese Treaty of
Alliance of 1373, published in English and Portuguese. It includes the following
papers: 'An old alliance past, present and future', by S. George West; and
'Anglo-Portuguese alliance 1373-1973, historical incidents (abridged)', by C. G.
Tait.

452 **The Anglo-Portuguese alliance 1373-1973.**
Edited by John Epstein. *World Survey*, no. 54 (June 1973), 18p.
This short account of the Anglo-Portuguese alliance is divided into sections
dealing with: an historical retrospect; Anglo-Portuguese relations today; Atlantic
relations; and Portugal in Europe.

453 **The intellectual relations between Portugal and Great Britain.**
Fran Paxeco, translated into English by Augusto Potier. Lisbon:
Editorial Império 1937. 39p.
A broad survey of the intellectual links between Portugal and Great Britain,
subdivided into sections on Classicism, Romanticism and Naturalism. Most
attention is paid to literature and in particular to translations of Camões *Os
Lusíadas* (The Lusiads).

454 **A true league: Portugal and Britain, 1373-1973.**
Jan Read. *History Today*, vol. 23, no. 7 (July 1973), p. 486-94.
A short account of the history of the political relationships between Britain and
Portugal.

455   **William Wordsworth's Convention of Cintra: a facsimile of the 1809 tract.**
Introduced by Gordon Kent Thomas.   Provo, Utah: Brigham Young University Press, 1983. 216p.

A facsimile of Wordsworth's 1809 tract entitled 'Concerning the relations of Great Britain, Spain, and Portugal, to each other, and to the common enemy, at this crisis; and especially as affected by the Convention of Cintra: the whole brought to the test of those principles, by which alone the independence and freedom of nations can be preserved or recovered'. This is the longest single work written by Wordsworth, and it strongly attacks the leadership of Britain's military forces who signed the Convention of Cintra in 1808 by which the French leader Junot agreed to evacuate Portugal.

456   **The Portuguese connection: the secret history of the Azores base.**
R. E. Vintras.   London: Bachman & Turner, 1974. 183p. map. bibliog.

An account of the author's role in the negotiations named Operation 'Alacrity' which led to the establishment of British maritime air bases in the Azores during the Second World War, together with a brief history of warfare in the Atlantic between 1564 and 1941. Fourteen appendixes provide the texts of various treaties between Britain and Portugal from the 14th to the 20th centuries, as well as other documents pertaining to the events described in the book.

457   **The British Factory in Lisbon, and its closing stages ensuing upon the Treaty of 1810.**
A. R. Walford.   Lisbon: Instituto Britânico em Portugal, 1940. 200p. bibliog.

Presents an account of the history of the Lisbon British Factory based on records in the British Museum Library, the Public Records Office in London and various archives in Lisbon. The Lisbon Factory was an assembly of merchants and factors which began to operate in the mid-17th century. Appendixes provide transcripts of several documents pertaining to the Factory.

Chapters in Anglo-Portuguese relations.
See item no. 180.

The commercial relations of England and Portugal.
See item no. 182.

Philippa: Dona Filipa of Portugal.
See item no. 198.

The English intervention in Spain and Portugal in the time of Edward III and Richard II.
See item no. 200.

The Methuens and Portugal 1691-1708.
See item no. 251.

A question of slavery: labour policies in Portuguese Africa and the British protest, 1850-1920.
See item no. 268.

The Portugal trade: a study of Anglo-Portuguese commerce 1700-1770.
See item no. 494.

Descriptive list of the State Papers Portugal 1661-1780 in the Public Record Office London.
See item no. 755.

Accession to the European Community

458 **Basic facts on Portugal's accession to the European Community.**
Prepared by the Foreign and Commonwealth Office, the British Overseas Trade Board and the Central Office of Information. London: Printed for HMSO, 1985. 12p. (Dd. 8831798, BOTB J0135).

An information booklet on Portugal's accession to the European Community covering the following issues: industry, taxation, banking and credit institutions, capital movements, agriculture, social questions and where to go for advice.

459 **The second enlargement of the EEC: the integration of unequal partners.**
Edited by Dudley Seers, Constantine Vaitsos with the assistance of Marja-Lisa Kiljunen. London: Macmillan Press, 1982. 275p. (Studies in the Integration of Western Europe).

An edited volume of papers investigating attitudes to the enlargement of the EEC by the addition of Greece, Portugal and Spain, their potential influence on economic structures in Western Europe and the likely impact on less developed countries.

460 **The European Community and its Mediterranean enlargement.**
Loukas Tsoukalis. London: Allen & Unwin, 1981. 273p.

A study of the entry of Greece, Portugal and Spain into the European Community and what this membership means for the three Mediterranean countries as well as for the future development of the Community. Most emphasis is laid on the problems of the three applicant countries, and considerable attention is paid to Portugal's agriculture, fiscal policy, banking sector, political change and relationships with its former colonies.

461   **Spain, Portugal and the European Community.**
University Association for Contemporary European Studies, and Iberian Centre, St. Anthony's College, Oxford.   London: University Association for Contemporary European Studies, no date [1979]. 62p.

These conference proceedings include the following papers related to Portugal: 'Political changes in the Iberian peninsula', by Robert Harvey; 'Portugal and the European Community: past, present and future', by Antonio Jose de Siqueira Freire; 'Portuguese agriculture and the EEC', by A. Trigo de Abreu; and 'Spain, Portugal and an enlarged Community: regional problems', by Vittorio Curzi.

462   **Does Europe still stop at the Pyrenees? Or does Latin America begin there? Iberia, Latin America and the second enlargement of the European Community.**
Howard J. Wiarda.   Washington, DC: American Enterprise Institute for Public Policy Research, 1981, 47p. (Occasional Papers Series, no. 2).

Examines the political, economic, socio-cultural and strategic relations of Iberia to Europe, and their implications for Latin America. The work presents an overview of Spain and Portugal in terms of their historical isolation, their recent social and economic transformations, the political changes that have taken place since the mid-1970s, and, in particular, the role of the European Community and the United States in these.

463   **Southern Europe transformed: political and economic change in Greece, Italy, Portugal, and Spain.**
Edited by Alan Williams.   London: Harper & Row, 1984. 295p. 3 maps.

Presents a review of the economic, political and social changes which have transformed southern Europe since the end of the Second World War, paying particular attention to the 1960s and 1970s. The chapters which discuss Portugal are 'The European Community and the Mediterranean region: two steps forward, one step back', by M. Blacksell; 'Urbanization: growth, problems and policies', by J. Gaspar; 'Capital accumulation: the industrialisation of southern Europe', by R. Hudson and J. R. Lewis; 'Agriculture: organisation, reform and the EEC', by A. R. Jones; 'Population mobility: emigration, return migration and internal migration', by Russell King; and 'Portugal: twenty years of change', by M. Porto.

Economy

464 ABECOR Country Report: Portugal.
London: Barclays Bank Group, 1981- . annual. 2p.

A summary sheet of information on Portugal covering: economy, agriculture, industry, money and finance, external position and accession to the EEC.

465 The economic transformation of Spain and Portugal.
Eric N. Baklanoff. New York; London: Praeger, 1978. 211p.
bibliog. (Praeger Special Studies).

Provides an account of the relationships between the political transformation of the countries of the Iberian peninsula and economic and social change therein. Part One is concerned with Spain and Part Three provides a comparative analysis of Spain and Portugal. Part Two, which is concerned specifically with Portugal, analyses the political economy of the old régime, structural change and growth between 1960 and 1973, and the economic consequences of the Portuguese revolution. An appendix provides a useful list of the main Portuguese economic policy measures taken between 1974 and 1977.

466 The political economy of Portugal's old regime: growth and change preceding the 1974 revolution.
E. N. Baklanoff. *World Development*, vol. 7, no. 8-9 (Aug.-Sept. 1979), p. 799-812.

This useful summary of the political economy of Portugal in the 1960s argues that on the eve of the 1974 revolution Portugal faced major economic problems associated with the concentration of political and economic power in the forty families oligarchy and the burdensome defence of the African territories.

467 **Bank of London and South America Review.**
London: Lloyds Bank Group Economics Department, 1966-83.
quarterly.

Presents a useful guide to economic change in Portugal and some of the countries
of Latin America. It provided current reviews of financial, economic and political
change in Portugal, together with a series of statistical tables.

468 **Growth, migration and the balance of payments in a small open
economy: Portugal.**
Manuel P. Barbosa.   New York, London: Garland, 1984. 212p.
bibliog.

A theoretical and empirical account of the economic effects of international
labour migration on Portugal. Following a discussion of two theoretical topics, a
long-run general equilibrium model of an economy with internationally mobile
labour and the behaviour of such a system in disequilibrium, it then applies this
econometric analysis to the example of Portugal.

469 **The third Portuguese empire 1825-1975: a study in economic
imperialism.**
Gervase Clarence-Smith.   Manchester, England; Dover, New
Hampshire: Manchester University Press, 1985. 246p. 8 maps.
bibliog.

Investigates the economic motivations behind Portugal's empire in the 19th and
20th centuries. It argues that the driving force behind its imperial expansion was
the search for markets associated with a constant preoccupation with the need for
foreign exchange.

470 **Economic planning in corporative Portugal.**
Freppel Cotta.   London: P. S. King, 1937. 188p. bibliog.

An early account of Portugal's economy at the time of Salazar's introduction of
the Corporative State, which is full of praise for Salazar's efforts. After
introductory chapters on the foundations, basic principles and organizations
involved in planning, it is divided into chapters on commodities: wheat, wine,
fruit, rice, codfish, sardines, forest products, manufacturing industry and services.
There are also chapters on the organization of agriculture and labour.

471 **Economic surveys by the OECD: Portugal.**
Paris: Organisation for Economic Co-operation and Development,
1964. 33p.

A summary of Portugal's economic position in the mid-1960s. The section on the
current economic situation covers trend in output and demand, prices and wages,
money and credit, public finance and balance of payments. There is also a survey
of some of Portugal's economic development problems, subdivided into parts on
manpower, the development plan and the 1965-67 investment plan.

472 **Portugal: current and prospective economic trends.**
Basil Kavalsky, Surendra Agarwal.   Washington, DC: World
Bank, 1978. 52p. map. (World Bank Country Study).

An account of the Portuguese economy in the 1970s divided into sections on
economic background, the Portuguese economy between the end of 1973 and
mid-1978, and the future. The central section is concerned with selected sector
developments, patterns of expenditure, financing of expenditure, public sector
budget and balance of payments. A statistical appendix provides a wide range of
economic data on Portugal related to population, national income and
investment, foreign trade and payments, external debt, money and credit, public
finance and agricultural production.

473 **Structure and growth of the Portuguese economy.**
V. Xavier Pintado.   Geneva: European Free Trade Association,
1964, 239p. bibliog.

A wide-ranging account of the Portuguese economy in the early 1960s, together
with an interpretation of its structure and growth. It has chapters on the
determinants of economic growth, resource use, agriculture, industrial development and foreign trade.

474 **Portugal: an Economic Report.**
London: National Westminster Bank, 1970-85. annual.

This report provides summary up-to-date information on Portugal divided into the
following sections: currency and exchange rate, politics, domestic economy,
external economy, prospects and economic statistics. From January 1986,
information on Portugal is included in the bank's *EEC: an Economic Report*,
which is published twice a year.

475 **Portugal: OECD economic survey.**
Paris: Organisation for Economic Co-operation and Development
(OECD), 1984. 73p.

This detailed economic survey of Portugal covers the labour market, inflation,
competitiveness and external disequilibrium, agriculture, the public sector, the
domestic economy, exchange rates and balance of payments, fiscal policy,
monetary policy, short-term prospects and economic policy conclusions. There is
a short statistical annex.

476 **The Portuguese Economy.**
London: Banco Totta & Açores, February 1975- . bimonthly.

Provides useful short summaries of changes in the Portuguese economy. Current
issues cover features such as: the primary sector; industry; prices, wages and
employment; money and banking; and trade and payment.

477 **Quarterly Economic Review of Portugal.**
London: Economist Intelligence Unit, May 1952- . quarterly, with annual supplement.

A useful quarterly review of Portugal's economic performance. Each issue is divided into an outlook section and a review, with the latter usually covering the political scene; production, demand and employment; prices, wages and finance; foreign trade and payments; and business news. The annual supplement provides a broad account of developments in each of the main sectors of the economy.

478 **Regional problems and policies in Portugal.**
Paris: Organisation for Economic Co-operation and Development, 1978. 69p. 3 maps.

A broad review of Portugal's regional problems and policies. Four detailed appendixes cover the country's background and context, regional imbalances, proposed regional policy objectives and industrial production measures.

479 **Economic stabilisation and growth in Portugal.**
Hans O. Schmitt. Washington, DC: International Monetary Fund, 1981. 24p. bibliog. (Occasional Paper, no. 2).

Presents an account of Portugal's economic stabilization in the late 1970s following the May 1978 austerity stabilization programme introduced by the government and supported by the IMF (International Monetary Fund). Three main sections in turn investigate the economic background in which disequilibrium arose during the 1970s, discuss the issues that had to be resolved in order to develop an effective programme, and evaluate critically the economic out-turn. An appendix provides fifteen statistical tables concerning Portugal's economy and financial sector.

480 **Underdeveloped Europe: studies in core-periphery relations.**
Edited by Dudley Seers, Bernard Schaffer, Marja-Lisa Kiljunen. Brighton, England: Harvester Press, 1979. 325p. (Harvester Studies in Development, no. 1).

This collection of papers was first presented at a workshop at the Institute of Development Studies at the University of Sussex in 1977, on whether or not concepts of core-periphery relations are applicable to underdeveloped Europe. Portugal is discussed in several papers, most notably that by Stuart Holland on 'Dependent development: Portugal as periphery'.

Area handbook for Portugal.
See item no. 16.

Spain and Portugal. Volume II: Portugal.
See item no. 37.

Economy and society in baroque Portugal, 1668-1703.
See item no. 254.

Economy

Corporatism and development: the Portuguese experience.
See item no. 311.

Portugal: twenty years of change.
See item no. 413.

The Portuguese industrial elite and its corporative relations: a study of compartmentalisation in an authoritarian regime.
See item no. 429.

Portugal: revolutionary change in an open economy.
See item no. 431.

Foreign economic trends and their implications for the United States: Portugal.
See item no. 489.

The Europa Yearbook: a World Survey.
See item no. 575.

Finance and Banking

481 Banking structures and sources of finance in Spain and Portugal.
Banker Research Unit. London: Financial Times Business
Publishing, 1980. 94p.

The section on Portugal within this survey of banking in Iberia covers the Central
Bank, commercial banks, savings and investment banks, savings credit institutions, deposits and credit operations, other services offered by the banking
system, bank interest rates, the capital market, export re-financing, foreign banks
and banking associations.

482 The man who stole Portugal
Murray Teigh Bloom. London: Secker & Warburg, 1967, 318p.

An account of how Artur Virgilio Alves Reis attempted to gain control of the
Bank of Portugal in 1924 and 1925 by arranging for Britain's leading security
printers, Waterlow and Sons, to print Portuguese 500 escudo banknotes. His
success ended in a twenty-year jail sentence in Lisbon, but it was one factor in
giving rise to the upheaval which brought Salazar to power, and it also came near
to ruining one of the world's major printing firms. At the time it was called the
crime of the century.

**483 The Portuguese bank-note case: the story and solution of a financial
perplexity.**
Cecil H. Kisch. London: Macmillan, 1932. 284p.

An account of the legal and banking repercussions following the fraud by which
580,000 notes worth almost £3 million were forged and more than 200,000 of them
were passed into circulation in Portugal in 1925. It is divided into three parts: the
first recounts the background to the crime; the second reproduces the substance
of the judgements of the three courts in London which dealt with the case
between the Bank of Portugal and the firm who printed the notes, Waterlow and

Finance and Banking

Sons; and the third scrutinizes the financial effects on the bank from an historical and economic standpoint.

Portuguese bankers at the court of Spain 1626-1650.
See item no. 241.

Trade

Contemporary

484 **Hints to exporters: Portugal, Madeira and the Azores.**
London: British Overseas Trade Board, 1985. 72p. 3 maps.
A useful publication aimed at British businesses exporting to Portugal. It has main sections on general information, travel, hotels, telecommunications, economic factors, import and exchange control regulations, and methods of doing business, covering continental Portugal, Madeira and the Azores. A final part provides a reading list and a section on British government and commercial organizations.

485 **Marketing opportunities in Portugal.**
London: Euromonitor Publications, no date [ca. 1981]. 143p. map.
Surveys marketing opportunities in Portugal in the early 1980s and is divided into sections on social and economic background, foreign trade and investment, marketing and distribution, standard of living and consumer markets.

486 **Overseas business reports: marketing in Portugal.**
Prepared by Ken Nichols. US Department of Commerce, International Trade Administration, Washington, DC: US Government Printing Office, [ca. 1974]. 25p. bibliog.
(International Marketing Information Series, OBR 80-18).
Surveys the marketing potential in Portugal covering its foreign trade outlook, distribution and sales channels, trade regulations, transportation and communications, advertizing and market research, investment in Portugal, taxation, labour relations, guidance for business visitors, sources of economic and commercial information, and a market profile of the country. First published ca. October 1974.

131

487 **Portugal – a country profile.**
London: Department of Trade, 1982. 61p. bibliog. (Export
Europe).

Presents a profile of the country for British exporters. The first section of the
work includes an introduction and chapters on trade and aid, trade between the
UK and Portugal, and new opportunities. The second is on doing business in
Portugal and covers such things as export conditions, marketing methods,
investment, work and residence in Portugal, and travel. The final part provides
other useful information including addresses.

488 **Technology exports from developing countries (1): Argentina and
Portugal.**
United Nations Industrial Development Organisation. New
York: United Nations, 1983. 66p. (Development and Transfer of
Technology Series, no. 17).

Portugal is discussed in Part Two (p. 45-66) of this volume, where there is an
analysis of its economic setting in the 1970s, a macro-analysis of technology
exports and an empirical assessment of technology exports. It suggests that
Portuguese industry has acquired enough experience to provide for the growing
technology exportation, but that its future development depends largely on its
cost competitiveness.

489 **Foreign economic trends and their implications for the United
States: Portugal.**
US Department of Commerce. Washington, DC: US
Government Printing Office, 1985. 14p. (International Marketing
Information Series).

A useful, irregularly updated, summary of economic trends in Portugal and their
implications for US exporters. It has sections on political developments, the
government's economic programme, balance of payments, foreign debt, economic
growth, fiscal policy, monetary performance and domestic credit, wages and
prices, labour management relations, public enterprises, liberalization, European
Community negotiations, increased import opportunities, Portuguese export
performance, Portuguese market for US exports, prospects for 1985, and foreign
investment. First published ca. August 1978.

Historic

490 **From Lisbon to Goa 1500-1750: studies in Portuguese maritime
enterprise.**
C. R. Boxer. London: Variorum Rerints, 1984. [not paginated].

A collection of ten of Boxer's papers on Portuguese maritime trade in the 16th,
17th and 18th centuries, all of which have previously been published elsewhere:

'The *Carreira da Índia* (ships, men, cargoes, voyages)' (1961); 'The principal ports of call in the *Carreira da Índia* (16th-18th centuries)' (1972); 'Moçambique island and the *Carreira da Índia*' (1961); 'Portuguese *Roteiros* 1500-1700' (1934); 'An introduction to the *História Trágico-Marítima*' (1957) some corrections and clarifications' (1979); 'On a Portuguese carrack's bill of lading in 1625' (1939); 'Admiral João Pereira Corte-Real and the construction of Portuguese East-Indiamen in the early 17th century' (1940); 'The naval and colonial papers of Dom António de Ataíde' (1951); and 'The sailing orders for the Portuguese East-Indiamen of 1640 and 1646' (1980).

491 **Sino-Portuguese trade from 1514 to 1644: a synthesis of Portuguese and Chinese sources.**
T'ien-Tsê Chang. Leyden, The Netherlands: E. J. Brill, 1933. 2nd. ed. 1969. 157p. bibliog.

First published in 1933, this volume presents a detailed analysis of trade between China and Portugal in the 16th and early 17th centuries. It traces the early contacts between Portugal and China, the subsequent expulsion of foreigners from China following clashes in Canton, the rise of Macao, the arrival of other Europeans in China and the later stagnation and decline of Sino-Portuguese trade.

492 **Twilight of the pepper empire: Portuguese trade in southwest India in the early seventeenth century.**
A[nthony] R. Disney Cambridge, Massachusetts; London: Harvard University Press, 1978. 220p. map. bibliog.

An account of Portuguese trade with Kanara and Malabar during the 17th century. These regions of south-west India were the principal sources of pepper which was the most important commodity sought by the Portuguese crown in Asia.

493 **Shipwreck and empire: being an account of Portuguese maritime disasters in a century of decline.**
James Duffy. Cambridge, Massachusetts: Harvard University Press, 1955. 198p. map.

An account of the fortunes of Portuguese shipping in the century from 1550 to 1650 divided into chapters on the ship, the complement, the voyage, the wreck and the march. It is based on an analysis of the Portuguese narratives of shipwrecks collected in the *História Trágico-Marítima* by Bernardo Gomes de Brito. This describes the events associated with the wrecks of the following ships: *São João* in 1552, *São Bento* in 1554, *Conceição* in 1555, *Aguia* and *Garça* in 1559, *Santa Maria da Barca* in 1559, *São Paulo* in 1561, *Santo António* in 1565, *Santiago* in 1585, *São Thomé* in 1589, *Santo Alberto* in 1593, *São Francisco* in 1596, *Santiago* in 1602, *Chagas* in 1594, *Conceição* in 1621, *São João Baptista* in 1622, *Nossa Senhora do Bom Despacho* in 1630-31, *Nossa Senhora de Belém* in 1635-36, *Sacramento* and *Nossa Senhora da Atalaya* in 1647, and *São Lourenço* in 1649.

494   **The Portugal trade: a study of Anglo-Portuguese commerce 1700-
1770.**
H. E. S. Fisher.   London: Methuen, 1971. 171p. 2 maps. bibliog.
Examines Anglo-Portuguese trade between 1700 and 1770, and of the commercial
links between the English North American colonies and Portugal at the time. It
concentrates on the export of textiles and foodstuffs from England to Portugal
and Brazil, and the return trade in wine from Portugal to England and its
colonies.

495   **The wine trade.**
A. D. Francis.   London: Adam & Charles Black, 1972. 353p. 3
maps. bibliog.
An account by the former Consul-General at Oporto, of the development of the
English wine trade. It concentrates on the period from the 17th century and on
the trade with Portugal. Particular attention is paid to port wine, treaties between
England and Portugal, the setting up of the Douro company in 1756 and the
Gladstone Acts of the 1850s and 60s which reduced duties on all wines and
eventually meant that lighter French wines could successfully compete with the
more alcoholic wines from Portugal.

The commercial relations of England and Portugal.
See item no. 182.

Industry

496 Portugal: Lloyds List special report.
Geoff Garfield. *Lloyds List*, 8 March 1984, p. 5-10.

Presents an account of recent changes in Portugal's shipping industry with sections on shipping companies, UK links, shipyards, the insurance market, energy, salvage and the ports of Lisbon and Sines.

497 Portugal's industrial policy in terms of accession to the European Community.
Klaus Esser, Guido Ashoff, Ansgar Eussner, Wilhelm Hummen. Berlin: German Development Institute, 1980. 90p. (Occasional Papers of the German Development Institute, no. 60).

A general survey of Portugal's industrial policy in the context of accession to the European Community. Case studies are undertaken of the following industries: textiles and clothing; shipbuilding and repairs; steel; and chemical fibres.

498 Portugal's industrial policy and crisis-hit industries of the European Community. Case study: shipbuilding and repairs.
Ansgar Eussner. Berlin: German Development Institute, 1980. 87p.

A detailed study of Portugal's shipbuilding and repair industry, and its development prospects. It puts forward recommendations on the shaping of the arrangements for the country's accession to the European Community and of Portuguese industrial policy.

499 **Regional variations in the rate of profit in Portuguese industry.**
João Ferrão. In: *Uneven development in southern Europe: studies of accumulation, class, migration and the state.* Edited by Ray Hudson and Jim Lewis. London, New York: Methuen, 1985. p. 211-45.

An exploration within a Marxist framework of the extent to which regional uneven industrial development in Portugal can be accounted for in terms of regional variations in the rate of profit. It provides a useful summary of the location of manufacturing industry within the country and includes a typology of industrial areas in 1970.

500 **Capital accumulation: the industrialization of southern Europe.**
R. Hudson and J. Lewis. In: *Southern Europe transformed: political and economic change in Greece, Italy, Portugal and Spain.* Edited by Allan Williams. London: Harper & Row, 1984, p. 179-206.

This account of industrialization in southern Europe notes that, of the four countries studied, Portugal has the highest percentage of GDP derived from industry. Particular attention is paid to the nature of capital flows and their influence on the forms of industrialization found. It provides a number of useful statistics relating to Portuguese industry.

501 **Industrial structure and regional development in Portugal.**
Christopher Jensen-Butler, Iva Maria Miranda Pires. Århus, Denmark: Geographical Institute Århus University, 1983. 45p. 7 maps. bibliog. (Arbejdsrapport, no. 13).

Analyses and considers industrial growth and regional development in Portugal within a regional policy framework. It uses a shift-share analysis of regional industrial employment growth in the period 1960-70, and a retrospective analysis of the extent to which results of this analysis could have been used to formulate regional policy in Portugal in the 1970s. This theoretical framework is compared with the actual course of regional development and industrial growth after 1970.

502 **The Sines project: Portugal's growth centre or white elephant?**
J. R. Lewis and A. M. Williams. *Town Planning Review,* vol. 56, no. 3 (1985), p. 339-66.

Reviews the objectives of the Sines project, which was chosen as a growth centre based on oil refining and steel production, and presents an evaluation of its economic influence in terms of the development of the Portuguese economy and regional planning issues.

Portugal in development: emigration, industrialization, the European Community.
See item no. 343.

Estatísticas Industriais (Industrial Statistics.)
See item no. 574.

Agriculture
and Fishing

General

503 **Portuguese agrarian reform and economic and social development.**
Afonso De Barros. *Sociologia Ruralis*, vol. 20 (1980), p. 82-96.
Surveys Portugal's agrarian reform following the political upheaval of 1974,
tracing its course; its role in economic and social development; and the political
and social constraints on reform.

504 **The hills of Alentejo.**
Huldine V. Beamish.   London: Geoffrey Bles, 1958. 224p. map.
Studies the lifestyles of the farmers of the Alentejo based on the author's own
experiences in running the farm of Relva near the Spanish border. The work
provides much information about the agrarian economy of the region and in
particular of its cattle and bullfights.

505 **Agrarian structures and recent rural movements in Portugal.**
M. V. Cabral. *Journal of Peasant Studies*, vol. 5, no. 4 (July
1978), p. 411-45.
A detailed account of the changing agrarian structure of Portugal between 1950
and the mid-1970s. It argues that emigration has been the most significant factor
in causing the stagnation of agriculture, and that there has been an increased
tendency for both the very small producers and the traditional latifundia to
become marginal to the benefit of small and medium-sized peasant farms. Much
attention is paid to land reform and the impact of the events following 25 April
1974.

506 **Portugal's agrarian reform: a process of change with unique features.**
Demetrios Christodoulou. *Land Reform, Land Settlement and Cooperatives*, vol. 2 (1976), p. 1-21.
A comprehensive survey of agrarian reform in Portugal between 1974 and 1976.

507 **Open boat whaling in the Azores: the history and present methods of a relic industry.**
Robert Clarke. Cambridge, England: Cambridge University Press, 1954. 63p. 3 maps. bibliog. (Discovery Reports, vol. xxvi, p. 281-354).
Following a short introductory account of the history of whaling in the Azores, this volume provides details of all aspects of whaling there, together with a short note on whaling in Madeira.

508 **A development model for the agricultural sector of Portugal.**
Alvin C. Egbert, Hyung M. Kim. Baltimore, Maryland; London: Johns Hopkins University Press for the World Bank, 1975. 97p. map. bibliog. (World Bank Staff Occasional Papers, no. 20).
This study uses mathematical programming to specify development strategies and investment requirements up to 1980, for homogenous agricultural production regions in Portugal. An introduction contains an overview of the study at a non-technical level.

509 **Selected agricultural statistics on Portugal.**
[William Gallagher] Washington, DC: United States Department of Agriculture, Economics and Statistics Service, 1981. 141p. map. bibliog. (Statistical Bulletin, no. 664).
A collection of statistical tables on Portuguese agriculture mainly at the district level. It covers the following broad subjects: population; labour force; economic indicators; farm numbers; land use; land area; crop areas, production and yields; livestock; supply utilization; per capita consumption, farm prices; crop prices; livestock prices; and farm inputs.

510 **Portugal: the greatest cork producing country in the world.**
Junta Nacional da Cortiça. Lisbon: Junta Nacional da Cortiça, 1939. 16p.
A short, illustrated account of Portuguese cork production in the 1930s.

Agriculture and Fishing. General

511   **The cork oak forests and the evolution of the cork industry in southern Spain and Portugal.**
James J. Parsons. *Economic Geography*, vol. 38, no. 3 (July 1962), p. 195-214.

A somewhat out-of-date account of the cultivation of the cork oak (*Quercus suber*) in southern Iberia, and of the development of the cork industry there from ancient times through to the 20th century.

512   **Portugal: agricultural sector survey.**
Washington, DC: World Bank, 1978. 323p. map. (A World Bank Country Study).

A report on the agriculture of Portugal based on the findings of a World Bank mission to the country in October and November 1976. The text is divided into six main sections: the changing role of agriculture; reforms in land distribution and tenure; building the institutional capability; major development prospects; implications for external assistance; and a strategy for agricultural and rural development. Statistical appendixes provide information on economic aggregates, agricultural imports and exports, population and employment, climate, area, yields and production, uses of major imports, prices, subsidies, staff and budgets. Ten annexes cover the following subjects: the role of agriculture in the economy; demand trends and projections for food; regional income inequalities and rural development; problems and prospects of agrarian reform; the present state and prospects of irrigation; livestock development; fisheries development; agricultural credit; the physical and economic characteristics of Portuguese farms; and prices and subsidies in agriculture.

513   **Land reform and the Portuguese revolution.**
I. Rutledge. *Journal of Peasant Studies*, vol. 5 (1977), p. 79-98.

Reviews three Portuguese books on agrarian change: B. H. Fernandes, *O que é a reforma agricola* (What is agrarian reform), Lisbon: Editorial Império, 1974; M. V. Cabral, *Materiais para a historia da questão agrária em Portugal* (Materials for the history of the agrarian question in Portugal); Porto: Editorial Nova, 1974; and E. de Freitas, J. F. de Almeida, M. V. Cabral, *Modalidades de penetração do capitalismo na agricultura* (Modes of capitalist penetration in agriculture), Lisbon: Editorial Presença, 1976. It provides an account of the relationships between Portuguese land reform and the events following 25 April 1974.

514   **Farmers' perceptions of agrarian change in north-west Portugal.**
Tim Unwin. *Journal of Rural Studies*, vol. 1, no. 4 (1985), p. 339-57.

Analyses the ways in which farmers in north-west Portugal perceive recent changes in the agrarian economy. It illustrates that, rather than being traditional and conservative, many of these farmers are indeed keen to adopt new farming techniques.

515 **Baleia! The whalers of Azores.**
   Bernard Venables.   London: Bodley Head, 1968. 206p. 2 maps.
Studies the people of the island of Fayal in the central group of the Azores, and in particular of the district of Horta, who in the 1960s still hunted the sperm whale with hand harpoons from small open boats.

Etat et paysannerie: politiques agricoles et stratégies paysannes au Portugal depuis la Seconde Guerre Mondiale. (State and peasantry: agricultural policies and peasant strategies in Portugal since the Second World War.)
See item no. 398.

New life in Portugal: impressions and pictures of a newly born cooperative farm
See item no. 567.

Estatísticas Agrícolas (Agricultural Statistics.)
See item no. 573.

Selected agricultural trade statistics for the European Community: Greece, Spain and Portugal, 1967-79.
See item no. 576.

Viticulture and wine

516 **Sherry and port**
   H. Warner Allen.   London: Constable, 1952. 215p.
Presents an introduction to the fortified wines of sherry and port. The latter is considered in the second half of the book, in four chapters on: 'The Englishman's wine'; making the wine; its maturation in the lodges; and the origins of port. In addition the volume includes several anecdotes of the author's experiences in Oporto, Vila Nova de Gaia and up the River Douro, and the last chapter also contains a short description of the history of port production.

517 **Good wine from Portugal.**
   H. Warner Allen.   London: Sylvan Press, 1957. 59p. map.
This brief sketch of Portuguese wines was published to celebrate the Royal visit of Queen Elizabeth II to Portugal in February 1957. It is divided into three main parts: the first is on port and regency madeira; the second on the wines of the mountains; and the third on the wines of the coastal region from Colares to Setúbal.

518 **The wines of Portugal.**
H. Warner Allen. London: George Rainbird in association with
Michael Joseph, 1963. 192p. 2 maps. bibliog.

Presents an introduction to the diverse wines of Portugal, concentrating mainly on
port. It provides an account of the history of Portuguese wines, the development
of vintage ports, great vintage ports, and the emergence of wood ports.
Concluding chapters cover Madeira, the wines of Setúbal, Colares and Bucelas,
and wines found between the Tagus and the Minho rivers.

519 **The wine of the Douro.**
Hector Bolitho. London: Sidgwick & Jackson, 1956. 23p.

A short, illustrated account of the production of port wine on the slopes of the
River Douro and the activities of the port shippers based at Oporto.

520 **The Englishman's wine: the story of port.**
Sarah Bradford. London: Macmillan, St. Martin's Press. 1969.
208p. 3 maps. bibliog.

Provides a detailed account of the production of port wine up to the end of the
1960s. The first section recounts the history of port and the second discusses the
contemporary port trade, paying particular attention to the growing of the grapes
in the Douro, the vintage, and the port lodges in Vila Nova de Gaia. Appendixes
list the vintage years since 1900 and the British port houses.

521 **The story of port: the Englishman's wine.**
Sarah Bradford. London: Christie's Wine Publications, 1983. 2nd
ed. 157p. 2 maps. bibliog.

A revised edition of the author's *The Englishman's Wine* (q.v.). It traces the
development of the port trade and the important role of Englishmen within the
business, and in so doing concentrates on the period since 1700. Considerable
attention is paid to the production of port wine today, from the cultivation of the
grapes in the Douro valley to the maturing of the wine in lodges in Vila Nova de
Gaia. Appendixes provide a glossary of technical terms, a port chronology and
vintage notes, and details of the English port houses.

522 **Oporto, older and newer, being a tribute to the British community
in the North of Portugal in continuation of 'Oporto old and new' by
Charles Sellers.**
Gerald Cobb. Chichester, England: Chichester Press, 1966. 110p.

An account of the British community of Oporto in the 20th century, written in a
somewhat lighter vein than Sellers' original volume *Oporto old and new* (q.v.). It
provides details of the community's social life, institutions and British families and
firms based in Oporto.

523 **Port wine and Oporto.**
Ernest Cockburn. London: Wine & Spirit Publications [1949].
132p.

A treatise on port wine based on the author's extensive experiences in the port wine trade. It begins with a general historical account of the development of port wine and the influence of phylloxera. This is followed by a series of annual notes on events concerning port and Oporto between 1860 and 1938. The remaining chapters cover the nature of different types of port, anecdotes concerning port, a summary of the position of the port trade ca. 1940, and finally some notes for the wine trade student.

524 **Madeira wine.**
Noel Cossart. In: *André Simon's wines of the world*. 2nd ed.
Edited by Serena Sutcliffe. London: Macdonald, 1981, p. 391-98.

A general account of the history, the vines, viticulture, vinification and the types of wine to be found in Madeira.

525 **A treatise on the wines of Portugal; and what can be gathered on the subject and nature of the wines, &c. since the establishment of the English Factory at Oporto, anno 1727: also a dissertation on the nature and use of wines in general, imported into Great Britain, as pertaining to luxury and diet.**
John Croft [Member of the Factory at Oporto, and wine merchant, York] York, England: printed by Crask & Lund, 1787. 27p.

The first seventeen pages of this treatise and dissertation relate the early history of port wine production and its export to England. It argues that the soil and distance from the sea make the upper Douro valley the best part of Europe for the production of red wine. It also provides details of the activities of the English merchants in Oporto and of the conflict between them and the Portuguese government under Pombal.

526 **Port.**
Rupert Croft-Cooke. London: Putnam, 1957. 219p.

Presents an account of the production of port wine, concentrating on its history, the cultivation and harvesting of grapes in the Douro valley, the activities of the English in the port trade from the 17th century to the mid-20th century, details of port shippers, the use of port in the kitchen, and the drinking of vintage port after dinner. Three short appendixes provide details of port shippers and vintages between 1900 and 1955.

527 **Madeira.**
Rupert Croft-Cooke. London: Putnam, 1961. 224p.

A general introduction to the wines of Madeira. The first eight chapters provide an account of the history of wine production on the island concentrating on the period since 1700, and the remaining eight chapters describe the contemporary vines, harvesting, blending, maturing and use of the wine as a drink and in the kitchen.

143

Agriculture and Fishing. Viticulture and wine

528 **The Factory House at Oporto.**
John Delaforce. London: Christie's Wine Publications, 1979.
108p. bibliog.

An account of the history, customs and contents of the British Factory House established at Oporto. The present building was constructed in 1789-90 and since 1814 it has been the headquarters of the British Association composed of British Port Wine Shippers, and their Partners and Directors as the individual members.

529 **Port: an introduction to its history and delights.**
Wyndham Fletcher. London: Sotherby Parke Bernet, 1978. 124p.

A straightforward introduction to port wine covering its history, the production of vintage and wood ports, vintage years, the Factory House and British Clubs, details of some port shippers and some anecdotal reminiscences of the author's career at Cockburns. Useful appendixes provide information on vintage ports and their shippers between 1870 and 1975, details of the register of vineyard properties in the Douro, a list of the main vine varieties grown in the demarcated port wine region and a diagram of the autovinification process.

530 **Port.**
Wyndham Fletcher. In: *André Simon's wines of the world.* 2nd ed. Edited by Serena Sutcliffe. London: Macdonald, 1981, p. 371-91.

Surveys the production of port wine, and provides descriptions of some of the 20th-century vintages and notes on the various port houses.

531 **Port wine: notes on its history, production and technology.**
A. Moreira da Fonseca, A. Galhano, E. Serpa Pimental, J. R.-P. Rosas. Oporto, Portugal: Instituto do Vinho do Porto, 1981. 175p.

A well-illustrated introduction to port wine, divided into sections on its history, the demarcated region, the wine district, the technology of port-making and principal State Papers published over the years which deal with the port wine trade.

532 **Mr. Forrester's vindication from the aspersions of the Commercial Association of Oporto; and his answer to the judge, and late member of the cortes, Bernardo de Lemos Teixeira de Aguillar. Being the 2nd part of 'Observations on the attempts lately made to reform the abuses practised in Portugal, in the making and treatment of port-wine'.**
Joseph James Forrester. Edinburgh: J. Menzies, 1845. 49p.

A continuation of Forrester's arguments concerning the adulteration of port wine in the 1840s.

533 **Observations on the attempts lately made to reform the abuses practised in Portugal, in the making and treatment of port wine: together with documents proving the existence of the abuses and letters on the same subject.**
Joseph James Forrester. Edinburgh: J. Menzies, 1845. 80p. map.
Forrester's exposition of his argument that the port wines of the Douro were adulterated and that their fermentation was checked by sweetening. It includes copies of numerous letters concerning the port trade in 1844 and 1845.

534 **The Oliveira prize essay on Portugal: with the evidence regarding that country taken before a committee of the House of Commons in May, 1852; and the author's survey of the wine districts of the Alto-Douro, as adopted and published by order of the House of Commons. Together with a statistical comparison of the resources and commerce of Great Britain and Portugal.**
Joseph James Forrester. London: John Weale; Edinburgh: John Menzies; Oporto, Portugal: Coutinho, 1853. 290p. map.
A comprehensive mid-19th-century survey of the Portuguese economy and trade between Portugal and Britain. In particular it concentrates on wine production and the duties on Portuguese wine. Appendixes give the minutes of evidence on import duties on wines given before a Select Committee of the House of Commons by the author as well as documents relating to his topographical works and maps of the wine district of the Alto-Douro.

535 **Portugal: a wine country.**
Francisco Esteves Gonçalves. Lisbon: Editora Portuguesa de Livros Técnicos e Científicos, Lda., 1984. 273p. 20 maps. bibliog.
An extensively-illustrated account of Portuguese viticulture. Following introductory sections on the history of the vine, pruning, vine-propping, wine and tasting, each of the demarcated and undemarcated regions is summarized in turn, with short sections on each region's history, legislation, area, soils, vinestocks, planting and vine-propping, climate, grape varieties, types of pruning and types of wines. It concludes with chapters on glass, bottles, cork, cellars and ageing. On the whole, however, this is a disappointing volume: although attempting to be comprehensive it actually says very little about each region.

536 **Rich, rare and red: the International Wine & Food Society's guide to port.**
Ben Howkins. London: Heinemann; International Wine & Food Society, 1982. 169p. map.
Provides a comprehensive introduction to port wine, covering its history, the vineyards and vines, port maturation in Vila Nova de Gaia, the port shippers' lodges, vintage port and tasting. There are also chapters on visiting the region, the city of Oporto, gastronomy, wines similar to port wine from other countries, and world markets. Appendixes provide a guide to further reading, a glossary of wine terms and a list of vintage ports and their shippers.

537 **Croft, a journey of confidence.**
Oliver Knox. London: Collins, 1978. 40p.

This book was commissioned by the directors of Croft & Company to celebrate the tercentenary of the company which was established in 1678. It consists of a number of anecdotes and short descriptive essays about the company, its vineyards in the Douro valley, its port wines, the lodges in Vila Nova de Gaia and the customs of the Factory House.

538 **Decanter Magazine wine guide: Madeira.**
Edited by Tony Lord. London: Decanter Magazine, 1984. 18p.

This account of the wines of Madeira is divided into chapters entitled: 'The burnt wines from the burnt island', by Tony Lord; 'Old Madeiras – wines of an almost indestructable nature', by Michael Broadbent; 'The Madeira process', by David Pamment; and 'A guide to Madeira producers', by Tony Lord; followed by a general chapter on tourist information.

539 **Wine trade of Portugal. Proceedings at the meeting of the nobility, wine proprietors and public authorities of the wine district of the Alto-Douro, held at the quinta of Messrs. Offley, Webber and Forrester, at Pezo-da-Regôa, 8th October, 1844; at the invitation of Joseph James Forrester.**
Hugh Owen. London: Pelham Richardson, 1845. 31p.

Notes on the meeting organized by Forrester in October 1844 to discuss the plight of Douro wine production and his method for making wines.

540 **Portuguese wine.**
Raymond Postgate. London: J M Dent, 1969. 102p. 5 maps.

An account of Portuguese wines written from the author's own wide-ranging experiences, with the majority of the wines discussed having been tasted by him on numerous occasions. The first two chapters are on the history and regulations concerning Portuguese wines. These are followed by a section on the demarcated wines of the Vinhos Verdes, Dâo, Bucelas, Carcavelos, Colares and Setúbal regions, and by a chapter on undemarcated and sparkling wines. The book concludes with chapters on rosé wines and brandies, madeira and port.

541 **The wines of Spain and Portugal.**
Jan Read. London: Faber & Faber, 1973. 280p. 4 maps. bibliog.

A detailed guide to the wines of Iberia. The section on Portugal is divided into chapters on port; Vinhos Verdes (green wines); Dão; the demarcated wines of the centre; rosé and undemarcated wines; Madeira; spirits; and sparkling and aromatic wines. Appendixes include figures on the production of Portuguese table wine in 1961, 1965 and 1970, and Portuguese wine exports in 1970.

542   **Guide to the wines of Spain and Portugal.**
Jan Read.   London: Pitman, 1977. 126p. 4 maps.
A short guide to the wine regions and production of Iberia. The section on
Portugal includes chapters on the land and history of the country, the various
types of wine to be found in Portugal, wine control and labelling, the regions of
the country and regional cooking.

543   **The tablewines of Spain and Portugal.**
Jan Read.   In: *André Simon's wines of the world.* 2nd ed. Edited
by Serena Sutcliffe. London: Macdonald, 1981, p. 333-58.
This introduction to the wines of the Iberian peninsula has major sections on
Vinhos Verdes, the Dão wines, demarcated wines of the centre and undemar-
cated wines.

544   **The wines of Portugal.**
Jan Read.   London: Faber & Faber, 1982. 190p. 3 maps. bibliog.
A well-illustrated survey of Portuguese wine. Following an historical introduction
and a short chapter on control and labelling, chapters are devoted to the wines of
Portugal on a regional basis, covering: port; madeira; the demarcated wines of the
centre; Vinhos Verdes or green wines; Dão; Bairrada; undemarcated wines of the
north; and wines of the south. The five concluding chapters cover wines in bulk;
rosé wines; sparkling and aromatic wines, together with spirits; a note on cork;
and food with wine. Appendixes give information on: production of Portuguese
table wines in 1974, 1978 and 1980; exports of bottled wine and wine products
from Portugal; and export of port by volume and value. There is also a glossary of
Portuguese and technical terms.

545   **Port.**
George Robertson.   London; Boston, Massachusetts: Faber &
Faber, 1978. rev. ed., 1982. 188p. 2 maps. bibliog.
A thorough and readable account of the production, places and people of port
wine. It is divided into chapters on historical background, the Douro, the vine,
viticulture in the Douro, the vintage, the lodges in Vila Nova de Gaia, shipping,
storing, decanting and drinking. Four appendixes provide information on: vintage
ports and their shippers, 1869-1977; exports of port, 1958-79; duties on port
imported into the United Kingdom, 1921-80; and a list of port shippers.

546   **The British Factory Oporto.**
Elaine Sanceau.   Oporto, Portugal: British Association, 1970.
128p.
An account of the British community in northern Portugal, the building of the
Factory House in the late 18th century and the vicissitudes of the 19th century.
An appendix provides a Portuguese view of the Factory House derived from an
account in the newspaper *O Primeiro de Janeiro.*

547 **Port and sherry: the story of two fine wines.**
Patrick W. Sandeman. London: George G. Sandeman, 1955.
63p. map.

Following a brief historical introduction to port wine and the House of Sandeman, this short book provides an outline of port and sherry production.

548 **Oporto, old and new. Being a historical record of the port wine trade, and a tribute to British commercial enterprize in the north of Portugal.**
Charles Sellers. London: Herbert E. Harper, 1899. 314p.

The bulk of this account of British involvement in the port trade consists of chapters providing details of the history and development of each of the British companies involved in the production and shipping of port wine. It also gives some information on travel and the 19th-century history of Portugal.

549 **Port.**
André L. Simon. London: Constable & Company, 1934. 130p.
(Constable's Wine Library).

A broad account of the history of port wine. Following a short chapter summarizing the nature of port wine, details are given of the old alliance between Portugal and England, the Methuen Treaty (1703), the Pombal régime, the Peninsular War (1808-14), the life of Baron J. J. Forrester, and the Burnay sale of port in 1892. Two final chapters provide a summary of port vintages between 1892 and 1933, and notes on the numerous port wine shippers.

550 **Landscapes of Bacchus: the vine in Portugal.**
Dan Stanislawski. Austin, Texas; London: University of Texas Press, 1970. 210p. 11 maps. bibliog.

A well-illustrated geographical account of viticulture in Portugal. Specific attention is paid to the Minho, Douro and Dão regions and there is also a chapter on the four minor demarcated areas of Setúbal, Colares, Carcavellos and Bucelas. Other chapters are concerned with the anomaly of the vineless south of Portugal, the bulk production of table wines and the early history of viticulture in the country.

551 **Facts about Port and Madeira, with notices of the wines vintaged around Lisbon, and the wines of Tenerife.**
Henry Vizetelly. London: Ward, Lock & Company, 1880. 211p.

A comprehensive 19th-century account of the wines of Lisbon, the Douro valley and Madeira, which first appeared in the columns of the *Pall Mall Gazette*. It is divided into three parts: the first covers the Lisbon wines, including those of Bucellas, Collares, Torres Vedras, the Termo, Camarate, Carcavellos and Lauradio; the second is concerned with port wine and includes descriptions of the area around Oporto, the Vinho Verde wines of the Minho, the production of port wine, some port wine *quintas* (estates), the vineyards of the Alto-Douro, the inhabitants of the Alto-Douro and the lodges in Vila Nova de Gaia; and the third considers the wines of Madeira and Tenerife. It is illustrated with a hundred sketches, mainly derived from those by Ernest A. Vizetelly.

552 **Guide to fortified wines.**
Pauline Wasserman, Sheldon Wasserman.   Morganville, New Jersey: Marlborough Press, 1983. 210p. 5 maps. bibliog.
The first two chapters of this general introduction to fortified wines cover most aspects of the production and consumption of port and madeira. One of the appendixes is a checklist of port shippers and vintages.

Lusitanian sketches of the pen and pencil.
See item no. 88.

The wine trade.
See item no. 495.

Children of the vineyards.
See item no. 678.

Transport
and Communications

553 Steam on the Sierra: the narrow gauge in Spain and Portugal.
Peter Allen, Robert Wheeler.   London: Cleaver-Hume, 1960.
203p. 6 maps.

Surveys the narrow gauge railways of Iberia, paying most attention to Spain. The single chapter on Portugal provides information on the Sabor, Tua, Corgo and Tamega lines, and the Oporto and Viseu networks. The volume also includes photographs of some of the locomotives.

554 Spanish and Portuguese military aviation.
John M. Andrade.   Leicester, England: Midland Counties
Publications, 1977. 120p. map.

An illustrated account of Iberian military aviation. The Portuguese airforce is discussed in the second half of the book which includes sections on the history of the Portuguese airforce, its organization and order of battle, Portuguese military aviation in Africa, the naval air arm, an aircraft review including markings and national insignia, Portuguese military aviation unit badges and serial numbers. Appendixes provide information on Portuguese paramilitary organizations and flying clubs, and a list of Portuguese military airfields.

555 The decline of Portuguese regional boats.
Octavio Lixa Filgueiras, edited by Eric McKee.   London:
Trustees of the National Maritime Museum, 1980. 39p. map.
bibliog. (Maritime Monographs and Reprints, no. 47).

An illustrated account of the regional boats of Portugal used for fishing and transport. It concludes with a table of Portuguese regional boats from the period 1890-1980.

150

556 **Last steam locomotives of Spain and Portugal.**
M. J. Fox. London: Ian Allan, 1978. 144p. map. bibliog.
A pictorial survey of the last years of steam operations on Iberian railways.
Following a short introduction the book consists entirely of black-and-white
photographs of the various locomotives, including eighty-two from Portugal.

557 **Portuguese shipping companies, paquebot & ship cancellations.**
Richard Greenwood, Romano Camara, Philip Cockrill. Newbury,
England: Philip Cockrill, 1983. 100p. (Cockrill Series Booklet, no.
40).
A handbook for collectors of paquebot and ship cancellations relating to Portugal
and its former colonies. The first part includes chapters on Portugal's historical
heritage, Portuguese shipping and mail services since 1978, and an appendix
providing details of Portuguese ships between 1797 and 1974. The second part
provides details of Portuguese maritime markings and illustrations of ship
cancellations.

558 **The tramways of Portugal: a visitors guide.**
B. R. King, J. H. Price. Broxbourne, Hertfordshire, England:
Light Rail Transit Association, 1983. 74p. 7 maps. bibliog.
Presents a comprehensive guide to the urban tramways of Portugal, with chapters
on Lisbon, Oporto, Coimbra, Sintra and Braga. There are also short chapters on
the Lisbon Metropolitan underground railway, the Estoril railway, the Transpraia
beach railway on the Atlantic coast south of the Tagus, narrow gauge railways
and other lines.

559 **Boats of the Lisbon river: the Fragata and related types.**
Manuel Leitão. London: Trustees of the National Maritime
Museum, 1978. 154p. (Maritime Monographs and Reprints, no.
34).
A thorough reference account of the various types of traditional boat in use on
the River Tagus at Lisbon, their construction and their uses. Specific chapters
provide details of the following main types of craft: the *fragata*, the *cangueiro*, the
bote and the *bote de meia-quilha*, the *bote fragata*, the *falua* and the *bote da
tartaranha* or the *batel de Seixal*.

560 **Portugal: the cameo stamps.**
Fred J. Melville. London: Melville Stamp Books, 1911. 90p.
Provides a survey of the Portuguese stamps issued between 1853 and 1887
presenting cameo portraits of the reigning Portuguese kings and queens.

561 **West coasts of Spain and Portugal pilot: from Cabo Ortegal to Gibraltar, Strait of Gibraltar, North coasts of Africa from Cabo Espartel to Ceuta, and Arquipelago dos Açores.**
Prepared by W. B. Monk. Taunton, England: Hydrographer of the Navy, 1972. 5th ed. 188p.

Admiralty Sailing Directions for the coast of Portugal and adjacent areas to the south. It provides a wealth of information, diagrams, panoramic views, illustrations and charts of the coasts and ports of the country. It is designed for use with the relevant Admiralty Charts of the area.

562 **World railways 1952-53.**
Edited by Henry Sampson. London: Sampson Low, Marston & Company, 1952. 550p.

The short section on Portugal (p. 398-400) in this survey of railways throughout the world in the early 1950s provides an historical note on the Companhia dos Caminhos de Ferro Portugueses (Portuguese Railway Company), and gives details of train control and signalling, named trains, running powers and other activities, track details, notable features, equipment, representative steam locomotives, and details of typical freight vehicles. It also has a brief note on the sixteen-mile Sociedade Estoril railway.

563 **A yachtsman's guide to the Atlantic coasts of Spain and Portugal El Ferrol to Gibraltar.**
A. A. Sloma, D. M. Sloma, G. C. Granger. St. Ives, England: Imray, Laurie, Norie & Wilson, 1983. 138p. 105 maps. bibliog.

A comprehensive guide for yachtsmen. After an introductory section on nautical background, formalities and documentation, regulations, amenities and sea creatures, each of the areas of the coastline is described in turn, with particular attention being paid to the ports. Each section of the coast is illustrated with maps and is subdivided into notes on passage, anchorage, formalities, amenities and information for the tourist, and, if relevant, there are details of ports covering position, charts, tides, approach lights and fog signals, radio, local port signals and weather and sea states. It concludes with appendixes of useful addresses and a glossary providing terms relevant to yachtsmen in English, Portuguese and Spanish.

564 **Stanley Gibbons stamp catalogue: part 9, Portugal and Spain.**
London: Stanley Gibbons, 1980, 313p.

The standard stamp catalogue for Iberia, noting all Portuguese stamps and the prices they are now worth.

565 **Railway holiday in Portugal.**
D. W. Winkworth. Newton Abbot, England: David & Charles, 1968. 158p. 4 maps. bibliog. (Railway Holiday Series, no. 9).

After an introductory description of newly-constructed lines in north-west Spain, this book proceeds to describe the railways of Portugal visited on a journey from

Valença do Minho to Oporto, Viseu, Coimbra, Lisbon and Setubal. Diversions off this main route included excursions to the Minho, up the Douro to Miranda, Bragança and Chaves, to Averio, and to Sintra. Appendixes provide lists of broad- and narrow-gauge steam locomotives, diesel and electric locomotives and some Portuguese railway terms.

Portugal: Lloyds List special report.
See item no. 496.

Employment
and Labour
Movements

566 The class struggle in Portugal: chronology and texts of 1976.
London: Red Notes, 1977. [not paginated]. 2 maps.

A loose collection of material concerning the class struggle in Portugal. An introduction provides a broad context for interpreting the working-class movement in 1976 and this is followed by a monthly chronology of events that took place during 1976. Appendixes provide short analyses of Portugal's agrarian reform, the cannery workers' strike, racism in Portugal, the economy and policy of the dominant class, nationalizations and class composition.

567 New life in Portugal: impressions and pictures of a newly born cooperative farm.
Regina Fischer, Cyril Pustan with photographs by Cyril Pustan.
London: Kay Beauchamp, 1976. 36p.

An account of the authors' visit in January 1976 to a cooperative farm in the Alentejo province during the period of agrarian reform following the revolution of 25 April 1974. It provides some insights into the fervour of hope engendered amongst the poor of southern Portugal by the events of 1974 and 1975.

568 Employment and basic needs in Portugal.
Co-ordinated by W. van Rijckegem. Geneva: International Labour Office, 1979. 228p.

Presents the report of a team of Portuguese and international 'experts' who had cooperated in the preparation of the Portuguese medium term economic plan for 1977-80. It is divided into three parts. The first is devoted to basic needs in Portugal, considering both methodological and substantive issues relating to food, housing, health and education. The second part provides a macro-economic framework, relating to consumption, employment and income. The final part considers sectors, regions and groups, paying particular attention to agriculture,

154

industry, regions and women. An annex gives an overview of the economic and social development of Portugal prior to 1975. The publication also provides numerous statistics relating to basic needs provision and requirements in Portugal.

569   **The employment of women in Portugal.**
Manuela Silva.   Luxembourg: Office for Official Publications of the European Communities, 1984. 218p. bibliog.

A broad survey of female employment in Portugal, subdivided into sections covering: women's employment – a statistical analysis; wages and earnings; legal status; demographic structure – factors affecting the employment of women; education and vocational training; employment departments; social services; the unionization of women and their involvement in union affairs; social security and taxation; women's employment, the crisis and economic change; social attitudes towards women's employment; and the future.

570   **From corporatism to neo-sydnicalism: the state, organised labor, and the changing industrial relations of southern Europe.**
Howard J. Wiarda.   Cambridge, Massachusetts: Center for European Studies, Harvard University, 1981. 76p. (Monographs on Europe, no. 4).

A preliminary report on the author's study of the state, organized labour and the changing labour and industrial relations systems of southern Europe. It focuses on the historic and continued influence of corporatism in shaping the labour relations systems of southern Europe, now expressed in more 'liberal' and 'neo-syndicalist' forms. The experiences of Portugal are compared with those of Greece, Italy and Spain.

Statistics

571 **Anuário Estatística** (Statistical Yearbook.) Lisbon: Instituto
   Nacional de Estatística, 1875- . annual.
The basic Portuguese official statistical yearbook covering all aspects of the
country's economy and demography. It has main sections on land and climate;
demography; health; employment and salaries; unions and syndicates; education,
culture and recreation; justice; agriculture, forestry and fishing; extractive
industries; manufacturing industries; energy and water; construction; housing;
transport and communications; tourism; external trade; corporations; commerce
and prices; monetary and financial market; public finance; and international
comparisons. The text is in Portuguese and French.

572 **Demographic Yearbook**
   New York: United Nations, 1948- . annual.
Provides a basic range of demographic statistics for most countries of the world,
including Portugal, for which details of population numbers, natality, mortality
and nuptiality are given.

573 **Estatísticas Agrícolas** (Agricultural Statistics.)
   Lisbon: Instituto Nacional de Estatística, 1965- . annual.
Portugal's official agricultural statistics, with main sections on the following
subjects: land, climate and population; property; landholding structure; fruit and
olive trees; agricultural machines; livestock production; commerce; consumption
and distribution; salaries and prices; agricultural insurance; industries directly
related to agriculture; development; health and hygiene; agricultural education;
economic accounts; and food balance. The text is in Portuguese and French.

574 **Estatísticas Industriais** (Industrial Statistics).
Lisbon: Instituto Nacional de Estatística, 1967- . annual.
Covers all aspects of Portugal's industry. It replaces *Estatística Industrial* (1945-66). The text is in Portuguese and French.

575 **The Europa Yearbook: a World Survey.**
London: Europa Publications, 1926- . annual.
The section on Portugal within this useful year-book includes an introductory survey, a statistical section and a directory. The introduction covers the country's geography, history, government and economy, while the statistical section provides data on area and population, agriculture, fishing, mining, industry, the country's finances, trade, transport, tourism, communications media and education. The directory includes information on the constitution, the government, the President and legislature, political organizations, diplomatic representation, judicial system, religion, the press, publishers, radio and television, finance, trade and industry, transport, tourism and atomic energy.

576 **Selected agricultural trade statistics for the European Community, Greece, Spain and Portugal, 1967-79.**
Compiled by Harold A. McNitt.   Washington, DC: United States Department of Agriculture, International Economics Division, Economic Research Service, 1982. 110p. (Statistical Bulletin, no. 692).
This report provides data on the agricultural trade of the European Community and of Greece, Spain and Portugal during the period 1967-79, paying particular attention to their trade with the USA. Trade is shown by value, commodity composition and country or region of origin or destination.

577 **Portugal**
Lisbon: Instituto Nacional de Estatística, 1969- . annual.
A useful statistical synopsis of Portugal in English and Portuguese editions. Recent issues have been thirty pages in length, and have covered the following subjects: geography and climate, population, health, education and culture, employment and wages, social security, agriculture, fisheries, construction, energy, housing, prices, transport, communications, tourism, foreign trade, national accounts, companies, finance, and international comparisons.

578 **Statistical Yearbook**
New York: United Nations, 1948- . annual.
Provides up-to-date summary economic, financial and social statistics relating to most countries in the world, including Portugal.

Portugal: a bird's eye view.
See item no. 28.

157

Statistics

Bank of London and South America Review.
See item no. 467.

Portugal: OECD economic survey.
See item no. 475.

Quarterly Economic Review of Portugal.
See item no. 477.

Selected agricultural statistics on Portugal.
See item no. 509.

Education, Science and Technology

579 **Swedish-Portuguese cooperation in the field of scientific and technical information and documentation: project identification mission to Portugal, 2-14 February 1976.**
Roland Hjerppe.   Stockholm: Royal Institute of Technology Library, 1976. 22p. (Stockholm Papers in Library and Information Science. Report TRITA-LIB-1072).
The report of a Swedish investigation into the introduction of modern methods for information services for research and development, based on the establishment of premises and prerequisites in Portugal.

580 **Revised programme proposal for the Swedish-Portuguese co-operation in the field of scientific and technical information and documentation.**
Roland Hjerppe, Carlos Pulido, Gabriela Lopes da Silva. Stockholm: Royal Institute of Technology Library, 1978. 43p. (Stockholm Papers in Library and Information Science. Report TRITA-LIB-1082).
A revision of the programme outlined by Hjerppe in the previous entry, made necessary by difficulties caused by the change of government. It provides the framework for the introduction of a modern information services system to Portugal.

581 **Long term development plan of scientific and technical research in Portugal.**
Lisbon: Ministério da Educação Nacional Gabinete de Estudos e Planeamento da Acção Educativa, 1968. 8 vols.

The report of a working group created according to an Agreement of November 1965 between the OECD (Organisation for Economic Co-operation and Development) and the Portuguese government to study the need for scientific and technical research in relation to the economic and social development of Portugal. Part One is an introduction and summary, Part Two presents an account of the situation of scientific and technical research in Portugal in the 1960s, Part Three is on Portuguese economic development and technical progress, Part Four is on development prospects and orientation of scientific and technical research, Part Five is a study of the demand and supply of research by sectors of activity, and Part Six presents a long term development plan for scientific and technical research in Portugal.

582 **Adult education in Portugal.**
Alberto Melo. Prague: European Centre for Leisure and Education, 1983. 100p. map. bibliog. (Studies and Documents, no. 16).

A broad survey of adult education in Portugal. Following a section on basic statistics about Portugal and a brief introduction, it is divided into three broad sections: the system of adult education; the personnel in adult education; and the theory and research on adult education. It concludes with a short list of addresses of adult education institutions in Lisbon.

583 **Experiments in popular education in Portugal 1974-1976.**
Alberto Melo, Ana Benavente. Paris: United Nations Educational, Scientific and Cultural Organization, 1978. 45p. bibliog. (Educational Studies and Documents, no. 29).

Studies the experimental educational activities in Portugal between 1974 and 1976 undertaken by the Life-Long Education Department. It is divided into three main chapters on historical and social factors influencing education, on seven grass-roots educational programmes, and on the development of a new administrative structure for adult education.

584 **A catalogue of 200 Type-I UFO events in Spain and Portugal.**
Vicente-Juan Ballester Olmos. Evanston, Illinois: Center for UFO Studies, 1976. 77p. map.

A summary of 200 UFO sightings in Iberia between 1914 and 1975, some of which are illustrated with line-drawings. Four of the sightings were from Portugal at the following locations: Alvito, 1954; Nazaré, 1957; Algoz, 1960; and Alportel, 1962.

585   **Reviews of national policies for education: Portugal.**
Organisation for Economic Co-operation and Development. Paris:
OECD, 1984. 110p.

This review of Portugal's education system was undertaken by a team of
examiners who visited the country at the end of 1982. The first section of the
volume is the examiners' report which covers recent socio-economic change in the
country, educational policy, the school system, vocational training and higher
education. The second section is a record of the review meeting held in Paris in
June 1983 and the third part is a summary of the education system in Portugal,
prepared by the country's Ministry of Education.

586   **Guide to world science: volume 9, Spain and Portugal.**
Edited by Robert A. C. Richards.   Guernsey: Francis Hodgson
(F. H. Books Ltd.), 1974. 2nd ed. 252p.

Although now somewhat out-of-date, this guide provides an introduction to the
organization and practice of science of all kinds in Portugal, as well as a directory
of scientific establishments in the country before the events of 1974.

587   **Pioneers in angiography: the Portuguese school of angiography.**
Edited by J. A. Veiga-Pires, Ronald G. Grainger.   Lancaster,
England; Boston, Massachusetts; The Hague: MTP Press, 1982.
131p. bibliog.

An edited volume of papers recounting the experimental and chemical
investigations by the team of Portuguese medical men led by the 1949 Nobel Prize
winner, Egas Moniz, who developed diagnostic angiography in the late 1920s. His
team undertook many experiments to discover a safe intra-arterial radiological
contrast agent and a suitable technique for clinical cerebral arteriography. It
includes surveys of the work of the Portuguese school of angiography as well as
translations of several of their original communications on angiography,
aortography, lymphography, angiopneumography, phlebography and porto-
graphy. It concludes with bibliographies of the work of Egas Moniz, Reynaldo
dos Santos, Lopo de Carvalho, Hernani Monteiro, João Cid dos Santos, A. de
Sousa Peréira.

Portuguese pioneers in India: spotlight on medicine
See item no. 190.

Literature

Literary history and criticism

588   **A Portuguese version of the life of Barlaam and Josaphat.**
Richard D. Abraham.   Philadelphia: University of Pennsylvania,
1938. 144p. bibliog.

An edition of the Portuguese text of the Barlaam and Josaphat story contained in
the manuscript volume *Codex Alcobacensis*, no. 266, together with a discussion of
its palaeography, orthography, phonology, morphology and syntax.

589   **Portuguese literature.**
Aubrey F. G. Bell.   Oxford: Oxford University Press, rev. ed.,
1970. 395p. bibliog.

A reprint of the 1922 edition with the addition of a select bibliography by B.
Vidigal. It provides detailed surveys of Portuguese literature divided into
chronological sections and includes chapters on the *Cossantes* and the
Cancioneiros of the period 1185-1325; the Galician poets; the dramatist Gil
Vicente (1470?-1536?): Luís de Camõs; *Quinhentista* prose; the *Seiscentistas*; and
the 19th-century Romantic School and the subsequent reaction to it. Two
appendixes provide information on the general folk literature of the people and
on the Galician revival of the 19th century.

590   **Two notes on Francisco de Holanda.**
J. B. Bury.   London: Warburg Institute, University of London,
1981. 45p. (Warburg Institute Surveys VII).

Two short articles on the 16th-century writer and painter Francisco de Holanda.
The first is on the authenticity of his *Roman dialogues* and the second is a
catalogue of his writings, drawings, paintings and architectural designs.

591 **Albor: mediaeval and Renaissance dawn-songs in the Iberian peninsula.**
Dionisia Empaytaz de Croome.   London: University Microfilms International, for the Department of Spanish and Spanish American Studies, University of London, King's College, 1980. 90p. bibliog.

Analyses the general theme of lovers' meetings and partings at dawn found in Iberian poetry. Most attention is paid to Spanish texts, but there is mention of some Galician-Portuguese and Portuguese poems.

592 **Theme and image in the poetry of Sá de Miranda.**
T. F. Earle.   Oxford: Oxford University Press, 1980. 153p.

Discusses the themes and images used by the 16th-century Portuguese poet Sá de Miranda, who was responsible for introducing the Italian hendecasyllabic line and other poetic forms into Portugal. The three chapters on 'themes' discuss Sá de Miranda's opinions on classical mythology, the philosophy of love and moral thought.

593 **The 'Brother Luiz de Sousa' of Viscount de Almeida Garrett.**
Viscount de Almeida Garrett, translated into English by Edgar Prestage.   London: Elkin Mathews, 1909. 137p.

A translation of the play by the 19th-century author Almeida Garrett. It is preceded by an extended introduction which discusses the author's life and work, and in particular his writing of *Brother Luiz de Sousa*, which concerns the religious, idealistic and chivalrous life of the period of union, from 1580-1640, between the Crowns of Spain and Portugal.

594 **Portuguese studies.**
Edward Glaser.   Paris: Fundação Calouste Gulbenkian, Centro Cultural Português, 1976. 277p.

An edited collection of papers by Glaser on Portuguese literature: 'A biblical theme in Iberian poetry of the Golden Age'; 'The *statio solis* (Joshua 10: 12-14) as a theme in Iberian letters of the Golden Age'; '*Se a tanto me ajudar o engenho e arte*: the poetics of the proem to *Os Lusíadas*'; 'Frei Heitor Pinto's *Imagem da vida Christã*'; 'Manuel de Faria e Sousa and the mythology of *Os Lusíadas*'; 'The Odyssean adventure in Gabriel Pereira de Castro's Vlyssea'; and 'Miguel da Silveira's *El Macabeo*'.

595 **Mediaeval and Renaissance studies on Spain and Portugal in honour of P. E. Russell.**
Edited by F. W. Hodcroft, D. G. Pattison, R. D. F. Pring-Mill, R. W. Truman.   Oxford: Society for the Study of Mediaeval Languages and Literature, 1981. 226p.

A collection of articles mostly written by past students of Peter Russell. Those with particular reference to Portugal include the following: 'The idea of kingship in the chronicles of Fernão Lopes', by L. de Sousa Rebelo; 'The life and humour of João de Sá Panasco, 'O Negro, former slave, court jester and gentleman of the Portuguese Royal Household (fl. 1524-1567)', by A. C. de C. M. Saunders; 'A Brazilian student at the University of Coimbra in the seventeenth century', by A. J. R. Russell-Wood; and 'The Middle Ages in fact and fiction: Alexandre Herculano's *O bobo*', by T. F. Earle.

596 **The Ocean Flower: a poem. Preceded by an historical and descriptive account of the island of Madeira, a summary of the discoveries and chivalrous history of Portugal and an essay on Portuguese literature.**
T. M. Hughes. London: Longman, Brown, Green & Longmans, 1845. 309p.

Preceding the poem, which is divided into ten cantos describing the island of Madeira, there is a lengthy introduction covering the history, discovery and present state of the islands in the mid-19th century. There is also an essay on Portuguese literature which includes translations of various Portuguese poems into English, and which refers to the following authors: Filinto Elizio; Manoel Maria Barbosa de Bocage, leader of the Nova Arcádia group of poets, Nicolao Tolentino satirist; Visconde de Almeida-Garrett; Antonio Feliciano de Castilho, leader of the Romantic movement; and J. A. Monteiro Texeira.

597 **Byron Portugal 1977.**
F. de Mello Moser, J. Paço D'Arcos, J. Almeida Flor, E. Santos Mattos, C. Estorninho. Coimbra, Portugal: Imprensa de Coimbra; sponsored by the Instituto de Cultura Portuguesa, 1977. 159p. bibliog.

This collection of four papers in both English and Portuguese, together with a bibliography on Byron's connections with Portugal, was published to mark the beginnings of the activities of the Portuguese Committee of the Byron Society. The papers are: 'Three approaches to Byron' by F. de Mello Moser; 'Rosa Corder, or an autograph of Lord Byron's', by J. Paço D'Arcos; 'A Portuguese review of Childe Harold's pilgrimage', by J. Almeida Flor; and 'A poet finds the new Eden', by E. Santos Mattos. The bibliography is by Estorninho. It includes some discussion of Byron's descriptions of Portugal, and in particular of Cintra, in Childe Harold.

598 **Three twentieth century Portuguese poets.**
John M. Parker. Johannesburg: Witwatersrand University Press, 1960. 43p. bibliog.

Presents an account of Portuguese poetry in the twentieth century. The generation of the *Orpheu*, a magazine first published in 1915, is represented by the work of Fernando Pessoa and Mário de Sá-Carneiro, and the *Presença* movement founded in 1927 around the review of that name by José Régio. It provides accounts of the lives and thoughts of these three poets, together with translated selections of their poems.

599   **D. Francisco Manuel de Mello.**
Edgar Prestage.   Oxford: Oxford University Press, London:
Humphrey Milford, 1922. 98p. (Hispanic Notes and Monographs,
Portuguese Series III).

An account of the life and works of the Portuguese writer Dom Francisco Manuel de Mello, who was born in Lisbon in 1608 and who belonged to the noble Spanish family of Manuel. Two of his works were translated into English: one under the title *The government of a wife* in the 17th century; and the other *Relics of Melordino* in the early 19th century. He died in 1666.

600   **Negritude as a theme in the poetry of the Portuguese-speaking world.**
Richard A. Preto-Rodas.   Gainesville, Florida: University of
Florida Press, 1970. 85p. (University of Florida Humanities
Monograph, no. 31).

Analyses the growth of racial awareness and the various aspects of Negritude (the awakening of Negro racial consciousness and pride) as poetic themes in the poetry of Negroes and mulattos of the Portuguese-speaking world.

601   **Garrett and the English muse.**
Lia Nóemia Rodrigues Correia Raitt.   London: Tamesis Books,
1983. 146p. bibliog.

An account of the influence of England and English writers on Almeida Garrett, the early 19th-century Portuguese author. Following an introduction there is a chapter on the role of England in Garrett's life then chapters on the influence of Addison, Byron, Scott, Sterne and Shakespeare on Garrett.

602   **The rediscoveries: major writers in Portuguese literature of national regeneration.**
Ronald W. Sousa.   University Park; London: Pennsylvania State
University Press, 1981. 192p. bibliog.

An account of the regenerationist literature of five Portuguese writers. The authors and works dealt with are Luís de Camões (1525?-80) and his epic poem *Os Lusíadas* (1572); Padre António Vieira (1608-97) and his expository *História do Futuro* (1647-63); Almeida Garrett (1799-1854) and his lyric-narrative poem *Camões* (1825); Eça de Queiroz (1845-1900) and his novel *A ilustre casa de Ramires* (1900); and Fernando Pessoa (1888-1935) and his volume of lyric poetry entitled *Mensagem* (1934).

603   **Studies in modern Portuguese literature.**
New Orleans, Louisiana: Tulane University, 1971. 104p. (Tulane
Studies in Romance Languages and Literature, no. 4).

A collection of five papers on modern Portuguese literature: 'The themes of Fernando Pessoa's English sonnets', by Robert D. F. Pring-Mill; '*A poesia portuguesa entre 1950 e 1970: notas para um estudo*' (Portuguese poetry 1950-70: notes for a study), by Alberto de Lacerda; '*O romance português contemporâneo*'

(The contemporary Portuguese romance), by Almeida Faria; '*Actualidade e circunstância de Eça de Queiroz*' (Actuality and circumstance of Eca de Queiroz), by Vianna Moog; and 'Realism and naturalism in western literatures, with some special references to Portugal and Brazil', by Jorge de Sena.

604 **Spanish and Portuguese romances of chivalry: the revival of the romance of chivalry in the Spanish Peninsula, and its extension and influence abroad.**
Henry Thomas.   Cambridge, England: Cambridge University Press, 1920. 355p. bibliog.
A comprehensive account of the Iberian romances of chivalry which emerged at the turn of the 15th century and spread over western Europe.

605 **Medieval lyrics in Spain and Portugal.**
J[ohn] B[rande] Trend.   Cambridge, England: R. I. Sivers, 1952. 25p.
Surveys traditional mediaeval lyrics and country poetry from Iberia.

606 **Twenty-five years of Portuguese fiction.**
Lisbon: Office of the Secretary of State for Information and Tourism, General Direction for Information, 1973. 41p. (Portugal Today Series).
A short, but quite useful, general introduction to Portuguese fiction between 1945 and 1972. It is divided into sections on: chronology and literature; the great traditional novel-writing current; Aquilino Ribeiro, Vitorino Nemésio and Tomás de Figueiredo; the influence of *Presença* (a Coimbra review founded in 1927); criticism of social customs; neo-realism; the generations of the fifties and the sixties; and women in Portuguese fiction.

607 **Juan de la Cueva and the Portuguese succession.**
Anthony Watson.   London: Tamesis Books, 1971. 280p. map. bibliog.
A piece of literary detective work in which the author sets out the evidence on which he came to the conclusion that Juan de la Cueva turned to the theatre in 1579 in order to express his views on the problem of the Portuguese succession. In so doing he discusses the following plays: the *Siege of Zamora, The sack of Rome*, the *Seven infantes of Lara, Bernardo del Carpio, Ajax and the arms of Achilles, The tyrant prince, Mucius Scaevola, The old man in love* and *The defamer*.

Portugal of the Portuguese.
See item no. 3.

Portugal and Brazil: an introduction.
See item no. 21.

Travels in Portugal, and through France and Spain, with a dissertation on the literature of Portugal, and the Spanish and Portuguese languages.
See item no. 91.

Lord Byron's Iberian pilgrimage.
See item no. 100.

Portugal.
See item no. 184.

Fernam Lopez.
See item no. 189.

Gaspar Corrêa.
See item no. 206.

Diogo do Couto.
See item no. 207.

João de Barros: Portuguese humanist and historian of Asia.
See item no. 211.

The Lisbon earthquake.
See item no. 255.

The downfall of a King: Dom Manuel II of Portugal.
See item no. 288.

The intellectual relations between Portugal and Great Britain.
See item no. 453.

Elementos para a historia da imprensa periódica Portuguesa (1641-1821).
(Elements for the history of the Portuguese periodical press (1641-1821).)
See item no. 721.

Bibliography of Hispanic women writers.
See item no. 747.

Portuguese bibliography.
See item no. 750.

Anthologies, novels and translations

608 **The love letters of a Portuguese nun, being the letters written by Mariana Alcaforado to Noël Bouton de Chamilly, Count of St. Leger (later Marquis of Chamilly) in the year 1668.**
Translated by R. H., with an introduction by Josephine Lazarus and a preface by Alexandre Piedagnel. New York: Cassell, 1890. 148p.

The first American translation of the five famous letters (reputedly) written by the nun, Mariana Alcaforado. It includes a short introduction on the background of her affair with Noël Bouton.

609 **Letters from a Portuguese nun written in the year 1667 by Mariana Alcaforado.**
Mariana Alcaforado, translated by Lucy Norten, with an introduction by Raymond Mortimer. London: Hamish Hamilton, 1956. 51p.

A translation of the five letters from the Portuguese nun Mariana Alcaforado to Noël Bouton de Chamilly, in the language of the Augustan Age. The fourth letter in the original edition is here presented first, followed by the first, the third and the second. There is a short introduction.

610 **English translations from the Spanish and Portuguese to the year 1700: an annotated catalogue of the extant printed versions (excluding dramatic adaptations).**
A[ntony] F[rancis] Allison. London: Dawsons, 1974. 224p.

An author catalogue of printed translations into English of Spanish and Portuguese works prior to 1701. Brief biographical notes are also given for each author. There are indexes of subjects and English titles and a biographical index of translators.

611 **I like it here.**
Kingsley Amis. London: Victor Gollancz, 1958. 208p.

A novel about an English family's visit to Portugal. It conveys a sense of the economic and social conditions as well as of the political intrigue of Salazar's régime.

612 **South of nowhere.**
Antonio Lobo Antunes, translated by Elizabeth Lowe. London: Chatto & Windus, 1983. 154p.

The first appearance in English of the novel by Antonio Lobo Antunes which was originally published as *Os Cus de Judas*, Lisbon: Editorial Vega, 1979. It is a first person narrative about colonial ambition and depravity in Angola, as well as a story of seduction and impotence.

613 **New Portuguese letters.**
Maria Isabel Barreno, Maria Teresa Horta, Maria Velho da Costa,
translated by Helen R. Lane, Faith Gillespie, Suzette Macedo.
London: Victor Gollancz, 1975. 432p.
The writings, letters and poems of three Portuguese women authors seeking to
reform the social patterns of their country. The book's unity derives from the
themes of the famous *Letters of a Portuguese nun*, and the book is in a sense a
meditation on the latter's relevance to the situation of women today. Three weeks
after it was first published (as *Novas cartas portuguesas*, Lisbon: Estudios Cor) in
April 1972 it was banned and the authors, who became known as the Three
Marias, were arrested and charged with 'offending public morals and abusing the
freedom of the press'. Following the events of 1974 the Three Marias were
acquitted. This volume also includes translations of the five original letters of a
Portuguese nun written by Mariana to the Marquis de Chamilly and translated by
Donald E. Ericson.

614 **Portugal through her literature: an anthology of prose and verse,**
with introduction, notes on authors, and parallel translation.
A. R. Barter. Glastonbury, England: Walton Press, 1972. 185p.
Presents an anthology of Portuguese literature after 1500. It includes prose by
thirty-five writers and poems by seventeen poets. There is a short biography of
each writer and the original Portuguese texts are published alongside the English
translations.

615 **Poems from the Portuguese (with the Portuguese text).**
Translated by Aubrey F. G. Bell. Oxford: Blackwell, 1913. 131p.
A collection of Portuguese poems together with translations, from the late 13th
century through to the end of the 19th century. It includes early poems illustrating
the influence of Provençal poetry, a selection of poems by Gil Vicente, poems by
Sá de Miranda and Camões illustrating the introduction of Italian metres into
Portuguese poetry, and lyric poems from the late 19th century such as those by
João de Deus.

616 **The Oxford book of Portuguese verse, XIIth century-XXth century.**
Chosen by Aubrey F. G. Bell, 2nd ed. edited by B. Vidigal.
Oxford: Clarendon Press, 1925. 2nd ed., 1952. 384p.
A collection of 256 untranslated Portuguese poems written prior to 1946. There is
a short introduction on Portuguese poetry, and the volume includes brief
biographical notes of each of the poets included in the anthology.

617 **Nostalgia: a collection of poems by J. Paço d'Arcos.**
Translated and with an introduction by Roy Campbell. London:
Sylvan Press, 1960. 51p.
Following a brief introduction, this volume includes translations of the twenty-
eight poems by J. Paço d'Arcos originally published in Portuguese as *Poemas
Imperfeitos* (Uncompleted poems).

618 **Ignez de Castro, a tragedy by Antonio Ferreira.**
Translated from the Portuguese by Thomas Moore Musgrave.
London: John Murray, 1825. 179p.

Presents a translation of the 16th-century tragedy by Ferreira recounting the story of the death of Ignez de Castro. An introductory memoir provides details of the author's life and work.

619 **The Portuguese letters: love letters of Mariana to the Marquis de Chamilly.**
Donald E. Ericson. New York: Crown Publishers, 1941. 66p.

A 'modern' translation of the five 'Portuguese letters' together with a short introduction.

620 **77 poems.**
Alberto de Lacerda, translated by Alberto de Lacerda, Arthur Waley. London: Allen & Unwin, 1955. 85p.

A collection of translations of poems by Alberto de Lacerda who was born in Mozambique in 1928 and lived there until 1946 when he went to Portugal.

621 **Selections from contemporary Portuguese poetry: a bilingual selection.**
Jean R. Longland, illustrated by Anne Marie Jauss. New York: Harvey House, 1966. 96p.

An anthology of forty-three short poems by Portuguese writers born in the 20th century. Emphasis is placed on younger poets who were not particularly familiar to foreign audiences in the mid-1960s.

622 **Modern poetry in translation 13/14: Portugal.**
Compiled by Helder Macedo. London: Modern Poetry in Translation, 1972. 48p.

This edition of *Modern poetry in translation* includes a selection of works by thirty modern Portuguese poets. There is a short biography of each poet whose work is represented.

623 **Contemporary Portuguese poetry: an anthology in English.**
Selected by Helder Macedo, E. M. de Melo e Castro. Manchester, England: Carcanet New Press, 1978. 182p.

An anthology of 130 poems by thirty-eight contemporary Portuguese poets, translated into English by eight different translators. There is a short biographical note about each poet represented. The poets with most poems in the anthology are Jorge de Sena, Sophia de Mello Breyner Adresen, António Ramos Rosa, Alexandre O'Neill, António Maria Lisboa and Pedro Tamen. An interesting introduction discusses the recent poetic background in Portugal.

624 **Thirteen days.**
Roger Mitton. London: Robert Hale, 1978. 224p.

A novel about the revolution of 25 April 1974, in which Celeste Zamora, although tortured and raped by the secret police, deceives them about the date of the revolution. It reflects the three-sided conflict that emerged between the Fascists, the liberators and the spirit of the Portuguese people.

625 **The letters of a Portuguese nun (Mariana Alcaforado).**
Translated by Edgar Prestage. London: David Nutt, 1893, 709p. bibliog.

This edition of the famous letters of a Portuguese nun includes a detailed introduction, an English translation, a French text, and an appendix of a verse translation printed in London in 1713. The bibliography includes the previous English translations of the work.

626 **Sixty-four sonnets.**
Anthero de Quental, translated into English by Edgar Prestage.
London: David Nutt, 1894. 133p.

In addition to the sixty-four sonnets included here, this volume provides an introductory essay on the poet Anthero de Quental (1842-91) and an autobiographical letter written by Anthero to Dr Storck, the German translator of his sonnets. His poetry is mainly psychological, reflecting a life of strife, which ended when he shot himself in the public square of Ponto Delgada having been told that the spinal disease from which he was suffering was incurable.

627 **Portuguese essays.**
Américo da Costa Ramalho. Lisbon: National Secretariat for Information, 1968. 2nd ed. 115p.

This collection of essays was based on talks given at New York University, a letter sent to a Belgian journal and a résumé of an article first published in Portuguese. The four main essays are on Portuguese culture in the era of expansion, the first explorers of the Congo, a new source for Sir Richard Grenville's last fight in the Azores in 1591 and the modern poet Fernando Pessoa. The volume also includes an essay on the Portuguese publications in the Library of Congress.

628 **When the wolves howl.**
Aquilino Ribeiro, translated by Patricia McGowan Pinheiro.
London: Jonathan Cape, 1963. 288p.

When this novel was first published, as *Quando os lobos uivam* by Livraria Bertrand in Lisbon in 1958, it was claimed a masterpiece but the author was arrested and charged with having attempted to discredit Portugal in the eyes of the world and of inciting action against State security. However, protests by writers from several countries secured his release. The novel concerns the return of Manuel Louvadeus from Brazil to his native village where he is elected to lead a revolt against a government afforestation scheme. As a result he is imprisoned and his father exacts a terrible revenge.

629 **The poetry of Jorge de Sena, a bilingual selection.**
Edited and with an introduction by Frederick G. Williams. Santa
Barbara, California: Mudborn Press, 1980, 316p.

A collection of poems by Jorge de Sena (1919-78) in Portuguese with adjacent
English translations. An introduction provides an account of Jorge de Sena's life
and work.

630 **An anthology of modern Portuguese and Brazilian prose.**
Edited by A. G. de Sousa, I. R. Warner. London: Harrap, 1978.
172p.

Although the anthology presents the works of the twelve authors discussed in
their original Portuguese language, there is a useful introduction in English on
Portuguese prose and there are also biographical details of each author. The
Portuguese authors whose works are included are Aquilino Ribeiro, Ferreira de
Castro, José Régio (José Maria dos Reis-Perreira), Vitorino Nemésio, Miguel
Torga (Adolfo Rocha) and José Cardoso Pires, and two examples of Portuguese
African prose are taken from the works of Castro Soromenho and Luandino
Vieira (José Vieira Mateus da Graça). Works of four Brazilian authors are also
included.

631 **Farrusco the blackbird and other stories from the Portuguese.**
Miguel Torga [pseudonym of Adolfo Correia da Rocha], translated
and with an introduction by Denis Brass, illustrations by Gregorio
Prieto. London: Allen & Unwin, 1950. 93p.

A collection of fourteen short stories set in Trás-os-Montes. The introduction
provides a commentary on the life and works of Torga.

632 **Portuguese poems with translations.**
J. B. Trend. Cambridge: printed by R. I. Severs Limited, 1954.
32p.

Provides a collection of seventeen short poems by Nuno Fernandes Torneol, El-
Rei D. Dinis, João Zorro, Francisco de Sousa, Camões, Afonso Lopes Vieira,
Francisco Bugalho, António de Sousa, Afonso Duarte and Fernando Pessoa,
together with a short concluding note about the poets.

633 **Mountain of the star – a story of Portugal.**
Evelyn Webster. London: Macdonald, 1947. 224p.

A novel developed around two love stories set in the region below the Serra da
Estrela in central Portugal.

634 **Portugal: an anthology, edited with English versions.**
George Young. Oxford: Clarendon Press, 1916, 168p.

An anthology of fifty Portuguese poems, together with their translations, divided
into the following sections: old ballads (1000-1500); King Diniz (1279-1325); Gil
Vicente (ca. 1470-1539); Camoens (1525-80); historical ballads (1576-1600);
modern ballads (1600-1700); popular songs and airs (1800-1900); João de Deus

Ramos (1830-96); young Portugal (the Revolution and the Republic); Anthero de Quental (1842-91); Sousa Viterbo (1845-1901); Theophilo Braga; and Guerro Junqueiro (1850).

The obedience of a King of Portugal.
See item no. 199.

Conquests and discoveries of Henry the Navigator, being the Chronicles of Azurara, Portuguese navigators and colonizers of the fifteenth and sixteenth centuries.
See item no. 203.

The tragic history of the sea 1598-1622: narratives of the shipwrecks of the Portuguese East Indiamen *São Thomé* (1589), *Santo Alberto* (1593), *São João Baptista* (1622), and the journeys of the survivors in south east Africa.
See item no. 209.

Further selections from the tragic history of the sea 1559-1565; narratives of the shipwrecks of the Portuguese East Indiamen *Aguia* and *Graça* (1559), *São Paulo* (1561), and the misadventure of the Brazil ship *Santa António* (1565).
See item no. 210.

Portuguese voyages 1498-1663.
See item no. 221.

A journal of the first voyage of Vasco da Gama 1497-1499.
See item no. 231.

Commentaries of Ruy Freyre de Andrada, in which are related his exploits from the year 1619, in which he left this Kingdom of Portugal as General of the Sea of Ormuz, and Coast of Persia, and Arabia until his death.
See item no. 238.

The Ocean Flower: a poem.
See item no. 596.

Luís de Camões

635 Memoirs of the life and writings of Luis de Camoens.
John Adamson. London: Longman, Hurst, Rees, 1820. 2 vols.

Presents a detailed account of the life and times of Camoens derived from his own writings and the works of earlier biographers. It provides information on the state of poetry in Portugal at the time Camoens was writing in the 16th century, and contains memoirs of his writings, a bibliographical account of translations of *Os Lusíadas* (The Lusiads) and a list of editions of Camoens' works.

636 The Lusiads.
Luis Vaz de Camoens, translated by William C. Atkinson. Harmondsworth, England: Penguin, 1952. 249p. map. Reprinted, 1980.

An easily accessible prose translation of *Os Lusíadas*. It includes a thirty-six page introduction on the themes of the book, the poet, the poem, a summary of the poem and the translation.

637 Camoens and the sons of Lusus.
W. C. Atkinson. London: Hispanic and Luso Brazilian Council, 1973. 18p.

The text of a lecture delivered at Canning House, London, to commemorate the 400th Anniversary of the first publication of *Os Lusíadas* (The Lusiads) by Camoens. It provides a short account of the writing and subject matter of the poem.

638 The Lusiads of Camoens.
Translated into English verse by J. J. Aubertin. London: Kegan Paul, Trench & Company, 1878, 2nd ed., 1884. 2 vols. map.

A translation of *Os Lusíadas* into English poetry, with the Portuguese and English text on facing pages. There is a short introduction.

639 Seventy sonnets of Camoens: Portuguese text and translation with original poems.
J. J. Aubertin. London: C. Kegan Paul & Company, 1881. 253p.

This volume contains the Portuguese texts and translations of seventy of Camoens' sonnets together with a selection of Aubertin's own work including sonnets, poems and several other short translations.

640 The Lusiads of Luiz de Camões.
Translated by Leonard Bacon. New York: Hispanic Society of America, 1950. 435p. map.

A translation of *Os Lusíadas* into modern American verse. It includes a thorough introduction on the author, extensive notes and concludes with a brief sketch of Portugal's history in the 14th and 15th centuries.

641 **Luis de Camões, the Lusiads, in Sir Richard Fanshawe's translation.**
Edited and with an introduction by Geoffrey Bullough. Fontwell, Sussex, England: Centaur Press, 1963, 352p. bibliog.

Presents a new edition of Fanshawe's 1655 verse translation of *Os Lusíadas*. It includes a short introduction on the poem, its author and on Richard Fanshawe who first translated it into English. This edition also includes Fanshawe's hitherto unprinted corrections to his own copy of his translation.

642 *Os Lusíadas* **(The Lusiads).**
Translated into English by Richard Francis Burton, edited by Isabel Burton. London: Bernard Quaritch, 1880. 2 vols.

Burton's verse translation of Camões' *Os Lusíadas*, which the translator claimed to be 'the most pleasing literary labour of my life'. It aims to give a word-for-word rendering of the original, and was completed over a period of twenty years.

643 **Camoens: his life and his Lusiads, a commentary.**
Richard F. Burton. London: Bernard Quaritch, 1881. 2 vols.

The extensive commentary to Burton's translation of *Os Lusíadas*, containing five main chapters. The first is on the life and poetry of Camoens; the second provides details of earlier translation of *Os Lusíadas*; the third is an account of the history of Portugal, paying particular attention to the period between the reign of D. João II 1481-95 and the death of Camoens in 1580; the fourth is a topographical and geographical account of Camoens' travels; and the fifth gives explicatory and philological details illustrating the text.

644 **Camoens: the lyricks (sonnets, canzons, odes and sextines).**
Translated into English by Richard F. Burton. London: Bernard Quaritch, 1884. 2 vols.

Translations of Camoens' 360 sonnets, twenty-one canzons, fourteen odes, and five sextines. As with Burton's translation of *Os Lusíadas*, he deliberately maintained archaisms and the eclectic style of the originals.

645 **The Lusiad of Camoens translated into English Spenserian verse.**
Robert Ffrench Duff. London: Chatto & Windus; Philadelphia: Lippincott; Lisbon: Mathew Lewtas, 1880. 506p.

A translation of Camoens' *Os Lusíadas* into Spenserian verse, together with a short biographical note on Camoens. It concludes with appendixes giving biographical information on people and places illustrated in the volume, details of the translation, a chronology of the kings of Portugal, the return of Vasco da Gama to Portugal, a list of Viceroys and Governors General of India and explanatory notes of all the proper names in the text.

646 **The Lusiad, or Portugals historicall poem: written in the Portingall language by Luis de Camoens; and newly put into English by Richard Fanshawe.** London: printed for Humphrey Moseley, at the Prince's Arms in St. Pauls Churchyard, 1655. 224p.

The first translation into English of Camoens' *Os Lusíadas*. Fanshawe's work reflects a certain amount of Italian influence and the work remained uncorrected when it was sent to the printers, but nevertheless this remained the standard translation for many years.

647 **The Lusiad by Luís de Camoens.** Translated by Richard Fanshawe, edited with an introduction by Jeremiah D. M. Ford. Cambridge, Massachusetts: Harvard University Press, 1940. 307p.

A new edition of Fanshawe's translation of *Os Lusíadas* by Luís de Camoens. The introduction provides an account of Fanshawe's life, his appointment as Ambassador to Portugal in 1662 and his work in translating *The Lusiads*.

648 **Dante, Petrarch, Camoens: CXXIV sonnets.** Translated by Richard Garrett London: John Lane; Boston: Copeland & Day, 1896. 147p.

This selection of translated sonnets includes forty by Camoens.

649 **Camões: some poems translated from the Portuguese by Jonathan Griffin. Essays on Camões by Jorge de Sena and Helder Macedo.** London: Menard Press, 1976. 41p.

This publication is in three parts: an essay by the poet Jorge de Sena placing Camões in his historical cultural and literary context; translations by Jonathan Griffin of eighteen sonnets and poems by Camões; and an essay on the principal themes in Camões' lyric poetry by Helder Macedo.

650 **Luis de Camoëns and the epic of the Lusiads.** Henry H. Hart. Norman, Oklahoma: University of Oklahoma Press, 1962. 335p. bibliog.

A detailed biography of Camoëns recounting his life in Portugal, his travels and sojourns in India and his eventual return to Portugal. Appendixes include translations of poems and lyrics referred to in the text.

651 **The purpose of praise: past and future in *The Lusiads* of Luís de Camões.** Helder Malta Macedo. London: King's College, University of London, 1983. 19p. (Inaugural Lecture in the Camoens Chair of Portuguese).

Evaluates the purpose of *The Lusiads*. It argues that the comparison between Gama and Aeneas is central to the conception of history embodied by Camões in his poem, and that he introduces a novel combination of epic celebration and pastoral regret into the epic tradition.

652 **The Lusiad, or, the discovery of India. An epic poem translated from the original Portuguese of Luis de Camoëns.**
William Julius Mickle. Oxford: Jackson & Lister, 1776. 484p.
The second major translation of *Os Lusíadas* into English verse. It includes a long introduction on Camoëns and Portuguese history during the 15th and 16th centuries particularly concerning the discovery of India.

653 *Os Lusíadas* **(The Lusiads).**
Luís de Camões, edited with an introduction and notes by Frank Pierce. Oxford: Oxford University Press, 1973. Reprinted in paperback with corrections, 1981. 271p. map. bibliog.
Probably the best and clearest edition of *Os Lusíadas* (The Lusiads) in Portuguese with notes in English. There is a thorough introduction in English covering the life of Camões, the literary significance of *Os Lusíadas*, a synopsis of the book, an evaluation of its contents and a discussion of the poet's erudition.

654 **Poems from the Portuguese of Luis de Camoens: with remarks on his life and writings, Notes, etc. etc.**
Lord Viscount Strangford [Percy Clinton Sydney Smythe].
London: printed for J. Carpenter by C. Whittingham, 1803. 159p.
Following an introduction on the life and writings of Camoens this collection of translations includes seven canzons, eight canzonets, five madrigals, a rondeau, four stanzas, twenty sonnets, part of the third elegy, and part of Canto VI of *The Lusiads*.

655 **Camoens in the periodical literature of the British Isles, 1771-1970.**
S. George West. Lisbon: Comissaõ Executiva do IV Centenário da Publicação de 'Os Lusíadas', 1973. 12p. bibliog.
Following a very short introduction, the author provides a bibliography of ninety-three items concerning Camoens in British periodical literature.

Eça de Queiroz

656 **The relic.**
José Maria Eça de Queiroz, translated by Aubrey F. G. Bell. London: Max Reinhardt, 1954. 231p.
A novel telling the story of the events befalling the narrator on his return to Portugal following a pilgrimage in 1875 to Jerusalem where he miraculously witnessed certain scandalous events.

657 **Eça de Queirós and European realism.**
Alexander Coleman. New York; London: New York University
Press, 1980. 330p. bibliog.

Examines Eça de Queiroz's major novels and also his essays in literary criticism.
These are discussed in the context of his life and geographical residence as well as
his relationship with Flaubert and other European authors. An appendix provides
a reprint of Richard Franko Goldman's translation of *José Matias* which contains
a summation of the obsessive themes that characterize all of the novels.

658 **Cousin Bazilio.**
José Maria Eça de Queiros, translated by Roy Campbell. London:
Max Reinhardt, 1953. 296p.

A novel unfolding the events following the reunion of Luiza with her first love,
Cousin Basilio, when her husband, Jorge, a mining engineer, is away.

659 **The city and the mountains.**
Eça de Queiroz, translated by Roy Campbell. London: Max
Reinhardt, 1955. 217p.

A novel set towards the end of the 19th century about Jacinto who has an estate
in the Alentejo and an extensive social life in Paris, which provide the framework
of the mountains and the city of the title.

660 **The sin of Father Amaro.**
Eça de Queiroz, translated by Nan Flanagan. London: Max
Reinhardt, 1962. 352p.

An English translation of the novel *O crime do Padre Amaro* first published in
1874. It traces the events following the arrival of a new priest, Amaro Vieira, in
the town of Leiria.

661 **The Mandarin and other stories.**
Eça de Queiroz, translated by Richard Franko Goldman. London:
Bodley Head, 1966. 186p.

An English translation of the novel *The Mandarin*, first published in 1880,
together with the three short stories 'Peculiarities of a fair-haired girl', 'A lyric
poet', and 'José Matias'.

662 **The Maias.**
Eça de Queiroz, translated by Patricia McGowan Pinheiro, Ann
Stevens. London: Bodley Head, 1965. 633p.

A dramatic account of incest and moral collapse in the Maia family set against the
background of a Lisbon peopled with poets, diplomats, politicians and dandies
living out the last years of a doomed monarchy.

663 **The sweet miracle.**
José Maria Eça de Queiroz, translated by Edgar Prestage. Oxford:
Blackwell, 1914. 4th ed. 35p.

A short story about Jesus who could not be found in Galilee by the rich and
powerful, but who revealed himself to a beggar's child.

664 **The illustrious house of Ramires.**
Eça de Queiroz, translated by Ann Stevens. London: Bodley
Head, 1968. 310p.

A novel in which the 19th-century Portuguese author Eça de Queiroz (1843-1900)
depicts Gonçalo Mendes Ramires, one of the last scions of an old family, trying to
resolve the conflicting pressures of his public and private lives. It suggests in
miniature the struggles of Portugal towards unity and consistency of purpose.

665 **Letters from England.**
Eça de Queiroz, translated by Ann Stevens. London: Bodley
Head, 1970.

These letters were begun in 1879 when Eça de Queiroz was Consul in Newcastle
upon Tyne, and they were published in the Rio de Janeiro *Gazeta de Notícas*.
They provide accounts of English life in the 1880s and include details of the
shooting and yachting seasons, the aristocracy, fashion, war, rebellion and the
death of Lord Beaconsfeld in 1881.

Fernando Pessoa

666 **Fernando Pessoa i-iv: Alberto Caeiro, Ricardo Reis, Alvaro de
Campos, Fernando Pessoa.**
Translated by Jonathan Griffin. Oxford: Carcanet Press, 1971, 4
vols.

A collection of poems translated into English in four booklets by the modern
Portuguese poet Fernando Pessoa, derived from the two collected editions of his
poetry: that of *Aticá* (Lisbon), and that of *Aguilar* (Rio de Janeiro).

667 **Selected poems: Fernando Pessoa.**
Translated by Jonathan Griffin. Harmondsworth, England:
Penguin Books, 1974. 2nd ed. with new supplement, 1982. 159p.

Fernando Pessoa (1888-1935) wrote poetry under the four names of Alberto
Caeiro, Ricardo Reis, Alvaro de Campos and Fernando Pessoa, and this selection
of his poetry gives examples of each style English translation.

668 **Selected poems by Fernando Pessoa including poems by his heteronyms Alberto Caeiro, Ricardo Reis, Alvaro de Campos, as well as some of his English sonnets and selections from his letters.** Translated by Edwin Honig, with an introduction by Octavio Paz. Chicago: Swallow Press, 1971.

A selection of Pessoa's poems in Portuguese with English translations. The introduction by Octavio Paz is entitled 'Pessoa or the imminence of the unknown'. It concludes with some biographical dates.

669 **The man who never was: essays on Fernando Pessoa.** Edited by George Monteiro. Providence, Rhode Island: Gávea-Brain Publications, 1982. 195p.

A series of essays in English on Fernando Pessoa (1888-1935), considered by many to be the greatest Portuguese poet since Luís de Camões. It includes the following articles: 'Fernando Pesoa: the man who never was', by Jorge de Sena; 'Presença's Pessoa', by João Gaspar Simoës; 'Pessoa and Portuguese politics', by Gilbert R. Cavaco; 'Ascendant romanticism in Pessoa', by Ronald W. Sousa; 'The quest for identity in Pessoa's orthonymous poetry', by Joanna Cousteau; 'The search for the self: Álvaro de Campos's "ode marítima"', by Francisco Cota Fagundes; 'The sun vs. ice cream and chocolate: the works of Wallace Stevens and Fernando Pessoa', by Catarina T. F. Edinger; 'Edwin Honig and Jean Longland: two interviews', conducted by Carolina Matos; 'The short happy life of Amadeo de Souza Cardoso', by Hellmut Wohl; and 'A biographical-bibliographical note on Pessoa', by José Martins Garcia.

670 **Fernando Pessoa: sixty Portuguese poems.** Introduction, selection, English translation of the poems and notes by F. E. G. Quintanilha. Cardiff: University of Wales Press, 1971. 141p. bibliog.

A selection of sixty of Fernando Pessoa's poems, with translations into English, together with an extensive introduction on his life and his work.

671 **Fernando Pessoa: selected poems.** Edited, translated by Peter Rickard. Edinburgh: University of Edinburgh Press, 1971. 189p. bibliog.

A collection of the poems of Fernando Pessoa (1888-1935) together with an extensive introduction covering his life and his work. The poems are given in the original Portuguese as well as in translation.

Gil Vicente

672 **Four plays of Gil Vicente edited from the editio princeps (1562), with translation and notes, by**
Aubrey F. G. Bell.   Cambridge, England: Cambridge University Press, 1920. 98p. bibliog.

This volume provides texts and translations of the following four 16th-century plays by Gil Vicente: *Auto da alma* (The soul's journey), *Exhortação da guerra* (Exhortation to war), *Farsa dos almocreves* (The carriers) and *Tragicomedia pastoril da Serra da Estrella* (Pastoral tragi-comedy of the Serra da Estrela). It has an extensive introduction about the author and his work and it concludes with notes, a list of proverbs in Gil Vicente's works, a table of his life and works, a bibliography of Gil Vicente and an index of persons and places.

673 **Gil Vicente.**
Aubrey F. G. Bell   Oxford: Oxford University Press; London: Humphrey Milford, 1921. 70p. bibliog. (Hispanic Notes and Monographs, Portuguese Series 1).

A critical biography of the court poet Gil Vincente who was also a goldsmith, musician, actor and dramatist, and who lived ca. 1465-1536.

674 **Lyrics of Gil Vicente.**
Aubrey F. G. Bell.   Oxford: Blackwell, 1921. 132p.

Translations of fifty-one lyric poems by Gil Vicente, who was the greatest 16th-century Portuguese dramatist. This volume also includes the original Portuguese texts of the poems, an introduction on Gil Vicente's lyrics and a section of detailed notes.

675 **Gil Vicente, farces and festival plays.**
Edited by Thomas R. Hart.   Eugene, Oregon: University of Oregon, 1972. 234p. bibliog.

This volume includes the texts of five of Gil Vicente's 16th-century farces and plays, without translations into English. However, there is a detailed introduction by the editor which provides useful background material on the work of Gil Vicente.

676 **The court theatre of Gil Vicente.**
Laurence Keates.   Lisbon: Livraria Escolar Editora, 1962. 154p. bibliog.

Studies the theatre of Gil Vicente with particular regard to the 16th-century society and audiences for which it was written and performed. A review of his general culture and the dramatic antecedents to his work precedes an analysis of his theatre and an estimate of his achievement.

Children's Books

677 **We go to Portugal.**
Sylvia L. Corbridge. London: Harrap, 1963. 186p. map. ('We go' Series).

The story of a family holiday in Portugal, written in a style suitable for children.

678 **Children of the vineyards.**
E. C. van Houten. London: Hutchinson, 1961. 32p. map. (This is Our Country Series).

A book for young children concentrating on the life of children in the Douro valley of northern Portugal.

679 **Manuela lives in Portugal.**
Camilla Jessel. London: Methuen 1967. 48p. (Children Everywhere Series).

An account of the life of a young girl, the daughter of a fisherman, in Lisbon. It is written for children and is extensively illustrated with photographs.

680 **Folk tales from Portugal.**
Alan S. Feinstein, illustrated by Diana L. Paxson. South Brunswick New York: A. S. Barnes; London: Thomas Yoseloff, 1972. 102p.

A collection of eighteen Portuguese folk-tales designed primarily for children.

681　**The young traveller in Portugal.**
Honor Wyatt.　London: Phoenix House, 1955. map. (Young
Traveller Series).

A fictional story of a holiday spent in Portugal by William and Patience, in a
series aimed at 12-16 year-olds. 'Based on fact', it provides a picturesque account
of Portugal in the 1950s as the family travel from Oporto to Braga, Chaves,
Bragança, Coimbra, Alcobaça, Nazaré, Caldas da Rainha, Obidos, Estoril,
Setúbal, Évora, Portimão, Sagres, Lisbon and Fatima.

Let's visit Portugal.
See item no. 35.

The sweet miracle.
See item no. 663.

Portuguese fairy tales.
See item no. 711.

The Arts

General

682 **Hispanic furniture: from the fifteenth through the eighteenth century**
Grace Hardendorff Burr   New York: Archive Press, 1964. 2nd ed. 231p. bibliog.

A history of Hispanic furniture from the Gothic to the end of the Rococo period. It concentrates on the 16th and 17th centuries when the cabinet makers of Portugal and Spain developed their own original style, and there is also a section on colonial furniture.

683 **Modern Portuguese tapestries: exhibition organised by the Ministry of Foreign Affairs and the Department of Culture Museu Nacional de Arte Antiga with the collaboration of the Calouste Gulbenkian Foundation on the occasion of the oficial (sic) visit to London of his Excellency the President of the Republic of Portugal General António Ramalho Eanes.**
Cécil Cotin, translated by J. M. Vaz, Teresa Amado.   Lisbon: Neogravura Lda, 1978. [not paginated].

The catalogue of an exhibition of Portuguese tapestry held at Kensington Palace, London in November 1978. It includes an account of 20th-century tapestry in Portugal, as well as details of the lives and activities of the twelve artists whose works are illustrated in the twenty plates.

684 **Afro-Portuguese ivories.**
W. P. Fagg. London: Artia for Batchworth Press, 1959. 92p.
bibliog.

An account of the collection of ivories at the British Museum produced by African craftsmen to Portuguese orders. It concludes with forty-six large photographs of items in the collection, each of which is briefly described.

685 **Traditional embroidery of Portugal, complete with designs.**
Clementina Carneiro de Moura. London: Batsford, no date [ca. 1950s]. 58p. map.

An illustrated account of the different regional traditions of embroidery in Portugal. It also provides details of how to make the embroidery, and it concludes with three printed patterns.

686 **A descriptive catalogue of printing in Spain and Portugal 1501-1520.**
F. J. Norton. Cambridge, England; London; New York;
Melbourne: Cambridge University Press, 1978. 581p. bibliog.

A catalogue of Spanish and Portuguese works from 1501-20 together with details of lost editions of which a reliable record exists. It includes forty-three Portuguese entries.

687 **The Wellington Plate Portuguese Service. (A baixela Wellington).**
Charles [Chichele] Oman. London: Her Majesty's Stationery
Office; Victoria and Albert Museum, 1954. 11p.

Describes the collection of plate given to the Duke of Wellington by the Portuguese in 1816. It also provides details of the background of the gift and it concludes with a series of thirty-nine pictures illustrating the collection. The Wellington Plate is one of the major examples of the work of the silversmiths of the neo-classical period and forms the largest commission ever executed at one time by Portuguese silversmiths.

688 **The golden age of Hispanic silver, 1400-1665.**
Charles Oman. London: Her Majesty's Stationery Office, 1968.
70p. map. bibliog.

A catalogue and description of the collection of Hispanic silver in the Victoria and Albert Museum. It includes examples of the work of many of the most important silver centres of Portugal in the 15th, 16th and early 17th centuries.

689 **The art of Portugal 1500-1800.**
Robert C. Smith. London: Weidenfeld & Nicolson, 1968. 320p.
bibliog.

The first major volume written in English devoted to the general history of Portuguese art. It is extensively illustrated and has chapters on architecture, the gilt-wood church interior, sculpture, painting, ceramics, silver, furniture and textiles.

690 **Portuguese needlework rugs: the time-honored art of Arraiolos rugs adapted for modern handcrafters.**
Patricia Stone. Mclean, Virginia: EPM Publications, 1981. 118p. bibliog.

A comprehensive survey of Portuguese needlework rugs covering their history, construction, patterns, materials, stitching, finishing, purchase and care of the rugs. It includes detailed patterns from which rugs could be made, and appendixes give information on retail outlets for Arraiolos rugs and museums where rugs from the 17th to the 19th centuries can be seen in Portugal.

Palácios portugueses: Portuguese palaces and castles; palais et châteaux portuguais, 1° volume.
See item no. 20.

Portugal and Brazil: an introduction.
See item no. 21.

Travels in Portugal: through the provinces of Entre Douro & Minho, Beira, Estremadura and Alem-Tejo in the years 1789 and 1790. Consisting of observations on the manners, customs, trade, public buildings, arts, antiquities, &c., of that kingdom.
See item no. 93.

Unknown Portugal: archaeological itineraries illustrated with photographs by the author.
See item no. 160.

Architecture

691 **Lusitania: a brief introduction to the material history of Portugal considered in its total environment.**
Harold N. Cooledge, Jr.; photographs: Frazer Pajak, Mary Frances Dodenhoff, Harold N. Cooledge, Jr.; edited by Blake Prator, L. Clark Wickliffe, Fred S. Buckner. Clemson, South Carolina: Clemson Architectural Foundation, College of Architecture, Clemson University, 1977. 76p. map.

A 'coffee-table picture book' placing the architecture of Portugal in its wider environment. Particular attention is paid to the towns of Chaves, Vila do Conde, Barcelos, Lamego, Coimbra, Tomar, Sintra, Évora, Vila Vicosa, Mafra, Pena.

692 **Art in Spain and Portugal.**
Marcel Dieulafoy. London: Heinemann, 1913. 376p. (Ars Una:
Species Mille, General History of Art).

This volume argues that Persia was not only the source of inspiration of the so-
called Mudejar architecture found mainly in the Toledo area of Spain, but also
that she played an important part in the elaboration of religious themes found in
the Asturias, Castille and Catalonia. The majority of the book is about Spain, but
a final chapter considers art in Portugal and covers the following main subjects:
religious, civil and military architecture, sculpture, painting, joinery, pottery and
the work of goldsmiths. It is illustrated by numerous small photographs.

693 **Portuguese plain architecture between spices and diamonds, 1521-
1706.**
George [Alexander] Kubler. Middletown, Connecticut: Wesleyan
University Press, 1972. 315p. bibliog.

An account of the development of Portuguese architecture between the 1520s,
when Manueline decoration was abandoned, and the resumption of surcharged
ornament in the years around 1700. It is well-illustrated with figures and 126
plates. The author concludes that Portuguese plain architecture corresponded to
an experimental attitude among designers who were nourished on Renaissance
theory and yet were able to disregard its prescription in the quest for useful and
inexpensive building.

694 **Art and architecture in Spain and Portugal and their American
dominions 1500 to 1800.**
George Kubler, Martin Soria. Harmondsworth, England:
Penguin Books, 1959. 445p. bibliog. (The Pelican History of Art,
no. Z17).

A thorough survey of Iberia and Iberian-influenced architecture, sculpture and
painting in the 16th, 17th and 18th centuries. Most attention is paid to Spain, but
Portuguese Manueline, Baroque, Rococo, and Neo-Classical architecture is
discussed, together with painting from the High Renaissance, through the
Mannerism and Baroque periods to the 18th century.

695 **Baroque in Spain and Portugal and its antecedents.**
James Lees-Milne. London: Batsford, 1960. 224p. bibliog.

An essay on the Baroque architecture of Spain and Portugal, with emphasis on
the origins of the style. The second half of the book is on Portugal with chapters
on the Manoeline (sic), Renaissance sculpture, Renaissance architecture, 17th-
century Baroque, the arts under João V, João Federico Ludovice (1670-1752) and
the Foreigners, and Rococo. It argues that in Portugal the Baroque was the
expression of a profound nationalism.

696 **Monuments of Portugal.**
Luis Reis Santos. Lisbon: National Secretariat of Information,
[no date]. 156p.

A short, illustrated account, first published in Portuguese in 1940, of the
architecture and monuments of Portugal, paying particular attention to the
churches, palaces and castles of the country. It concludes with a list of national
monuments and buildings of public interest classified up to September 1940.

697 **Portuguese architecture.**
Walter Crum Watson. London: Archibald Constable, 1908. 280p.
map. bibliog.

A thorough survey of architecture in Portugal prior to the 20th century. The
introduction provides a general survey of Portuguese history and accounts of
painting, church plate and tiles. The remaining nineteen chapters provide a
generally chronological survey of the development of architecture in the country.
Three of these chapters are devoted to the influence of the Moors. Particular
attention is paid to Alcobaça, Batalha, Thomar and Belém, although details are
given of all the major buildings in the country.

Painting

698 **Exhibition of Portuguese art, 800-1800: Royal Academy of Arts
Winter Exhibition 1955-86.**
London: Royal Academy of Arts, 1955-56. 114p. bibliog.

The catalogue of the Royal Academy's exhibition of Portuguese art held in the
winter of 1955-56. After an introduction by Sir James Mann there is a chapter on
'The art of Portugal, its character and development', by Professor Reynaldo dos
Santos. Each of the 572 exhibits is then described in turn.

699 **Trends in modern Portuguese art.**
José Augusto França. *Apollo* new series, no. 199, vol. 108 (Sept.
1978), p. 190-95.

An illustrated overview of the different currents that have existed in Portuguese
art in the 20th century, beginning with Cubism and Futurism and finishing with
the Surrealism of the 1950s.

700 **Medina.**
Switzerland: Fretz Frères, [no date]. 72p.

A collection of the work of the portrait painter Henrique Medina de Barros, born
in Oporto in 1901. After an introductory text in Portuguese, French and English
there are seventy-two full-page reproductions of Medina's paintings, two of which
are in colour.

701 **Portuguese video art.**
Lisbon: Secretaria de Estado da Cultura, 1981. 31p. bibliog.
The catalogue of an exhibition held in April and May 1981 and organized by J. M.
Vasconcelos at Corboree: Gallery of New Concepts (School of Art and Art
History, The University of Iowa). It provides profiles and bibliographies of the
fourteen exhibiting artists: Helena Almeida, José Barrias, José de Carvalho, José
Conduto, Abel Mendes, Leonel Moura, António Palolo, Silvestre Pestana,
Cerveira Pinto, Joana Rosa, Julião Sarmento, Henrique Silva, Ernesto de Sousa
and João Vieira.

702 **The early Portuguese school of painting, with notes on the pictures
at Viseu and Coimbra, traditionally ascribed to Gran Vasco.**
J. C. Robinson. London: printed by John Childs, 1866. 30p.
(Extracted from the *Fine Arts Quarterly Review*).
A general account of the emergence of a Portuguese school of painting at the
close of the 15th century and the beginning of the 16th century. Considerable
attention is paid to the pictures in the cathedral at Viseu and the church and
monastery of Santa Cruz at Coimbra.

703 **Nuno Gonçalves the great Portuguese painter of the fifteenth
century and his altar-piece for the convent of St. Vincent.**
Reynaldo dos Santos, translated by Lucy Norton. London:
Phaidon, 1955. 18p.
An account of the work, style and significance of Nuno Gonçalves, the 15th-
century court painter to Alfonso V of Portugal, paying particular attention to his
altar-piece which, as well as being one of the great 15th-century paintings of
Iberia, is of interest since it depicts the members of the Portuguese court and
church of his day.

704 **Portuguese 20th century artists: a biographical dictionary.**
Michael Tannock. Chichester, England: Phillimore, 1978. 188p.
This dictionary of Portuguese art between 1900 and 1974 provides biographical
information about 2,150 Portuguese artists, including details of their exhibitions,
and it concludes with ninety-four colour plates and 287 black-and-white plates.

705 **Portuguese art since 1910.**
Introduction by Helmut Wohl. London: Royal Academy of Arts
in collaboration with the Anglo-Portuguese Society and the
Calouste Gulbenkian Foundation, 1978. 178p.
The catalogue of an exhibition of 20th century Portuguese art held in September
1978. It includes a short introduction on the subject followed by illustrations of
the 162 paintings. The artists represented are Almada Negreiros, Fernando
Azevedo, Eduardo Batarda, Carlos Botelho, Lourdes Castro, Costa Pinheiro,
Cruzeiro Seixas, João Cutileiro, António da Costa, D'Assumpção, Mário Eloy,
Ana Hatherly, Hogan, Fernando Lanhas, Menez, Luis Noronha da Costa, Júlio
Pomar, Paula Rego, Júlio Resende, Santa Rita, Bartolomeu dos Santos, Ângelo

189

de Sousa, Amadeo de Souza Cardoso, Vespeira, Eduardo Viana and Vieira da Silva, and there are short accounts about the work of most of these artists.

Portuguese panorama.
See item no. 105.

Music and dance

706 Dances of Portugal.
Lucile Armstrong. London: Max Parrish, 1948. 2nd ed., 1950. 40p. map.
Describes the regional dances of Portugal together with their music and costumes.

707 Baroque organ cases of Portugal.
Carlos de Azevedo. Amsterdam, The Netherlands: Uitgeverij Frits Knuf, 1972. 130p. bibliog. (Bibliotheca Organologica, Vol. 50).
Following short chapters on organists, organ builders and the development of organ cases, this volume provides an illustrated catalogue of fifty-six major and positive Baroque organ cases in Portugal.

708 Feasts and folias: the dance in Portugal.
José Sasportes. *Dance Perspectives*, no. 42 (Summer 1970), 50p.
A history of Portuguese dance from the mediaeval period to the mid-20th century, concentrating mainly on the period 1450-1800.

The Azores: or Western Islands.
See item no. 286.

Primeiro esboço duma bibliografia musical portuguesa com uma breve notícia histórica da musica no nosso pais. (First sketch for a Portuguese musical bibliography with a short historical note on the music of our country.)
See item no. 767.

Folklore

709 **Portuguese folk-tales.**
Collected by [Zophima] Consiglieri Pedroso, translated by
Henriqueta Monteiro with an introduction by W. R. S. Ralston.
London: published for the Folk Lore Society by Elliot Stock, 1882.
124p.

A compilation of thirty folk-tales from Portugal collected by the author. The main theme represented is that of the supernatural spouse who is temporarily condemned to assume an unattractive appearance. The supplanted bride theme occurs four times and other themes include undeserved suffering and enchantment.

710 **Portugal: a book of folk-ways.**
Rodney Gallop. Cambridge, England: Cambridge University
Press, 1936. Reprinted 1961. 291p. bibliog.

This is an interesting general review of Portuguese folklore, written at a time when much of it still survived. It is divided into three parts. The first provides what the author calls a 'personally conducted tour of the country' touching on various aspects of its culture and environments. The second section on traditional beliefs and customs covers subjects such as: magic and superstition; birth, marriage and death; spring magic; summer saints; and the death of the year. The final section is on folk-music and literature, and includes chapters on folk-songs, ballads, the popular quatrain, the fado, and folk-tales and proverbs.

711 **Portuguese fairy tales.**
Maurice Michael, Pamela Michael, illustrated by Harry Toothill,
Ilse Toothill. London: Frederick Muller, 1965. 185p.

A collection of twenty-four Portuguese fairy tales. It illustrates how the Moors became the ogres of Portuguese folk-tales following the Arab conquest of the Iberian peninsula.

712 **Tales from the lands of nuts and grapes (Spanish and Portuguese folklore).**
Charles Sellers. London: Field & Tuer; Leadenhall Press, 1888.
178p.

A collection of twenty-one Iberian folk-tales. Unfortunately it gives no indication of the origins of the stories, but many are derived from the north of Portugal, where the author was born and grew up. This part of the country is especially rich in folklore, particularly concerning enchanted Moors and warlocks.

Cuisine

713 A Portuguese-American cookbook.
E. Donald Asselin.   Rutland, Vermont; Tokyo: Charles E.
Tuttle, 1966. 102p.

A cookery book of 218 recipes designed mainly for Americans of Portuguese descent. It is divided into sections on bread, rice dishes, sweetmeats, egg dishes, fish, meat, sauces, soups, salads and vegetables.

714 Good food from Spain and Portugal.
Susan Lowndes Marques.   London: Frederick Muller, 1956. 247p.

In this book of Spanish and Portuguese recipes the part on Portugal covers soups, eggs and sauces, fish and shellfish, meats, poultry and game, vegetables, desserts and cakes, and Portuguese drinks.

715 The home book of Portuguese cookery.
Maite Manjón.   London: Faber & Faber, 1974. 164p.

An extensive cookery book on Portuguese food divided into chapters on sauces and dressings, appetizers, soups, eggs, fish, meat, poultry and game, rice and vegetables, and desserts. In addition, there is a section on marketing, cooking and eating out in Portugal, and a short chapter on Portuguese wines by Jan Read.

716 The cooking of Spain and Portugal.
Tony Schmaeling.   Ware, Hertfordshire, England: Omega Books,
1983. 144p. map.

A collection of recipes divided into two parts: those from Spain and those from Portugal. It is illustrated with coloured photographs of the countries and the food, and the section on Portugal is divided into recipes on soups, vegetables, fish, poultry and game, meats, and desserts and cakes.

192

717 **The Oporto ladies' secrets.** *Os segredos das 'senhoras Inglesas' do Porto.*
Compiled by Angela Sellers, Julie Miles.   Oporto, Portugal: Fraternidade de Sameiro, 1981. 288p.

A collection of recipes and household hints started by the Ladies' Guild of Oporto in the 1960s and written in both English and Portuguese.

718 **Portuguese food.**
Carol Wright.   London: J. M. Dent, 1969. 214p. 10 maps.

This book includes over 200 recipes of Portuguese food anglicized for preparation in England, as well as a guide to where and what to eat in Portugal. It is divided into chapters on each of the main regions of the country, and within each of these it relates the topography and way of life of the people to their food.

719 **Self-catering in Portugal: making the most of local food and drink.**
Carol Wright.   London, Sydney: Croom Helm, 1986. 132p. bibliog.

This guide provides details of the local fruit, vegetables, meat and fish available at different seasons in Portugal, and includes a variety of regional menus. There are also chapters on what it is important to bring with you when self-catering in Portugal, and on wines and spirits. It concludes with a short glossary.

Mass Media and the Press

General

720 **Arquivos do Centro Cultural Portugues.** (Archives of the
Portuguese Cultural Centre.)
Paris: Fundação Calouste Gulbenkian, 1969- . annual.
This annual cultural volume publishes studies on the history, literature and arts of
Portugal, most of which are in Portuguese. It is in three parts. The first comments
on academic studies, the second provides details of notes and documents of
historical use, and the third is an annotated bibliography of material on
Portuguese cultural history.

721 **Elementos para a historia da imprensa periódica Portuguesa (1641-
1821).** (Elements for the history of the Portuguese periodical press
(1641-1821).)
Alfredo da Cunha.   Lisbon: Academia das Ciências, 1941. 324p.
A Portuguese-language history of periodical publications between 1641 and 1821.

722 **The press and the rebirth of Iberian democracy.**
Edited by Kenneth Maxwell.   Westpoint, Connecticut; London:
Greenwood Press, 1983. 198p. bibliog. (Contributions in Political
Science, no. 99, Global Perspectives in History and Politics).
A collection of eight papers resulting from a conference at Columbia University
sponsored by the Graduate School of Journalism and the Institute of Latin
American and Iberian Studies. While most of the papers discuss Portugal to some
extent, the following three are directly concerned with the country and its press:
'Newspapers and democracy in Portugal: the role of market theatre', by Jorge
Braga de Macedo; 'The Portuguese media in transition', by Jean Seton and Ben

194

Pimlott; and 'Democracy and authoritarianism and the role of the media in Portugal, 1974-75', by Francisco Pinto Balsemão. Another recent study of the Portuguese mass media is provided by 'A frustrated fourth estate: Portugal's post-revolutionary mass media' in *Journalism Monographs* (1984, no. 87 p. 1-53) by Warren K. Agee and Nelson Traquina. This article outlines the history of the press in Portugal and looks at the changes which followed the revolution of 1974, with an analysis of the press, radio and television.

723　**Portugal and the press 1961-1972.**
Lisbon: Panorama Books, 1973. 586p.

A collection of press articles from a wide range of international newspapers about Portugal in the period 1961-72. They are mainly concerned with Portugal's African wars. It is prefaced with the following statement: 'Since 1961 Portugal has proved a fruitful topic in the world press. Throughout those twelve years there has been a constant flood of criticism, baseless charges, objective analyses and some praise. We have now brought together some of these many articles, our hope being to contribute to a better understanding of the problems at stake. In so doing, we have not forgotten that we are Portuguese ourselves.'

Newspapers

724　**A Capital.** (The Capital.)
Lisbon: Empresa Pública dos Jornais Notícias e Capital, 1968- .
daily.

A forty page independent Lisbon daily evening tabloid concentrating on current affairs. It has a circulation of around 40,000.

725　**O Comércio do Porto.** (The Commerce of Oporto.)
Oporto, Portugal: O Comércio do Porto SARL, 1854- . daily.

One of the three main morning papers of Oporto, it has a circulation of approximately 50,000 and normally consists of fifty-six pages covering national, international, regional, local and sporting issues, with a liberal tendency.

726　**Correio da Manhã.** (The Morning Post.)
Lisbon: Correio da Manhã, 1979- . daily.

An independent morning newspaper with a circulation figure of 50,000.

727　**O Dia.** (The Day.)
Lisbon: O Dia, 1975- . daily.

A Lisbon morning newspaper. Its circulation is around 46,800.

Mass Media and the Press. Newspapers

728   **O Diário.** (The Daily.)
Lisbon: Editorial Caminho, 1976- . daily.
A Lisbon morning newspaper of between twenty-four and thirty-two pages covering all subjects from a communist viewpoint. Its circulation averages 37,000.

729   **Diário de Lisboa.** (Lisbon Daily.)
Lisbon: Diário de Lisboa, 1921- . daily.
An independent Lisbon tabloid evening daily paper distributed throughout the country. It covers general political, economic, labour and sporting information, and also has weekly supplements on literature and weekend events. Circulation is approximately 30,000.

730   **Diário de Notícias.** (News Daily.)
Lisbon: Empresa Publica dos Jornais Notícias e Capital, 1864- . daily.
A Lisbon morning paper with a circulation figure of around 55,000, which was nationalized following the revolution in 1974. It has a long tradition and gave its name to the street where it was born. In 1982 it introduced a photocomposition system, and in 1984 its format was changed to tabloid.

731   **Diário Popular.** (Popular Daily.)
Lisbon: Empresa Publica do Jornal Diário Popular, 1942- . daily.
A Lisbon evening paper, nationalized following the revolution in 1974. It is a politically independent daily tabloid of thirty-six pages or more, mainly covering Portuguese and international news, and current affairs. It has a circulation of around 50,000.

732   **Jornal de Notícias.** (The Paper of News.)
Oporto, Portugal: Jornal de Notícias, 1888- . daily.
The biggest of the three main morning papers of Oporto generally supporting the left. It has a circulation figure of 79,466.

733   **Notícias da Tarde.** (Evening News.)
Oporto, Portugal: Empresa de Jornal de Notícias, 1981- . daily.
An evening paper from Oporto.

734   **O Primeiro de Janeiro.** (The First of January.)
Oporto, Portugal: O Primeiro de Janeiro, 1868- . daily.
An independent liberal/right-wing morning paper from Oporto with a circulation figure of 40,293.

735   **A Tarde.** (The Afternoon.)
Lisbon: A Tarde, 1979- . daily
A small Lisbon evening paper with a circulation of 32,500.

English-language periodicals

736 **British bulletin of publications on Latin America, the Caribbean, Portugal and Spain.**
London: Hispanic and Luso-Brazilian Council, 1949- . semi-annual.
Lists recently-published material in English on Portugal and the other regions mentioned in the title. Each book mentioned is provided with a short annotation and a selection of periodical articles is also included. This is one of the best sources of accessible information on recent publications about Portugal.

737 **Bulletin of Hispanic Studies.**
Liverpool, England: Liverpool University Press, 1923- . quarterly.
Originally entitled *Bulletin of Spanish Studies* this journal is devoted to the study of the languages, literature and civilization of Spain, Portugal and Latin America.

738 **Iberian Studies.**
Keele, England: University of Keele, 1972- . bi-annual.
A journal concentrating on the anthropology, economics, geography, history, politics and sociology of Portugal and Spain.

739 **Lisbon Letter.**
Coggeshall, England: Hawkins Publishers, 1983- . bi-monthly.
A bi-monthly economic newsletter published in English and Portuguese.

740 **Luso-Brazilian Review.**
Madison, Wisconsin: University of Wisconsin Press, 1964- . semi-annual.
A journal concerned with a wide range of affairs related to Portugal and Brazil, but concentrating on literature and language. It is divided into sections on articles, review articles, reviews, news and notes, research in progress and books received.

741 **Portuguese Studies.**
Edited by the Department of Portuguese, King's College London.
London: Modern Humanities Research Association, 1985- . annual.
An annual journal devoted to the literature, culture and history of Portugal, Brazil and the Portuguese speaking countries of Africa. It concludes with a section of reviews and a list of bibliographic and research information.

742   **Vida Hispánica: Journal of the Association of Teachers of Spanish and Portuguese.**
York, England: Association of Teachers of Spanish and Portuguese, 1953- . 3 times per year.
A journal on all aspects of Hispanic civilization, language-teaching, and linguistics written in English, Spanish or Portuguese.

743   **Portuguese Studies Newsletter.**
Edited by Douglas L. Wheeler.   Durham, New Hampshire: International Conference Group on Modern Portugal. Spring 1976- . irregular.
The newsletter of the International Conference Group on Modern Portugal which includes details of the Group's activities and also bibliographical material on Portugal and the Portuguese-speaking countries of the world.

Bibliographies and Catalogues

744 **Bibliografia geral portuguesa: seculo XV** (General Portuguese Bibliography: 15th century.)
Academia das Ciências, Lisboa.   Lisbon: Imprensa Nacional de Lisboa, 1941-44. 2 vols.
A wide-ranging bibliography of 15th-century works pertaining to Portugal. Many of the manuscripts are illustrated. Volume Two includes works of Portuguese authors published outside Portugal prior to the end of the 15th century.

745 **Bibliografia hidrológica do Império português.** (Hydrological bibliography of the Portuguese Empire.)
Luis de Menezes Acciaiuoli.   Lisbon: Direcção Geral de Minas e Serviços Geológicos, 1949-50. 2 vols.
A hydrological bibliography of Portugal, subdivided by chronological period.

746 **Geologia de Portugal: ensaio bibliográfico.** (Geology of Portugal: bibliographical essay.)
Luis de Menezes Acciaiuoli.   Lisbon: Direcção Geral de Minas e Serviços Geológicos, 1957. 3 vols.
A bibliography of the geology of Portugal, subdivided by subject matter.

747 **Bibliography of Hispanic women writers.**
Norma Alarcón, Sylvia Kossnar.   Bloomington, Indiana: Chicago-Riqueño Studies, 1980. 86p.
A bibliography of Hispanic women writers which also includes some Portuguese material, particularly relating to Maria Isabel Barreno, Maria Teresa Horta, and Maria Velho da Costa. There is a short index by chronology.

Bibliographies and Catalogues

748 **Bibliografia das bibliografias portuguesas.** (Bibliography of
Portuguese bibliographies.)
António Anselmo. Lisbon: Oficinas Gráficas da Biblioteca
Nacional, 1923. 158p.
A collection of 1,030 entries for general, special and serial bibliographies on
Portugal published prior to 1923. There are author, subject and archive indexes.

749 **Bibliografia das obras impressas em Portugal no século XVI.**
(Bibliography of works published in Portugal in the 16th century.)
António Joaquim Anselmo. Lisbon: Oficinas Gráficas da
Biblioteca Nacional, 1926. 367p.
An annotated bibliography of works published in Portugal in the 16th century
including 1,277 items in the main text and thirty in a supplement. Biographical
details are given of most of the authors and there is an author and title index.

750 **Portuguese bibliography.**
Aubrey F. G. Bell. Oxford: Oxford University Press, London:
Humphrey Milford, 1922. 381p. (Hispanic Notes and Monographs,
Bibliography Series).
A bibliography mainly relating to Portuguese literature divided into sections on
general works, texts, anthologies, folklore and popular poetry, Portuguese
language, dictionaries and authors, of which the last section is by far the largest.
It includes few works in English and there is no index. It was intended to
accompany the author's *Portuguese literature*, (q.v.).

751 **Portugal in Rymer: a chronological reference index to all documents
relating to Portugal or to Portuguese affairs in Rymer's 'Foedera',
based upon T. D. Hardy's 'Syllabus to Rymer'.**
William A. Bentley. Streatham, England: no publisher, 1926.
38p.
A chronological précis of documents dating from 1200 to 1653, relating to
Portugal.

752 **Bibliografia e Informação** (Bibliography and Information.)
Lisbon: Centro de Investigação Pedagógica, Fundação Calouste
Gulbenkian, 1972-73. biannually.
A bibliography of material held by the Departamento de Documentação e
Informação of the Fundação Calouste Gulbenkian in Lisbon. It is broadly divided
into sections on philosophy, psychology, sociology and education. From Vol. 7,
1968 there is an author index. Each volume also includes some information about
the activities of the Departamento de Documentação e Informação. The
bibliography was previously entitled *Boletim Bibliográfico e Informativo*
(Bibliographical and Informative Bulletin) and appeared from 1964-71 under that
name.

753   **Boletim Bibliográfico.** (Bibliographical Bulletin.)
Lisbon: Fundação Calouste Gulbenkian, Biblioteca Geral, Nov.
1976- . monthly (except Aug. Sept.).

A monthly bibliography of new material held by the Library of the Fundação
Calouste Gulbenkian, which concentrates mainly on a wide range of aspects of
art. It is divided into sections on books and periodical articles, and although
including material from all over the world there are several useful references on
Portugal.

754   **Boletim Internacional de Bibliografia Luso-Brasileira** (International
Bulletin of Luso-Brazilian Bibliography.)
Lisbon: Fundação Calouste Gulbenkian, Jan-Mar 1960-73.
quarterly.

A register of publications in books and journals on Portugal and Brazil, published
throughout the world. It is divided into main sections on the land and the people,
language, literature, fine arts, history, society, politics, economy, law, mediaeval
science, research documents and culture, and unclassified studies. Each volume
also includes a range of appendixes and an index, and four special numbers have
been concerned specifically with providing a bibliography of the history of the
great sea routes.

755   **Descriptive list of the State Papers Portugal 1661-1780 in the Public
Record Office London.**
Prepared by C. R. Boxer, J. C. Aldridge.   Lisbon: Academia das
Ciências de Lisboa, with the collaboration of the British Academy,
the PRO, 1979. 2 vols.

Provides a list of the State Papers Portugal (S.P. 89/. . .) in the Public Record
Office, London, with Volume One referring to the period 1661-1723 and Volume
Two to 1724-65. It begins with the circumstances surrounding the marriage of
Charles II to Catherine of Braganza in 1661 and ends with the arrest and
imprisonment of Lt. James MacNamara R. N. who went to Lisbon with the
intention of challenging Capt. Roberts in the Portuguese naval service to a duel in
1765. There is unfortunately no index of subjects or names.

756   **Catalogue of books in the library of the British Association, Oporto.**
British Association (Oporto).   Oporto, Portugal: Tipografia
Nunes, 1925-6   2 vols.

An alphabetical catalogue of books in the British Association Library in Oporto
in the 1920s, divided into two parts. The first is on general literature and the
second on fiction. It provides a few references for books on Portugal, but most of
the material is that which one would expect to have been of interest to British
people living overseas at this time.

757 **Special Anglo-Portuguese collection: books and periodicals.**
British Council Libraries in Portugal. Lisbon: British Council
Libraries in Portugal, 1958. 69p.

This list of books and periodicals held in the British Council Library in Lisbon is
divided into sections on English works on Portugal; English translations of
Portuguese works; Portuguese works on Britain; and Portuguese translations of
English works.

758 **Canning House Library, Luso-Brazilian Council, London: author
catalogue A-Z and subject catalogue A-Z.**
Boston, Massachusetts: G. K. Hall, 1967. 2 vols. First supplement,
1973. 288p.

Reproduces the card catalogues of the materials held by the Luso-Brazilian
Council in the Canning House Library, London. It provides a wealth of material
on Portugal classified by subject and author.

759 **Emerging nationalism in Portuguese Africa: a bibliography of
documentary ephemera through 1965.**
Ronald H. Chilcote. Stanford, California: Hoover Institute on
War, Revolution and Peace, Stanford University, 1969. 114p.

A thorough bibliography on nationalism and related subjects in the Portuguese
African territories. It is divided into sections on general Portuguese Africa;
Angola and Cabinda; Portuguese Guiné, Cape Verde, São Tomé and Príncipe;
Moçambique; United Nations documents on Portuguese Africa; and joint
publications research service documents. There are no indexes.

760 **Bibliografia de textos medievais portugueses publicados.**
(Bibliography of published mediaeval Portuguese texts.)
Maria Adelaide Valle Cintra. Lisbon: Centro de Estudos
Filológicos, 1951. 40p.

Provides details of mediaeval Portuguese texts that have appeared in published
form. Reprinted from *Boletim de Filologia*, vol. XII (1951).

761 **A alimentação do povo português: bibliografia prefaciada e
coordenada.** (The food of the Portuguese people: prefaced and
coordinated bibliography.)
Antonio Augusto Mendes Corrêa. Lisbon: Centro de Estudos
Demográficos, 1951. 251p.

A bibliography on the food and alimentation of the Portuguese people, preceded
by a short introduction on the history of research into the subject and its findings.
The bibliography provides a survey of the findings of each publication mentioned.

762 **Diccionario bibliographico portuguez: estudos de Innocencio
Francisco da Silva applicaveis a Portugal e ao Brasil, continuados e
ampliados por Pedro V. de Brito Aranha, revistos por Gomes de
Brito e Álvaro Neves.** (Portuguese bibliographical dictionary:
studies of Innocencio Francisco da Silva related to Portugal and
Brazil, continued and amplified by Pedro V. de Brito Aranha, and
revised by Gomes de Brito and Alvaro Neves.)
Lisbon: Imprensa Nacional, 1858-1923. 22 vols.

A bio-bibliography of Portuguese books prior to the 19th century providing
detailed information on authors and their works.

763 **Latin America, Spain and Portugal: an annotated bibliography of
paperback books.**
Compiled by Georgette M. Dorn.   Washington, DC: Library of
Congress, 1971. 180p. (Hispanic Foundation Bibliographical
Series, no. 13).

An annotated bibliography of 1,512 paperback books on Latin America, Spain
and Portugal. It also includes a section on dictionaries, grammars, readers and
textbooks, and there is a list of publishers and addresses. Each section is
organized by author and there is a short subject index.

764 **Catalog of Luso-Brazilian material in the University of New Mexico
libraries.**
Compiled by Theresa Gillett, Helen McIntyre.   Metuchen, New
Jersey: Scarecrow Press, 1970. 961p.

A catalogue of the 10,085 items in the Luso-Brazilian collection of the University
of New Mexico library, about half of which are on Portuguese subjects. It is
divided into main sections: general; language; literature; history and allied
subjects; fine arts; philosophy; religion; education; social sciences; science and
technology; and miscellany. The alphabetical index is primarily an author index.

765 **Modern Iberian language and literature: a bibliography of homage
studies.**
Herbert H. Golden, Seymour O. Simches.   Cambridge,
Massachusetts: Harvard University Press, 1958. Reprinted,
Millwood, New York: Klaus Reprints, 1971. 184p.

A bibliography of material on Catalan, Portuguese and Spanish that has appeared
in various *Festschriften*. It includes 141 items on Galician and Portuguese
language, 120 items on Galician and Portuguese literature, 8 items on Portuguese
and Galician folklore, and 20 items on literary and intellectual relations in
Portugal. There is an author index.

Bibliographies and Catalogues

766 **Portuguese-speaking Africa 1900-1979: a select bibliography. Volume I: Angola.**
Susan Jean Gowan.   Braamfontein, South Africa: South African Institute of International Affairs, 1982. 346p. map.
(Bibliographical Series, no. 9).
A predominantly Portuguese and English bibliography providing 2,329 references to material on Angola. There are four identical sections for pre- and post-independent Angola: a general section, which includes bibliographies; politics and government, which includes the liberation movements and the civil war; foreign relations, negotiated by Portugal during the pre-independence period; and all aspects of economics and development including agriculture. There is an author index and a subject guide.

767 **Primeiro esboço duma bibliografia musical portuguesa com uma breve notícia histórica da musica no nosso pais.** (First sketch for a Portuguese musical bibliography with a short historical note on the music of our country.)
Bertino Daciano R. S. Guimarâes.   Oporto, Portugal: Imprensa Portuguesa, 1947. 173p.
An introductory bibliography on Portuguese music organized alphabetically by author.

768 **An annotated bibliography of publications relating to the Portuguese Revolution of the 25th April 1974 held in the Sheffield University Library.**
Robert Howes.   Sheffield, England: Sheffield University, 1976. 99p.
An annotated bibliography of 267 books and pamphlets mostly published in the immediate aftermath of April 1974. Following an introductory essay the work is divided into twenty-two subject categories and there is an author index.

769 **The Portuguese Pamphlets Microfilm 82/5800 MicRR: introduction and comprehensive guide to contents.**
Library of Congress Preservation Microfilming Office. Washington, DC: Library of Congress, 1983. [not paginated].
A detailed guide to the Library of Congress Portuguese Pamphlets Collection. The introduction describes the contents and organization of the collection, which was brought together mainly by António Augusto de Carvalho and consists of 3,602 items. This is followed by an article by Américo da Costa Ramalho on the Portuguese Pamphlets which was originally published in *The Library of Congress Quarterly Journal*, vol. 20, no. 8 (June 1963). There are two summary guides to the subject categories and reels, then the bulk of the volume lists principal bibliographic data for each of the 3,602 items.

770 **Revolution in Portugal: 1974-1976 a bibliography.**
William Lomax. Durham, New Hampshire: University of New
Hampshire, International Conference Group on Modern Portugal,
1978. 37p.
An alphabetical bibliography of works in a variety of languages, but mainly
Portuguese and English, on the Portuguese revolution of 1974. It concludes with a
list of Portuguese newspapers and magazines.

771 **The Portuguese manuscripts collection of the Library of Congress: a
guide.**
Compiled by Christopher C. Lund, Mary Ellis Kahler, edited by
Mary Ellis Kahler. Washington, DC: Library of Congress, 1980.
187p. bibliog.
A annotated listing of 537 Portuguese manuscripts in the Library of Congress.
Three main subjects are represented: Sebastianism; Luís de Camões; and the
military orders of knighthood. There is an index providing names of persons,
places and some titles.

772 **Early Portuguese books 1489-1600 in the library of His Majesty the
King of Portugal.**
H. M. King Manuel [II of Portugal]   London: Maggs Bros., 1929-
35. 3 vols. bibliog.
Describes the early books and manuscripts of Portugal in the library of Manuel II
relating to the period of the great discoveries. Volume One, concerning the
period 1489-1539, describes thirty-eight books, one manuscript and one
illuminated miniature; Volume Two treats a further eighty publications up to
1569; and Volume Three describes 294 other works produced prior to 1600. The
text is in English and Portuguese.

773 **Manual bibliográfico portuguez de livros raros, classicos e curiosos
revisto e prefaciado pelo Camillo Castello Branco. Catálogo
descritivo em ordem alfabético sob autores, com notas biográficos
descrevendo em detalhe suas obras com anotacoes criticas, desde o
século dezesseis até o meio do século decimo nono.** (Portuguese
bibliographical manual of rare, classical and unusual books
reviewed and prefaced by Camillo Castello Branco. Descriptive
catalogue in alphabetical order by author, with biographical notes
describing in detail their works with critical annotations, from the
16th century to the middle of the 19th century.)
Ricardo Pinto de Mattos.   Amsterdam, The Netherlands: Gérard
Th. van Heusden, 1971. 582p.
A bibliography of old and rare Portuguese books listed by author, also giving
brief biographical details of the authors.

774 **The Portuguese in the United States: a bibliography.**
Leo Pap. New York: Center for Migration Studies, 1976. 80p.

A thorough listing of books and articles accessible in libraries in the USA which make some explicit reference to the Portuguese element in that country. Coverage extends from the 15th century to the present, and from New England to Hawaii. The first part provides a listing of items of reference to the Portuguese in the United States subdivided on a regional basis. The second part concerns background material on the Portuguese in Portugal. The volume contains 800 references, but there is no index.

775 **Bibliografia analítica de etnografia portuguesa.** (Analytical bibliography of Portuguese ethnography.)
Benjamin Enes Pereira. Lisbon: Imprensa Portuguesa, 1965. 670p.

An annotated bibliography of 3,834 items on the ethnography of Portugal, the vast majority of which are in Portuguese. There is an author index only.

776 **Periódicos portugueses de ciências, letras e artas.** (Portuguese periodicals on science, letters and arts.)
Lisbon: Instituto para a Alta Cultura, Serviço de Inventariação da Bibliografia Científica, 1946. 28p.

A list of Portuguese periodicals subdivided by subject matter.

777 **Portugal and the War of the Spanish Succession: a bibliography with some diplomatic documents.**
Edgar Prestage. Cambridge, England: Cambridge University Press, 1938. 42p.

A short bibliography on Portugal's role in the War of the Spanish Succession, together with translations of six related diplomatic documents from the beginning of the 18th century.

778 **Brazil, Portugal, and other Portuguese-speaking lands: a list of books primarily in English.**
Francis M. Rogers, David T. Haberly. Cambridge, Massachusetts: Harvard University Press, 1968. 73p.

A list of the books, mostly in English, on Brazil and Portugal which were published between 1945 and 1968. The Portuguese section is divided into the following categories: general descriptions of Portugal; general background books; The Portuguese language; early Portugal to 1640; Bragança Portugal (1640-1910); Republican Portugal since 1910; the Inquisition; general books about the expansion beyond the seas; Prince Henry the Navigator and the times in which he lived; the Portuguese in Africa; the Portuguese in South and East Asia; the Portuguese in North America; the Portuguese in Insulindia and the Pacific; the overseas provinces yesterday and today; books about literature and writers; literary texts in translation; and the other arts.

779 **Bibliography of Goa and the Portuguese in India.**
Henry Scholberg, with the collaboration of Archana Ashok
Kakodker, Carmo Azevedo. New Delhi: Promilla, 1982. 413p.

A bibliography about Goa and the Portuguese in India divided into sections on
general works, bibliography and other sources, history, biography, early historical
accounts, the people, government and politics, humanities, journals and religious
life. There is an author and subject index, and the volume concludes with five
essays on Indo-Portuguese history by M. G. L. Alvares Meneses, E. R. Hambye,
Archana Ashok Kakodker, Lambert Mascarenhas and Henry Scholberg.

780 **Manuscritos portugueses ou referentes a Portugal da Biblioteca
Nacional de Paris.** (Portuguese manuscripts or those referring to
Portugal in the National Library of Paris.)
Joaquim Veríssimo Serrão. Paris: Fundação Calouste Gulbenkian
Centro Cultural Português, 1969. 187p.

An account and listing of Portuguese manuscripts and those referring to Portugal
in the National Library in Paris.

781 **Spain.**
Graham J. Shields. Oxford; Santa Barbara, California; Denver,
Colorado: Clio Press, 1985. 340p. map.

A comprehensive bibliography of Spain, which also includes eighty-eight items
concerning Portugal.

782 **The Jews in Spain and Portugal: a bibliography.**
Robert Singerman. New York, London: Garland, 1975. 364p.

A bibliography of a wide range of published material pertaining to the Jewish
presence in Spain and Portugal from antiquity to the present day. It includes 839
references on Portugal and is divided into sections mainly in a chronological
order. There is an author index.

783 **Spain, Portugal and Latin America.**
Utrecht, The Netherlands: Library of Utrecht University in
cooperation with the Spanish, Portuguese and Ibero-American
Institute, Utrecht University, 1965. 70p.

A bibliographical catalogue of the collection of works in the field of Ibero-
American literature and of works relating to the Spanish and Portuguese speaking
countries, published in Eastern Europe and the property of the Spanish,
Portuguese and Ibero-American Institute of Utrecht University. It is divided into
main sections on bibliography; philosophy; history; history of civilization and arts;
linguistics; literature; legal, political and economic studies; geography and travel;
and ethnography, archaeology and folklore. There is no index and this severely
limits its use.

784 **Subsidíos para a bibliografia da história local portuguesa.** (Material for a bibliography of Portuguese local history.)
Lisbon: Biblioteca Nacional, 1933. 425p.

A bibliography on Portuguese local history. Following short sections on the theory of local history and general works, the bibliography is divided up on a regional basis, and provides details of local monographs relating to individual towns and villages. Most of the works are in Portuguese and there are name and place indexes.

785 **Short-title catalogue of Portuguese books printed before 1601 now in the British Museum.**
Henry Thomas. London: British Museum, 1940. 43p.

A new edition of the Portuguese section of the combined short catalogues of the British Museum's collection of Portuguese works published unofficially in 1926 together with the additions to date.

786 **A catalog of the William B. Greenlee Collection of Portuguese history and literature and the Portuguese materials in the Newberry Library.**
Compiled by Doris Varner Welsh. Chicago: Newberry Library, 1953. 342p.

A catalogue of the extensive Greenlee Collection of Portuguese material divided into sections on general reference works, Portugal's political history, its ecclesiastical history, its economic history, its military history, its naval history, its social history, its cultural history, its local history, and the Portuguese colonies. It provides a very useful bibliography of material on Portugal published before the 1950s and there is an author and title index.

787 **Latin America, Spain and Portugal: a selected and annotated bibliographical guide to books published in the United States, 1954-1974.**
A. Curtis Wilgus. Metuchen, New Jersey; London: Scarecrow Press, 1977. 910p.

An annotated bibliography of works published in the USA between 1954 and 1974 on Latin America, Spain and Portugal, subdivided by regions and countries. The section on Portugal includes seventy-six items subdivided into four sections: description, travel, geography; history, government, foreign relations; economy, society, culture; and biographies, autobiographies, memoirs. There is an index of names.

Area handbook for Portugal.
See item no. 16.

History of Portugal.
See item no. 174.

English translations from the Spanish and Portuguese to the year 1700: an annotated catalogue of the extant printed versions (excluding dramatic adaptations).
See item no. 610.

Index

The index is a single alphabetical sequence of authors (personal and corporate), titles of publications and subjects. Index entries refer both to the main items and to other works mentioned in the notes to each item. Title entries are in italics. Numeration refers to the items as numbered.

American Air Force Base, Lajes Field
120
Amis, K. 611
Amorim Girão, A. de 46
Ancient languages of Spain and
Portugal 363
And yet they came: Portuguese
immigration from the Azores to the
United States 348
Andersen, Hans Christian 69
Andrada, Ruy Freyre de 238
Andrade, J. M. 554
André Simon's wines of the world 524,
530, 543
Angiography 587
Anglican Church 386, 394
Anglo-Brazilian Society, London 259
Anglicans abroad: the history of the
Chaplaincy and Church of St.
James at Oporto 386
Anglo-Portuguese 289
Anglo-Portuguese alliance 450
Anglo-Portuguese alliance 1373-1973
452
Anglo-Portuguese Treaty of Alliance
(1373) 448, 450-452
Angola 268, 312-313, 322, 327, 330,
336, 339, 612, 759
bibliographies 766
guerrilla war 339
nationalism 330
Portuguese settlement 313
revolution 330
slavery 268
Angola under the Portuguese: the myth
and the reality 313
Angolan revolution: volume 1, the
anatomy of an explosion (1950-
1962); volume 2, exile politics and
guerilla warfare (1962-1976) 330
Anne of Austria 252
Annotated bibliography of publications
relating to the Portuguese
Revolution of the 25th April 1974
held in the Sheffield University
Library 768
Anselmo, A. J. 748-749
Anthologies 610, 614-617, 621-623,
630-632, 634
bibliographies 750
Anthology of modern Portuguese and
Brazilian prose 630

Anthropology 341, 400
periodicals 738
Antilla 225
Antiquities 93, 259
António, M. 246
Antunes, A. Lobo 612
Anuário Estatística 571
April 25, 1974 174, 296, 303, 413, 415-
440, 465, 505, 513, 567, 613, 624,
721, 768, 770
Arabic influence on Portuguese
language 365
Aranha, P. V. de Brito 762
Araújo, N. de 1
Arbitration Agreement (1904) 450
Archaeological sites 159, 161
Lisbon 158
Archaeology 121, 157-161
Bell Beaker culture 158
Castro culture 157
Celtic Iron Age 161
citânias 159
East Africa 387
Lisbon 158
Palaeolithic 161
photographs 160
Roman bridges 159
Roman temples 159
Roman towns 159
Spain 157-159, 161
Architecture 21, 25, 34, 93, 115, 123,
156, 160, 590, 689, 691-697
Azores 76
Baroque 694-695
civil 692
history 692-695, 697
Lisbon 18
Manueline 693-695
military 692
Moorish influence 697
Mudejar 697
Neo-classical 694
photographs 692
plain 693
religious 692
Renaissance 695
Rococo 694-695
Arcos, J. P. d' 617
Area handbook for Portugal 16
Armed forces 16, 420, 434
Armed Forces Movement 419, 423,
425, 428, 434, 440

Armstrong, A. Oursler 380
Armstrong, L. 706
Armstrong Jr., M. F. 380
Army
  18th century 83
  19th century 266, 273, 275, 279, 283
  British 96, 272, 277, 455
  French 271-272, 280, 282
  uniforms 275, 283
Arquivos do Centro Cultural Portugues
  720
Arrábida, Serra da 91
Arraiolos 91
  rugs 690
Arrifana 18
Arriscado Nunes, J. 401
Art and architecture in Spain and
  Portugal and their American
  dominions 1500 to 1800 694
Art of Portugal 1500-1800 689
Art in Spain and Portugal 692
Arts 16, 22, 25-27, 93, 139, 150, 155-
  156, 162, 220, 326, 442, 682-708,
  720
  architecture 21, 25, 34, 93, 115, 123,
    156, 160, 590, 689, 691-697
  bibliographies 753-754, 764
  drawings 590
  history 689
  influence on Japanese civilization
    442
  music 21, 34, 81, 706, 708, 710, 767
  painting 21, 123, 590, 689, 692, 694,
    697-700, 702-705
  periodicals 720
  rural 81
  sculpture 34, 689, 692
  Spain 26
  video 701
Ashoff, G. 497
Ashok Kakodker, A. 779
Asia 163, 165, 181, 211, 492
  discoveries in 228, 329
  missionaries in 395
Asselin, E. D. 713
Assumpção, D' 705
Asta 126
Ataide, A. de 323, 490
Aticá 666
Atkinson, W. C. 21, 162, 449, 636-637
Atlantic islands: Madeira, the Azores
  and the Cape Verdes in seventeenth

century commerce and navigation
  248
Atlantic islanders of the Azores and
  Madeiras 32
Atlantic Ocean
  discovery of 212, 216, 222, 225, 228,
    329
Atlantic warfare
  history 456
Atlas de Portugal 46
Atlases 46
Atomic energy 575
  directories 575
Aubertin, J. J. 638-639
Augusto França, J. 699
Australia
  discovery of 223
Auto da Alma 672
Automobile Club of Portugal 52
Avelos Naar, M. E. de 360
Aveiro 69, 77, 91, 119, 565
Aviation 37, 554
Axelson, E. 204, 312
Axem 337
Azevedo, C. 779
Azevedo, C. de 21, 707
Azevedo, F. 705
Azevedo, M. M. 350
Azores 8-9, 32, 38-39, 54, 107, 120,
  217, 229, 248, 348, 456, 627
  17th century 248
  19th century 76, 78, 286, 441
  administration 38
  agriculture 76, 125
  architecture 76
  beetles 61
  birds 61
  botany 61
  British maritime air bases 456
  butterflies 61
  climate 78, 120, 125
  commerce 38, 76
  culture 32
  discovery of 212, 229
  economy 9, 32, 133, 286
  education 32
  emigration 32, 348
  exploration 39
  fauna 38, 61, 125
  Fayal 515
  flora 38, 61, 125
  geography 76, 286

Bragança (Braganza), Catherine of 247, 249, 258, 755
Bragança (Braganza), House of 168
Bragança - Cunha, V. de 164
Branco, A. de Castelo 31
Brandão, M. F. 341
Brandy 540-541
Branner, J. C. 388
Brass, D. 6, 631
Brazão, E. 450
Brazil 34, 165, 174, 263, 317, 323-324, 449, 494, 740-741, 754
  16th century 323
  18th century 331
  bibliographies 754, 778
  colonization 325, 329
  culture 325
  discovery of 212, 217, 221, 225, 229
  economy 331
  granting of independence 317, 329
  literature 630
  periodicals 740
  Portuguese emigration to 344
  relations with Portugal, 19th century 287, 316, 325, 329, 331
  slaves 325
  social history 325
  sugar 329
  trade with Portugal 187, 331
Brazil, Portugal, and other Portuguese-speaking lands: a list of books primarily in English 778
Brazilian-Portuguese language 21, 367
Brazilian studies 449
Brearley, M. 385
Brettel, C. S. 343, 420
Bridge, A. 124
Britain
  commercial relations with Portugal 182, 251
  maritime air bases, Azores 456
  reaction to Portuguese slave trade 268
  relations with Portugal 167, 180, 187, 295, 386, 448-457
  relations with Portugal, 17th century 445, 448
  relations with Portugal, 18th century 251, 448
  relations with Portugal, 19th century 70, 268, 331, 448
  relations with Portugal, mediaeval 200

trade with Portugal 182, 484, 487, 495, 521, 545, 548
trade with Portugal, 18th century 75, 251, 494, 525
trade with Portugal, 19th century 68, 70, 534
treaties with Portugal 180, 450-452, 456
Britannia sickens: Sir Arthur Wellesley and the convention of Cintra 271
British army 95-96, 272, 277-278, 455
British Association (Oporto) 756
British Association Library, Oporto 756
British batallion at Oporto: with adventures, anecdotes, and exploits in Holland; at Waterloo; and in the expedition to Portugal 277
British bulletin of publications on Latin America, the Caribbean, Portugal and Spain 736
British Community Council of Lisbon 451
British contributions to Portuguese and Brazilian studies 449
British Council Libraries in Portugal 757
British Council Library, Lisbon 757
British exporters 484, 487
British Factory in Lisbon, and its closing stages ensuing upon the Treaty of 1810 457
British Factory Oporto 546
British government 484
British Factory, Lisbon 457
British Factory House, Oporto 386, 525, 528-529, 546, 548
British Museum 223, 684, 785
British Museum Library 457
British navy 102
British Overseas Trade Board 458
British Port Wine Shippers 528
British residents 18, 521-522, 525, 546, 548
Brito, Bernardo Gomes de 209, 493
Brito, G. de 762
Broadbent, M. 538
Brochado, C. 212-213
Brockwell, C. 165
Bromley, W. 77
Brooks, L. 146
Brooks, M. E. 242

218

223

226

227

Economy *continued*
  foreign payments 472, 489
  forty families oligarchy 466
  impact of return migrants 343, 345
  impact of Catholic Church 382
  and imperial expansion 469
  implications for USA 489
  and industrial development 473
  inflation 475
  influence of USA 462
  investment 472
  Madeira 13, 17, 19, 23-24, 32, 106,
    133
  May 1978 stabilization programme
    479
  monetary policy 475
  national income 472
  planning 470
  and population 472
  public finance 471-474, 475
  regional 478
  role of colonies 320
  Salazar régime 292, 294-296, 300,
    302-303, 311, 465, 470
  statistics 6, 331, 467, 472, 474-475,
    479, 571, 573, 578
  wages 471, 476-477, 489
*Economy and society in baroque
  Portugal, 1668-1703* 254
Edge, B. L. 55
Edinger, C. T. F. 669
Edmund of Cambridge 200
Education 12, 16, 27-28, 35, 568-569,
    582-583, 585
  adult 582-583
  Azores 32
  bibliographies 752, 764
  government policy 585
  higher 585
  influence on Japanese civilization
    442
  Madeira 32
  Salazar régime 302
  statistics 571, 575, 577
  structure 585
Edward, Black Prince 200
Edward III of England 200, 448
Edward Reynolds, W. 224
EEC (European Economic
    Community) 343, 421, 431
  Greek accession to 412, 459-460, 463
  impact on economy 462

  impact on politics 462
  impact on society 462
  impact on Spain 462
  Portuguese accession to 343,
    458-464, 489, 497-498
  Spanish accession to 412, 459-461, 463
EEC: an Economic Report 474
EFTA (European Free Trade
    Association) 413, 431
Egbert, A. C. 508
Egerton, F. C. C. 291
Eight centuries of Portuguese monarchy
    164
El Macabeo 594
El-Ksar el-Kebir 237
el-Malek, Abd 237
Elcock, W. D. 353
Elections 420, 432
*Elementos para a historia da imprensa
    periódica Portuguesa (1641-1821)*
    721
Eliot Morison, S. 225
Elizabeth II 517
Elizio, F. 596
Ellingham, M. 148
Elliot, W. Granville 269
Eloy, M. 705
*Elsevier's dictionary of personal and
    office computing: English,
    German, French, Italian,
    Portuguese* 378
Elsna, H. 249
Elvas 70, 72, 79, 86, 91, 97, 142
Embleton, C. 50
Embroidery 685
  Madeira 13
*Emerging nationalism in Portuguese
    Africa: a bibliography of
    documentary ephemera through
    1965* 759
Emigration 23, 32, 343-347, 404, 413,
    420, 463, 505
  from the Azores 348, 441
  to Brazil 344
  to Canada 344
  to France 343-344
  to GFR 344
  impact on agriculture 505
  and industrialization 343
  statistics 166
  to USA 32, 166, 343-344, 348, 441,
    774

229

H

235

241

Photographs 1, 4, 11, 20, 22, 29-31, 36, 40, 44, 114, 118-119, 147, 435, 556, 692
  archaeology 160
  architecture 692
  children's books 679
  ivories 686
  Lisbon 1
  locomotives 553, 556
  Madeira 17, 23, 41
  royal family, Portuguese 298
  towns 407
Phrase books 152, 354, 361-362
Phylloxera 523
Physical environment 16, 29
Piedagnel, A. 608
Pierce, F. 653
Pilgrimages 392
Pillement, G. 160
Pimental, E. Serpa 531
Pimlott, B. 421, 722
Pina-Cabral, J. de 341
Pinheiro, C. 705
Pinheiro, P. McGowan 295, 628, 662
Pintado, V. X. 473
Pinto, C. 701
Pinto, F. M. 221
Pinto de Mattos, R. 773
Pintor, F. H. 594
Pioneers in angiography: the Portuguese school of angiography 587
Pires, I. M. M. 501
Pires, J. C. 630
Pivka, O. von 283
Plays 3, 593, 607, 672-673, 675
Pliny 157
Poemas imperfeitos 617
Poems from the Portuguese of Luis de Camoens: with remarks on his life and writings. Notes, etc. etc. 654
Poems from the Portuguese (with the Portuguese text) 615
Poetry 7, 80, 97, 122, 591-592, 596, 598, 600, 602, 605, 615-617, 625, 629, 632, 634, 635-655, 666-671, 673-674
  anthologies 614-617, 621-623, 632, 634
  bibliographies 750
  dawn-songs 591
  Galician-Portuguese 589, 591
  lyric 602, 605, 674

modern 598, 603, 620-623
  Nova Arcádia movement 596
  Presença movement 598
  Provençal 615
  sonnets 639, 644, 648-649, 654
  Spanish 97, 591
Poetry of Jorge de Sena, a bilingual selection 629
Police 308, 624
Police state 294-296
Political constition of the Portuguese Republic approved by the National Plebiscite of 19th March 1933 . . . 302
Political economy 465-466
Political forces in Spain, Greece and Portugal 412
Political organizations
  directories 575
Political parties 412, 421, 423, 425, 428, 432-433, 435, 575
  PCDS 412
  PCP 412, 415
  PPD 412
  PS 412
  PSD 412
Political posters 435
Political prisoners 414
Political structure 399
Politics 12, 16, 27-28, 120, 177, 295-297, 299-301, 303-311, 332, 411-440, 460, 462-463, 465, 467, 474, 477, 489, 503, 575, 611
  18th century 66, 75, 79
  19th century 71, 88
  Azores 32
  bibliographies 754, 787
  colonies 320
  forty families oligarchy 466
  history 165, 177, 184, 263
  impact of Catholic Church 382
  influence of USA 462
  Madeira 32
  periodicals 738
  Republican 310
  role of the military 310, 420
  role of religion 382
  Salazar régime 290-291, 295, 301-303
  statistics 467
Politics. A Portuguese statesman 300
Polunin, O. 62
Pomar, J. 705

251

252

S

260

Whitehead, H. G. 230
Whiteway, R. S. 338
Wiarda, H. J. 311, 420, 462, 570
Wickliffe, L. Clark 691
Wild flowers of Spain and Portugal 64
Wilgus, A. Curtis 787
*William Wordsworth's Convention of
    Cintra: a facsimile of the 1809 tract*
    455
Williams, A. M. 344, 406, 408-410,
    413, 463, 500, 502
Williams, C. H. 180
Williams, E. B. 366
Williams, F. G. 629
Williams, J. R. 348
Willis, R. Clive 367
Windsor, Treaty of 182, 198
Wine 7, 118, 123, 144, 155-156, 182,
    248, 470, 494-495, 516-552, 715,
    719
    17th century 495
    18th century 91, 525
    19th century 68, 70, 81, 88, 532-534,
        551
    Algarve 140
    Bairrada 544
    brandy 540-541
    Bucelas 518, 540, 550
    Camarate 551
    Carcavelos 540, 550
    Colares 517-518, 540, 550
    Dão 540-541, 543-544, 550
    Douro valley 18, 519-521, 525-526,
        529, 534, 537, 539, 545, 551
    exports 525, 541
    history 516, 518, 520, 523, 525, 527,
        529, 531, 535-536, 540, 549
    Lauradio 551
    Madeira 13, 54, 106, 134, 517-518,
        524, 527, 538, 540-541, 544,
        551-552
    port 33, 80, 88, 92, 116, 123, 144,
        156, 495, 516-523, 525-526,
        528-537, 539-542, 544-545, 547-552
    rosé 540-541, 544
    Setúbal 517-518, 540, 550
    sherry 516
    Spain 542-543
    sparkling 540-541, 544
    statistics 520-521, 526, 529, 534, 536,
        541, 544-545, 552
    Tenerife 551

Termo 551
Torres Vedras 551
trade 182, 248, 494-495, 520-523,
    525, 531
Vinhos Verdes 540-541, 543-544,
    550-551
Wine of the Douro 519
Wine trade 495
*Wine trade of Portugal. Proceedings at
    the meeting of the nobility, wine
    proprietors and publick authorities
    of the wine district of the Alto-
    Douro . . .* 539
Wines of Spain and Portugal 541
Wines of Portugal 518, 544
Winius, G. D. 217
Winkworth, D. W. 565
*Winter in the Azores and a summer at
    the baths of the Furnas* 78
Winter holiday in Portugal 104
Wise, A. 440
Witwatersrand University 400
Wohl, A. 44
Wohl, H. 44, 669, 705
Women 163, 404, 568-569, 613
    bibliographies 747
    employment 569
    in fiction 606
    historical experience in Iberia 402
    in prison 414
Wood sculpture 34
Wool trade 182
Woolf, S. J. 301
Wordsworth, William 455
Workers' movements 440, 566
Working classes 566
World Fertility Survey 342
World railways 1952-53 562
World War I 187
World War II 38, 304, 456, 463
Wright, C. 45, 718-719
Wright, D. 140-142
Wuerpel, C. 143
Wyatt, H. 681
Wyatt, S. S. 193
Wynn, M. 408

Y

Yachtsman's guide to the Atlantic coasts

Map of Portugal

This map shows the more important towns and other features.

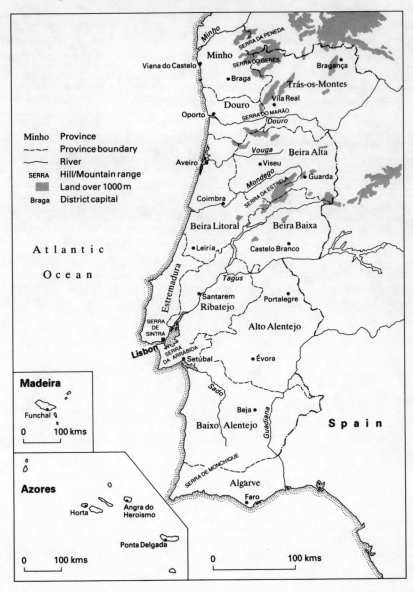

Minho Province
- - - Province boundary
⌇⌇⌇ River
SERRA Hill/Mountain range
▨ Land over 1000 m
Braga District capital

Atlantic Ocean

Madeira

Funchal

0   100 kms

Azores

Horta
Angra do Heroismo
Ponta Delgada

0   100 kms

0   100 kms

Minho
Viana do Castelo
Braga
SERRA DA PENEDA
SERRA DO GERÊS
Bragança
Trás-os-Montes
Douro
Vila Real
Oporto
SERRA DO MARÃO
Douro
Vouga
Beira Alta
Aveiro
Viseu
Mondego
SERRA DA ESTRELA
Guarda
Coimbra
Beira Litoral
Beira Baixa
Leiria
Castelo Branco
Tagus
Estremadura
Santarem
Ribatejo
Portalegre
SERRA DE SINTRA
Alto Alentejo
Lisbon
SERRA DA ARRABIDA
Setúbal
Évora
Sado
Beja
Guadiana
Baixo Alentejo
Spain
SERRA DE MONCHIQUE
Algarve
Faro